CARL WILLIAMS

Adam Shand is a journalist with nearly thirty years' experience in television, print and online media. As a freelance reporter, he covered the rise to power of Nelson Mandela in South Africa, the aftermath of the genocide in Rwanda and the corruption of Zimbabwe's democracy. Since 1997 he has been an investigative reporter. He is the author of five books, including *Big Shots: Carl Williams and the Gangland Wars – the Inside Story* and *The Skull: Informers, Hit Men and Australia's Toughest Cops*.

CARL WILLIAMS

ADAM SHAND

PENGUIN BOOKS

PENGUIN BOOKS

Published by the Penguin Group
Penguin Group (Australia)
707 Collins Street, Melbourne, Victoria 3008, Australia
(a division of Penguin Australia Pty Ltd)
Penguin Group (USA) Inc.
375 Hudson Street, New York, New York 10014, USA
Penguin Group (Canada)
90 Eglinton Avenue East, Suite 700, Toronto, Canada ON M4P 2Y3
(a division of Penguin Canada Books Inc.)
Penguin Books Ltd
80 Strand, London WC2R 0RL England
Penguin Ireland
25 St Stephen's Green, Dublin 2, Ireland
(a division of Penguin Books Ltd)
Penguin Books India Pvt Ltd
11 Community Centre, Panchsheel Park, New Delhi – 110 017, India
Penguin Group (NZ)
67 Apollo Drive, Rosedale, Auckland 0632, New Zealand
(a division of Penguin New Zealand Pty Ltd)
Penguin Books (South Africa) (Pty) Ltd
Rosebank Office Park, Block D, 181 Jan Smuts Avenue, Parktown North, Johannesburg, 2196, South Africa
Penguin (Beijing) Ltd
7F, Tower B, Jiaming Center, 27 East Third Ring Road North, Chaoyang District, Beijing 100020, China

Penguin Books Ltd, Registered Offices: 80 Strand, London WC2R 0RL, England

First published by Penguin Group (Australia), 2012
This edition published by Penguin Group (Australia), 2014

10 9 8 7 6 5 4 3 2 1

Text copyright © Adam Shand 2012

The moral right of the author has been asserted

All rights reserved. Without limiting the rights under copyright reserved above, no part of this publication may be reproduced, stored in or introduced into a retrieval system, or transmitted, in any form or by any means (electronic, mechanical, photocopying, recording or otherwise), without the prior written permission of both the copyright owner and the above publisher of this book.

Cover design by Alex Ross © Penguin Group (Australia)
Front cover photograph by Fairfax / John Woudstra. Back cover photograph by Shutterstock.com / Neale Cousland
Typeset in Sabon by Penguin Group (Australia)
Printed and bound in Australia by Griffin Press, an accredited ISO AS/NZS 14001 Environmental Management Systems printer

National Library of Australia
Cataloguing-in-Publication data:

Shand, Adam, author.
Carl Williams / Adam Shand.
9780143569169 (paperback)
Williams, Carl (Carl Anthony), 1970-2010.
Criminals–Victoria–Melbourne.
Organized crime–Victoria–Melbourne.
Criminal investigation–Victoria–Melbourne.
Murder–Victoria–Melbourne–Case studies.
Gangs–Victoria–Melbourne.

364.1099451

penguin.com.au

CONTENTS

Introduction 1

1. Who's a Shitman Now? 5
2. Camp Hell 10
3. Mummy's Boy 18
4. Criminal Royalty 27
5. The Princes of Darkness 36
6. Shane and Deana 41
7. Heading Uptown 53
8. Clandestine Cops 58
9. The Betrayal 64
10. Keepsakes 69
11. A Tattslotto Moment 79
12. Benji 93
13. Turncoats and Lionhearts 99
14. Lead Rain 110
15. A Whole Lotta Love 115
16. Wife and Baby 119
17. Plotting 128
18. The Godfather 132
19. Common Cause 136
20. Murder Incorporated 141
21. On the Ball 147
22. Grand Final Day 155
23. Spotlight 159
24. Beach Bail 169
25. Guns for Hire 177
26. A Dynasty Done and Dusted 186
27. Loose Ends 190
28. Behind Bars 196
29. Hotel Acacia 202
30. Deal or No Deal 211
31. Judgement Day 216
32. The Solo Sailor 223
33. Swan Island 231
34. A Secret Foe 238
35. Code Black 242
36. Violence and Mercy 246

Casualties of Melbourne's
Gangland War 1998–2010 251

Acknowledgements 255

'No criminal's story is worth
repeating unless in its depiction there
can be something of value to society.'

J. EDGAR HOOVER, 1938

INTRODUCTION

In death, Carl Williams' cult-hero status has been secured.

Melbourne's gangland war has become the most widely reported, and dissected, series of crimes in Australia's history. Millions more people around the world know Carl's story through having watched the top-rating *Underbelly* TV series.

In *Underbelly*, the actor Gyton Grantley portrays Carl as an ordinary man who prevails in a struggle against an evil criminal elite that tries to keep him and his family down. And that is the image that has stuck with Carl's fans, rather than that of a greedy, slothful coward who acquired a taste for blood.

The phenomenon came full circle when in 2009 *Being Carl Williams* was named as a finalist in Sydney's Tropfest short-film festival. In the film, two crooks confuse *Underbelly*'s Grantley for the real Carl. They kidnap him and make Grantley participate in an underworld killing. Even the victim is convinced that Carl has managed to escape Barwon Prison to do him in.

In nine years of covering this story as a reporter, I have swung between both views of Carl – as the hero and the coward. We see what we want to see.

In 2003, approaching this story as a journalist, I saw Carl as a product of the state's failed 'war on drugs'. He was supplying an unquenchable thirst for narcotics, aided and abetted by corrupt police. Drugs had poisoned society at all levels and the bloody gangland war taking place was a consequence. It was time to examine how the drugs prohibition model had created and enriched the dramatis personae of this story.

I accept that this approach tended to overlook some of the players' culpability. But, let's face it, they were killing people we didn't like. Melbourne crooks are fond of saying: 'We catch and kill our own.' On that basis, things ran quite smoothly in the Garden State for a long time. The public didn't care about the dozens of unsolved underworld murders. It made for great tabloid copy, nothing more.

Melbourne's gangland war was my first crime-writing assignment, undertaken for *The Bulletin* magazine and the Nine Network's *Sunday* program. From that work emerged a book, *Big Shots*, which recorded the time I spent with Carl Williams and his cohort as events moved towards their bloody crescendo in 2003–04.

The saturation media coverage of the saga, followed by the screening of *Underbelly*, and later the frenzy over his death, has turned Carl into an icon. There is a need to reclaim the fact of his life, before the fiction takes over.

In early 2012, a Higher School Certificate student from Sydney contacted me to say she was doing her major artwork on Carl. 'Silvy' came all the way to Melbourne with her mother in tow to interview me. She was going to turn Carl's life into 'a postmodern work capable of individual interpretation'.

'The origins of the concept are an interest in exploring the stories and background of individuals who have had a public image created by the media. The public image is often an artificial or superficial façade, and their stories and history are a more complex layering of human emotions,' Silvy told me earnestly.

Silvy had been only ten when the real Carl went on his murderous rampage, but the Carl portrayed by Gyton Grantley in *Underbelly* had captured her imagination. The lines between fact and fiction were blurred. The day the real Carl died had been one of the most intense experiences of her young life.

INTRODUCTION

'I had fifty text messages that day from my friends. We were all in shock that Carl, this person we felt so close to, had been killed. We felt we knew him because we identified with his struggle,' she said.

'Carl was just an ordinary person. People can relate. Carl seems like someone living a life that anyone could, but [he] became a rebel and underdog. While I wouldn't want to be him (too risky), when watching the TV show, I felt as though I was cheering for him.

'I suppose that the whole story is like watching a reality TV show – we are interested in ordinary people who become famous for simply being on TV. But would I want to be on the show? No way. With Carl's murder, the story has now finished and like movie stars that have died young, Carl's image will not age.'

For his critics, this immortality is rather inconvenient. *Herald Sun* columnist Andrew Bolt suggested that authorities put Carl's body on show to counter his folk-hero status.

'Let's see that famous "baby face" now. Let's see what Carl Williams looks like after being bashed to death,' Bolt wrote.

'Show the body, as we used to do when a killer was finally dead and we needed to kill his legend, too. The trouble is, Williams is not really dead. Not yet. Not in the way it matters to the rest of us.'

Some people would only believe Carl was dead after they saw him stretched out on a slab, his skull shattered like an eggshell. A grisly post-mortem picture of Carl's face was duly posted on Twitter. And still he lives on, at least in the virtual world.

On 13 October 2011, what would have been Carl's forty-first birthday, a female fan posted on one of several Facebook tribute sites.

'Happy Birthday, have a great day. X'

1

WHO'S A SHITMAN NOW?

On 3 March 2012, George Williams stood waiting in a bluestone city lane, minding his own business as usual. The image of his late son Carl was seared into the public mind but George could move about the city in relative anonymity. It was something he had practised over a long period of time, an attitude more than a physical thing.

At the height of the gangland war, when Carl had fronted the media outside court, George had always stayed a few paces behind, never stepping into his son's spotlight. It had been Carl's moment, after all.

George had spent most of his life going unnoticed, being underestimated. These were the key attributes of the successful pool shark and card player, the only things George had made a success of.

To the big shots of Melbourne crime, George was a 'shitman' (pronounced *shitm'n*), a nobody. To be someone in Australia's underworld, a man has to meet a strict set of criteria. For more than a hundred years, the top crooks always traced their roots to the abattoir, the docks or two-up ring and the starting price bookmaking game. The slaughtermen and the dockies did the muddy, bloody jobs that most decent people wouldn't do on a basic wage. The SP bookies and two-up men had the smarts to survive in a sometimes vicious world that always included a bent cop or two. If you didn't have one of these three bloodlines in your pedigree, you didn't rate. Until drugs changed everything, there had only been 300 or 400 nationwide who were recognised as 'good crooks'. The rest were shitmen, like George, who existed on the fringe of crime, eking out a living from whatever rorts they could pull, in between working straight jobs, perish the thought.

George had worked as a debt collector, repossessing fridges and TVs from working families. George was shifty and more than a little cunning, but not at all ruthless. He would have been happy to finish up with just a little more than when he started, having expended the bare minimum of effort. Certainly, he did not expect the gods of crime were ever going to bestow any opportunities on him.

But then George had fallen on a product and everything changed. The product was methamphetamine and it had made the family's name as it changed the face of the underworld. Suddenly, money spoke louder than ever before.

Some say he and Carl had made the best ecstasy pills in Melbourne. No one, except their competitors, had ever complained about the Williamses' product, which they branded as FUBUs or UFOs. They had been a cheap mix of speed and ketamine guaranteed to bring synthetic joy to Melbourne partygoers in the hundreds each weekend. It wasn't something that George had gone looking for. In fact, it was Carl that had brought this new business home to his father. But George didn't feel it was right to reject it. Compared to some other options, manufacturing pills seemed to be a victimless crime. They would just be meeting a demand that already existed, he reasoned. If you let such an opportunity pass, someone else would grab it. It was like a wad of banknotes left in a busy street. You'd be a mug to walk past.

However, success had also turned George's gentle, lazy boy into a gangster who got to decide whether people lived or died. This cold-blooded capacity was not something George had anticipated but he never condemned it. In fact, he was immensely proud that Carl had defended his family. His enemies had underestimated Carl and paid the price in blood. Carl had singlehandedly taken down the powerful

Moran faction and exposed their links to corrupt police. The underdog had come out on top. George still felt like one of the good guys.

In a perverse way, he admired Carl for making something of himself, or at least achieving his ambition. He had become a real gangster, a good one too: calculating, shrewd and without pity. Carl had showed everyone he wasn't a shitman, and neither were his family. Carl had spoken for all of them, so George didn't have to.

So he had shambled along behind Carl's media show outside court. Carl had loved playing up to the cameras. Clad in his favourite Ralph Lauren leisurewear, he had put on his best 'boob walk', the swaggering waddle of the real tough guys he had seen in jail.

And there was George, ready for our lunch meeting, his eyes downcast, his thinning hair slicked into an unfashionable quiff. George had chosen jeans and a high-visibility orange shirt, like you see on building sites. I wondered why; he hadn't been to work in years. In the sunlight, the shirt stood out like a beacon there in the lane. I remarked on it.

'I wouldn't want them to mistake you for me, would I?' he said with a crooked smile.

'They might miss me and hit you.' He did not have to say who 'they' were. We both knew there would always be someone out there who might take a pot shot at him.

Even bad guys had family and friends who might still harbour a desire for revenge. When you order the killing of seven or more, as Carl was reputed to have done, that leaves a lot of grieving people with a powerful reason to have you knocked.

There were all the lunatics with *Underbelly* fetishes to contend with too. There might be one out there who would listen to the voices inside his head.

Let them come, said George. His survival instinct was strong but it was a daily struggle to remember just what he was living for. There was no pleasure in life any more, he said as he ordered his meal. He could enjoy a steak and a Crown lager but that wasn't the same as enjoying life. He would always return to that dark hollow place.

He had been seeing a psychiatrist but George could never open up and share his feelings. There was no one who could really understand. How could they? He had watched his family die one by one, directly or indirectly, because of drugs. His eldest boy, Shane, was the first – a heroin overdose in 1997. His first love, Barbara, had committed suicide in November 2008 when she realised that Carl was never coming home from jail.

And then in April 2010, Carl had been murdered by fellow inmate Matty Johnson. His family's demise had been served up as entertainment by the media for the past decade.

If that wasn't enough, the Australian Tax Office was chasing him for $800 000, an estimate of what George had earnt from the family drug business. It looked as though he'd lose the family home in Broadmeadows and the townhouse he had bought for Barbara in Essendon. He started life with nothing and would more than likely finish up that way.

And he had brought it all on himself, he said. Was he suggesting that he should have stopped Carl from murdering everyone? No, his regret was that he had been the one who advised Carl to plead guilty.

'None of this would have happened had we gone to trial. We should have fought them charges, every last one of them,' he said ruefully.

Despite Carl's convictions on four murders, one attempted murder and various drug charges, George was able to dismiss everything as simply 'an allegation'.

In close to a decade of reporting on the Williamses' family saga, I'd heard this tortured logic many times before, but as usual I let it go. From past experience, I knew that by the end of lunch George would be more or less declaring all Carl's 'alleged victims' had deserved what they got.

He would work his way around to the proposition that Carl was, in fact, the victim. He was bad, but not as bad as the people he had killed. And at the end he had tried to put things right. He had agreed to give evidence against corrupt coppers and they had killed him for it.

And this was how George justified the heinous things Carl had done. The murders, the drug dealing, the betrayals and all the lies could be wrapped up and buried. The 'baby-faced assassin' of public repute could be turned back into his gentle, fun-loving son.

2

CAMP HELL

It took a long time for outsiders to fully understand Carl Williams' story. The more people analysed the events of the gangland war, the less sense they seemed to make. Here was a family at odds with the law and the state, but also with the criminal elites that ran the underworld. They seemed to have emerged from the suburban ether, white trash from nowhere. But there was a streak of rat cunning and resentment in the Williams clan that made them push back against much greater forces.

They built a small empire in the space of a single generation and Carl was fully prepared to slaughter anyone who crossed the family. What people couldn't be expected to understand was that the bloody feud with the Morans and the gods of Melbourne crime was the climax of an untold history. One characterised by ingrained poverty and disappointment, of generations beaten down, neglected and despised. The descent into crime and murder that followed speaks of what happens to the self-esteem of people denied the opportunities that others regard as their birthright. It's a situation born of the bitter realisation that the Australian ethos of 'the fair go' is in fact a cruel joke. It's the story of what happens when the have-nots finally get a grip on the main chance.

The Williamses' journey to infamy began in the squalor of a camp for the homeless and destitute on the northern fringe of Melbourne's Royal Park. In the years after World War Two, Camp

Pell was a place to hide what many regarded as the detritus of Melbourne society. It's almost forgotten now. It's a memory that jars with the postwar prosperity story that most Australians learn in schools these days. This place has been transformed into an 'Urban Camp', a quiet patch of cultivated bushland nestling between busy Flemington Road and the State Hockey Centre. Teenagers come here now for school excursions. Nice people from the adjoining suburbs walk their dogs among the eucalypts and wattles, enjoying this oasis in the urban jungle. It seems benign and peaceful.

In the 1940s, when Carl's grandparents on both sides of the family came here, it was far from that. Camp Pell was their last resort. It was a choice between this fetid sinkhole or the street for the Williams and the Denman clans. To George Williams, it seemed that everyone he knew had come from Camp Pell. It was his first memory. And his bride, Barbara Denman, had been born there too.

The sprawling shantytown had begun as a camp for Taskforce 6814, the forces that US Supreme Commander General Douglas MacArthur had thrown together after the Japanese had attacked Hawaii's Pearl Harbour in December 1941. The soldiers had stayed in tents or Nissen huts, igloo-shaped iron sweat boxes with dirt floors and no insulation. As a military camp, it had been suitably hard and uncomfortable, but it was only ever meant to be temporary.

The place had a sinister reputation from the beginning. Over the space of two weeks in May 1942, an American serviceman stationed there, Private Eddie Leonski, had murdered three local women, gaining the sobriquet 'the Brownout Strangler'. On MacArthur's orders, Leonski was hanged at Pentridge in November 1942, but the scandal cast a pall over Camp Pell. Later, a rumour swept Melbourne that American military police had shot and killed a number of GIs and some locals who had been involved in a vicious mass brawl outside the Flinders Street Railway Station in December. The story went that the incident was covered up on MacArthur's orders and the corpses were secretly cremated at Camp Pell, the ashes spread across the grounds. It was apocryphal but helped cement public notions that there was something sinister about Camp Pell.

After the war, the grounds were turned into a transit camp for homeless families, who moved straight into the Nissen huts the Americans had vacated. It was supposed to be a one-year arrangement while the Victorian government built new state housing for the poor. However, it stayed open for ten years amid government inaction and growing public revulsion.

At any one time, more than three thousand people lived at Camp Pell, sharing communal washing and cooking facilities. When it rained, the camp became a quagmire, a dismal playground for hordes of children with no shoes and ragged clothes. In summer the iron huts were so intolerably hot many took to sleeping out in the open. There were frequent outbreaks of diseases of poverty and overcrowding, like diphtheria and whooping cough.

Camp Pell kids were ostracised at local schools for being unclean and spreading illness and head lice. Carl's uncles and aunts found even the teachers gave them a hard time for their dirty appearance. In 1947, the Building Trades Federation wrote to government, stating that living conditions at Camp Pell were 'worse than the worst slums in Melbourne'.

Despite occasional half-hearted attempts by authorities to tidy it up, Camp Pell remained 'a breeding ground of physical and spiritual disease . . . an evil intolerable plague spot', according to an April 1953 editorial in *The Argus* newspaper.

'Nobody with eyes to see could bring himself to call any such monstrosity as this "a housing settlement". Camp Pell is, in plain language, nothing but a dump for human beings.'

Little wonder then that the settlement became known as 'Camp Hell'.

Privately, the state's leaders could only agree the conditions were disgraceful but there was simply nowhere else to house these poor families. A slum reclamation program had begun after the war and many families had been displaced from cheap rental accommodation across the inner city. A wave of middle-class European migrants had bought up many of the old tenements in inner-city suburbs like Richmond, Fitzroy, St Kilda and Carlton. The original inhabitants, including many who had been living there for generations on cheap rent, were given their marching orders.

There had always been a shortage of housing for the poor in Melbourne but by the late 1940s, the situation was dire: evictions were running at 100 a month. There was little sympathy for those forced to live at Camp Pell and a number of other transit camps around the state. It seemed to them that the migrants got a better deal than the poor families of the city, many of whom had sent sons and daughters to fight and die for King and country in the war. While migrants were praised by civic leaders for their work ethic and family values, the Anglo-Celtic poor were reviled for their moral degeneracy.

In 1949, the Victorian state housing minister complained his 'big problem was the provision of accommodation for habitual drunkards, sex perverts and sub-normal people living in emergency camps'.

Barbara's parents, Bill and Mary Denman, were none of those things, just decent hardworking people battling to survive in Melbourne. Mary's family had come from Glenrowan, Ned Kelly country, in Central Victoria. Bill's people were inner-city knockabouts. Bill Denman was a qualified welder but as work was scarce and accommodation virtually non-existent, the only alternative was Camp Pell. With a growing brood of children, they tried to make the best of what they hoped would be a short-term solution. They stayed for nearly five years. By that time seven children were crammed into the Denmans' iron hut.

George's family, his mother, two sisters and a brother, lived a few rows away from the Denmans. His father, who'd been a wharfie, spent little time with the family. In fact, George was not sure that the man was even his father. 'You only know your mother for sure, don't you?' he liked to say later.

George had fond memories of Camp Pell. It was a hard life but they were together. George had cousins living nearby and they formed a gang of urchins who were always getting into trouble, cutting down trees for fun and generally running amok in the camp. They had their own catch cry: 'Camp Pell kids. Camp Pell kids. Camp Pell kids are we. We're always up to mischief, wherever we may be.'

Yet the camp was an extremely dangerous place for adults, especially under the cover of night. The newspaper archives are full of stories of murders, robberies, rapes and incidences of domestic violence that were commonplace at Camp Pell. Police regarded the camp as the epicentre of crime in Melbourne.

By 1953, there were 1300 children under sixteen, like George Williams and Barbara Denman, living at Camp Pell. There were fears that 'this evil pernicious place' might poison its inhabitants and the city in general. That same year, *The Argus* mounted a strident campaign to have the camp demolished.

'First, the camp holds many hundreds of decent, hardworking men and their families, who want homes but can't get them. Second it holds an unhealthy number of work-shy parasites who wouldn't move out of Camp Pell at any price.'

The social consequences of the moral contagion that had flourished in Camp Pell would be felt later, the newspaper warned.

'We can't expect people, basically decent people, to go on living there for four, five, six years, as some of them have done, without contracting the moral diseases that Camp Pell breeds. We cannot expect children, basically decent children, to grow up in the miasma of this foul place as children are without becoming Dead-End kids – and graduating as Dead-End men and women.'

Families in the adjoining areas would warn their kids to stay out of Camp Pell as if the contagion of poverty could somehow be transmitted by contact with 'the inmates', as the residents were described.

The public condemnation of Camp Pell brought the residents closer together. In 1954, they formed an association to correct the public perception that everyone living in there was 'an undesirable'.

'Every suburb has its undesirables – even Toorak,' one resident, A.F. Gelsi, told *The Argus*.

'But 99 per cent of residents at Camp Pell are good clean families who care for their homes and their families and behave as well as anyone,' he said.

In July 1955, the Labor government of John Cain issued mass eviction notices to the residents without any plan for re-housing them. With the Olympic Games coming to Melbourne the following year, the state government had built 800 houses for the competitors in the Games Village but apparently could not find funds to accommodate the residents of Camp Pell. Instead, the residents had been told to move their belongings out as soon as possible so the decrepit hovels could be razed. The indignity of their treatment goaded the people into action. Protest meetings were held to complain of their inhumane handling.

'No self-respecting person wants to live in this filth and squalor but most of us have to,' the chairman of the Emergency Housing Tenant Committee told a meeting of residents.

'We don't want to live here. None of us with any decency would. But we have to have shelter for children.'

When the authorities came to forcibly evict residents, members of the Communist Party and trade unions helped families stand their ground, wresting back furniture and personal belongings and returning them to the huts.

Eventually sense prevailed and the camp was given a reprieve while government worked out what to do with the 600 families who stubbornly refused to move until offered proper housing. Despite all the outrage there was still nowhere to put these destitute people who seemed to threaten the moral health of the city.

In 1955, Liberal Party leader Henry Bolte came to power in Victoria and made a vow to dismantle Camp Pell one of his top election promises. The last family left Camp Pell on 31 May 1956, giving the Public Works Department enough time to clear away the remaining fifty huts before the Olympic Games came to Melbourne in November. It was not from a sense of pity or compassion. Bolte privately said that he could not allow Queen Elizabeth and her husband Prince Philip to gaze on the eyesore as they came in from the airport for the Games.

While the Denmans had already left Camp Pell in 1954 when Barbara was six, George's family had been among the last to vacate.

Most families had been shifted to housing commission dwellings while others had found their own housing. George's family had ended up in a worker's cottage in North Richmond that was marginally more salubrious than what they had just left.

But families who had lived at Camp Pell could never remove the stain, at least in the eyes of the good middle-class folk of Melbourne. While they abhorred the conditions and castigated the government for its inaction, there was a sense that the people living in Camp Pell were beyond redemption. Soon the chickens would come home to roost in the form of crime and social dysfunction. The vermin would infect the city.

'We hear of marriages breaking, men turning to crime, children becoming tough young dead-end delinquents under the ugly spell of Camp Pell,' one editorialist thundered.

'Is it surprising? The family that spends months or years in Camp Pell and comes out untarnished must be of uncommonly strong moral fibre. Men, women and children are not only physically ravaged by life in Camp Pell; they are also irreparably damaged in spirit.'

More than fifty years later, the moral arbiters were still passing judgement on the families who had passed through Camp Pell.

Even though society had been tainted by drugs, violence and official corruption at the highest levels, the blame could still be sheeted home to individuals, as if everything was perfect up on the high moral ground. In response to Carl's death in 2010, radio broadcaster Derryn Hinch declared him nothing more than 'a piece of greedy human flotsam'.

'Carl Williams is dead and believe me the world is better for his passing. It's one more vote for a cleaner Australia. He was scum and don't let TV shows like *Underbelly* ever fool you otherwise,' he said.

How laughable it was that Hinch and others could wish away half a century of social exclusion with the death of one man. There were thousands of people who recognised their own lives in Carl's story. To them, it was hardly surprising, even admirable, that Carl had put family before the law or society's norms.

3

MUMMY'S BOY

On 13 October 1970, from the moment she held her newborn boy in her arms, Barbara knew that Carl Anthony Williams was someone very special. She and George had another son, Shane, born four years earlier, whom she loved but this emotion was deeper. She knew it was wrong to love one kid more than the other, but she couldn't help it. People would later say only half-jokingly that Barbara didn't just love Carl, she was *in* love with him.

She couldn't keep her eyes off Carl. He was the most beautiful thing she had ever seen, Barbara told people. In hospital she wouldn't let anyone else hold the baby. She resolved to give him everything she could, even if that meant forgoing her own needs. Life had not given Barb much more than a pretty face, a sense of humour and a strong notion of family. After leaving Camp Hell, Bill and Mary Denman added another four children to the family, making a total of eleven. The extra mouths had made the Denmans even poorer, though at least they had escaped the squalor of emergency accommodation. It wasn't until the older kids hit working age and started chipping in that the family's circumstances began to improve.

On a typical day, the only food the kids might get would be a serving of bread and dripping, says Barb's older brother Bill. He first tasted meat at fourteen years old.

'We ate in relays, we slept in relays,' he jokes. But no matter how hard life was they would never go back to emergency housing.

For Mary Denman, gambling was both a pastime and a means

of survival. The early years had been filled with incidences of hurriedly moving house at all hours to escape the rent collector and the sheriff. The punt offered a chance at something more. Mary firmly believed they were just one red-hot tip away from redemption: when that winner came home, their lives would change forever. This fervent hope kept her shelling out the family's money to the bookies. There were many weeks when the punt kept food on the table; on a bad week, Barb's mum simply didn't pay the rent. One day they would beat the system, and the small wins along the way were a kind of confirmation of that. The more she gambled, the more she felt entitled to that big win. It never came.

When they were old enough to afford it, all of Mary's surviving offspring followed her example. The Denmans may have only produced one gang boss, in Carl, but every one of them learnt to play the odds.

Harness racing was the family favourite. 'The trots' revelled in its reputation as the most corrupt of all racing forms. Each week, the big syndicates in Sydney and Melbourne would fix the results of key races, with the connivance of the leading drivers. If you were in the know as a punter, you could make a bundle without getting off your bar stool, but the Denmans weren't among that select group who knew when a 'boat race' was on. It was always the same heads that got the mail first and grabbed the best odds. It was unfair, but there was no point complaining when you were that low on the food chain. Besides, one day you might be on the winning side.

In 1961, the Denmans welcomed a boarder into their crowded household. George Williams' parents had split up when he was fourteen, and his mother had organised for her son to move in with the Denmans.

George quickly became part of the family, even if he never really got on with some of Barb's brothers. There had been terrible fights between George and the Denman boys when the boarder started showing interest in their sisters. At first, George had taken a shine to Barb's older sister Kathleen, who was the straitlaced sort. Kath liked George but didn't think he was the kind of man she should marry. There was something shifty and sly about him that didn't sit properly with her. But Barbara was much more game for a laugh and so George suited her. He was no matinee idol but she liked his cheeky ways and ready smile. And, like her, George was gentle and self-deprecating.

Living under the same roof was George's biggest advantage in courting the pretty and popular Barb, and soon they were inseparable. At eighteen, she fell pregnant with Shane and that was it: Barb would be tied to George for life. There were dramas between George and Barb's family over the pregnancy. For a time, George had to leave Melbourne, heading up to the Riverina to go fruit picking.

To her family, Barb was still a kid herself; some say she never grew up. Like 'Little Audrey' jumping rope in the neon sign at the Skipping Girl vinegar factory on Victoria Street, Barb would always be stuck in her youth: forever fun-loving and playful.

By the time Carl came along in 1970, they were a proper family. She and George were married and they both had jobs. Neither was glamorous – George dug ditches in the Richmond sewer for the Melbourne & Metropolitan Board of Works, and Barb worked in a Collingwood cigarette factory – but it meant Barb could look to the future with optimism. They had managed to get away from the domineering influence of Barb's mother and brothers, and spent the early years living in Collingwood and Richmond on top of shops or in tiny units.

George was a low-key presence in those areas. Ask the old criminal lags of the Richmond crime scene and few will admit to having known George. He was just another face in the crowd at his favourite local pub, the Earl of Lincoln, in North Richmond. The Earl was a notorious haunt of Richmond knockabouts and heavies from the Federated Ship Painters and Dockers Union. For a decade or so from the late 1960s onwards, the Kane brothers, Brian and Leslie, were the power in Richmond. With strong links to the union movement, the Labor Party and the local constabulary, the Kanes were a force to be reckoned with.

Brian was a cool operator, friendly and intelligent, able to network at different levels of society. His younger brother, Les, was a firebrand, an unpredictable and violent character who cultivated a reputation as a gangster. The brothers' skills were complementary and they drew into their orbit some of the most dangerous and resourceful crooks of the era.

To be accepted into this clique provided an entree to a wide range of rorts: stand over, armed robbery, paid election thuggery for political candidates, the distribution of stolen goods, whatever was going. And the Earl of Lincoln was a hub for much of that.

The Kanes themselves were not usually found hanging around in pubs. That was beneath them, but if you wanted to make contact, then the Earl was the place to do it. There were always a few Kane cronies propping up the bar, maintaining the communications network in the days before mobile telephones. Whatever you wanted could be found or arranged in the Earl, if you were onside.

George's family lived a few hundred metres away from the pub and he had seen the network in action. He had seen the up-and-coming big shots of the day in that front bar – men like Graham 'the Munster' Kinniburgh, Lewis Moran, Leo 'the Lout' McDonald and a host of others in the Kane mob. He wasn't even on nodding terms with men like that but the Earl was a broad church and George took advantage of what opportunities were available.

It was in the Earl that George learnt to supplement his meagre income playing cards, pool and snooker. On a good day, he could make four or five hundred dollars hustling unsuspecting marks. He practised hard and made himself almost unbeatable on the pool table, but it was his guile combined with an unassuming manner that brought the money in.

He would let a mug win a few games to get their ego going while they only were playing for beers. But when they were drunk enough and the money had come out, George would turn on his A-game and clean them out. On a bad day, when the mug cut up rough, George might get a flogging and come home with nothing. When things got too hot, George would take his show on the road to other Melbourne pubs and snooker rooms. But he would always return to the Earl.

To Barbara, George was a good provider who shared her passion: giving their kids everything they never had growing up.

George was not a violent man and that suited Barb too. She hated brutality.

They needed to stick together if they were going to make something of themselves. Anyway, they were in love and the hard scrabble of their early lives was gradually receding.

The Williamses seemed like a tight, cohesive family, but it wasn't long before the cracks began to appear. Barb's sister Kathleen had married and started her own family. However, her husband was a hopeless drunk who bashed and terrorised her.

Between the births of Shane and Carl, Kathleen came to stay with George and Barb for a short period to escape her husband's cruelty. She was vulnerable and George couldn't help himself: the pair began a torrid affair. It might have gone unnoticed had it not been for Kath falling pregnant. There was no way that Kath would put herself through the agony and risk of a backyard abortion, so she had the baby, another boy, a half-brother to Carl and Shane.

After much soul-searching and heartache, Barb decided the best way to deal with it was not to deal with it. The affair would be swept under the carpet as if it never happened. The boy would be raised by Kath and her husband as their own child. Barb decreed that under no circumstances were Shane and Carl to be told that their cousin was in fact their half-brother, even though as he grew he came to closely resemble Shane and Carl. The secret was kept from outsiders for two decades, but the wedge remained between Kath and the rest of the family.

In 1973, when Carl was three, the family made the big move to Broadmeadows. 'Broadie' was a world away from Richmond: sitting on a vast ancient plain at the northern edge of the city.

The area had been settled by Presbyterian Scots in the 1850s but it was low-lying, marshy territory. Hopeful speculators had begun subdivisions in the 1880s but a slump in property prices had put paid to that.

For years the area marked time, the old derelict subdivisions disappearing into the grass. In 1949, the State Housing Commission bought up 2270 hectares to create a residential estate and over the next thirty years built about 1000 houses.

In the early 1970s, the Housing Commission was offering tenants the chance to own their own homes with rent to go against the purchase price. The brick house George and Barb signed up for was a revelation compared to the cramped places they were used to. For just $9000 they got three bedrooms and a generous allotment of land. Their block was on a little hill set back from busy Pascoe Vale Road. On warm summer nights, the young parents could sit on their new verandah, overlooking a vista of farmland and meadows, rather than the blank wall of the neighbour's house as they had in Richmond. It was the first time any of their family had ever owned their own home, modest as it was.

There were a number of families who had over fifteen years wound their way from Camp Pell through the inner-city slums and out to Broadie. So the society George found in Broadie was familiar, even if the location was new; these were old cards reshuffled into a new hand.

The population of Broadie was rising steadily, too fast for the state government to keep pace in building schools, hospitals and other public amenities. There were only a few shops and pubs so far, but they would come, the new residents believed. The Ford Motor Co. had set up a manufacturing plant in 1959 and other employers were now following.

Out on the northern fringe, there wasn't Richmond's hierarchy. A man could make something of his life without a bunch of big shots telling him what to do; here, they could live on their own terms, away from Barb's family.

While George was working his way into the local rorts, Barb busied herself turning the new house into a home. Faded black-and-white photographs from the early 1970s show Barb out the back planting trees with the help of Carl and Shane. George put in cypress hedges at the front like he had seen in the posh suburbs south of the river. They saved their money and put in an above-ground pool. And there was a garage, which the two growing boys made their own. Both George and Barb still returned each morning into town for work but the long train ride was worth it for the peace and serenity of their new home.

In the mid-1970s, George left the Board of Works after suffering a back injury and turned his hand to debt collecting for a Richmond white-goods retailer, repossessing fridges and stoves from families who had fallen behind in the payments. Barb had left the poisonous atmosphere of the tobacco factory and got a job in the TAB in Pascoe Vale, the only legacy of her former employment being a lifelong addiction to cigarettes.

As well as holding down a job, Barb was always the homemaker and doting mother. In her eyes, the men in her life could do no wrong, and they barely had to lift a finger around the house. Barb would do everything for Shane and Carl and spoilt them rotten, within their limited means. At the same time, she taught them to be polite and respectful, to get on with people.

At school, both Williams boys were bullied. Neither could fight to save himself, so they compensated with generosity, buying their friends with money and gifts. They drew boys to them whom they believed would be useful. Carl, in particular, blond and cherubic-looking, discovered early on the value of surrounding himself with those of greater physical abilities. Shane and Carl became popular and there was always a crowd of kids around at the Williamses' house. George set up the garage as a games room with pool and ping-pong tables. All summer, the pool was alive with the sound of kids playing and splashing.

Every Sunday morning, Barb would throw on a cooked breakfast and a horde of kids would descend. Many of them came from broken, unhappy homes, where alcohol, drugs and unemployment had hardened them at a young age. The Williamses' home was a sanctuary for them.

In every family snap, George bears an expression of quiet contentment. Things were travelling nicely for him. If he were up to mischief, then it was all low-key and self-contained. There were plenty in Broadie who had a fiddle or two going on the side – it was almost expected of a bloke – but George wasn't on anyone's radar and that's how he operated. George wasn't one to make enemies. He wasn't a big talker or a flashy dresser; there were no shiny suits or big cars. That kind of man came unstuck sooner or later. George knew of a few examples.

In the mid-fifties, Joseph Patrick 'Joey' Turner had been the main man in Richmond and wanted everyone to know it. A Painter and Docker, Turner had swaggered around the pubs of Richmond dressed like a Hollywood gangster, down to the diamond in one of his front teeth. It hadn't ended well for him. In 1959, local police lowered the boom, allegedly planting an arsenal of weapons in Turner's Collingwood house, including six handguns and some homemade nail bombs. Turner was effectively finished as a power after that and survived only by informing on other crooks in his brief stints outside jail. In this jealous and often vicious milieu, it wasn't a good idea to stand out too much. The Kanes, who had deep links with police and politicians, were a notable exception, though their story too was to end in blood by the early 1980s. George relied on the fact that if he didn't step on other people's toes, they would stay off his.

But all that was in the future. For now, George was just doing his best, making connections that would help him get ahead. Life was all about what you got, not what you gave. He and Barb had started life on the scrap heap and he wasn't going back to that. If he had to, George would fight for what he believed was his, and he could justify anything if it was done for the sake of family. In these years, George took what opportunities came along, if it was moving some stolen goods, growing a bit of marijuana, it was all part of surviving. In the early 1980s, police caught George with some electric fans that had gone missing from a warehouse, but he got off lightly with a good behaviour bond.

But then something changed in George. The circumstances leading up to the change have been shrouded in mystery for a long time. Nobody in the family ever talked about it openly, least of all George. There was a dispute with a cocky young man in a Richmond pub over a game of pool. Apparently, the man had accused George of cheating or hustling him. Then, without warning, the man glassed George, destroying the sight of his left eye. The story goes that soon after the incident, the young man was found dead from a heroin overdose, the syringe still in his arm. There were never any charges laid and it's doubtful whether police ever connected it with George, if indeed he had anything to do with it.

A pool player values his eyesight more than anything else. George was never quite the same player again. Whether this was enough to inspire him to revenge is uncertain.

To his son Carl, George's experience showed that minding one's own business might not be enough. Even winning fair and square might not protect you from the wilful stupidity and jealousy of others. Who knows how that seed of revenge was planted in Carl, but one wonders what he saw when he looked in his father's dead eye.

4

CRIMINAL ROYALTY

'So this is how the great and notorious Moran crime family ends,' Bert Wrout is fond of saying.

'In the greater scheme of things, in 100 years' time, what's going to be remembered? Nothing . . . fuckin' nothing, maybe a line in a book or two. A postscript in Melbourne's bloody social history – "The Morans were dominant criminal figures in the 1980s to the '90s and were wiped out in a gangland war."'

They had paraded around, thinking they were criminal royalty, says Wrout. They had looked down on people like Carl Williams and his family. Scum and shitmen from Broadmeadows, they had called them, as if they were something much better.

Looking back on his life, Herbert Wrout says his greatest regret is that he stuck to the Moran family until the end. Perversely, it is a source of pride too. Even if the Morans were nothing more than dogs, rats and give-ups, Wrout still holds his head high. When everyone else was dead or long gone, Bert stuck by Lewis Moran's side. He had been in the sweets with Lewis, and on 31 March 2004 it was time to taste the sours.

That night, two masked gunmen, Evangelos Goussis and Noel Faure, had run into Sydney Road's Brunswick Club, where Wrout was propping up the bar with Lewis. He and Lewis had known someone was coming for them. Carl had promised as much in telephone calls to Lewis over the preceding months.

The police had offered Lewis protection and advised him to change his routine, but he wouldn't have it. They would rather have died than give Carl the satisfaction of seeing them cower behind the cops like dogs, says Wrout.

So at the usual time they were standing in their appointed places at the bar. Lewis had his back to the wall in the corner, with one eye on the races on the telly and the other watching the front door for the approach of his executioner, as always.

For Wrout, even eight years on, those moments still come back to him every day. He remembers the cry of fear that Lewis had made when Goussis ran into the bar, the shotgun raised to his shoulder. 'Looks like we're off here,' said Lewis, Wrout recalls.

He remembers Lewis's desperate attempt to escape, running through to the back of the club where the pool tables and poker machines were. The club's CCTV footage showed Moran had pushed over a bar stool to impede his pursuer but Goussis had just vaulted it and was right on Lewis's tail. Lewis had then crashed into the club manager Sandra Sugars coming from the other direction. Goussis had Lewis cornered but his shotgun had jammed so he drew a handgun from his pocket and from point-blank range had shot Lewis in the left side of the head. He had put another in him for good measure. This was, after all, a $150 000 job. It wouldn't have done to leave anything to chance.

After the shots, Wrout remembers running for the front door, only to be confronted by the sound of the second gunman, Faure, coming in to back up his mate. Faure said, 'Gotcha now, old man,' as he levelled a 9-mm handgun at him.

'Go and get fucked, you weak cunt,' Wrout shouted back. He began to charge at the gun; he wasn't going to die without a fight. That's when Faure let off the first shot.

Getting shot is like being hit by a freight train, Wrout says. The bullet had ripped through his right arm, just below the elbow, and blasted out two centimetres of bone before ploughing into his chest cavity. The terrible impact spun him around and pushed him backwards towards the bar.

Wrout remembers trying to hold himself upright, clinging to the bar as long as he could. If he went down, he was as good as dead, he'd thought. Everything was swimming before his eyes. As his body went into shock, the scene took on a surreal sense. Wrout's ears were still ringing from the gunshot so the screams of the terrified witnesses seemed far away and muffled. The gunman morphed into a terrifying phantasm, a slavering, furious creature, half-man half-dog, barking at him over and over: 'WOOAAH! WOOAAH! WOOAAH! WOOAAH! WOOAAH!'

'What the fuckin' hell . . .' thought Wrout before he finally slumped to the floor. Later, Wrout learnt that Faure had not been barking but spraying shots all around him. Miraculously, five rounds had missed, hitting instead the brass rail of the bar, a statuette on the counter and the wall behind.

Wrout's next memory is of being loaded onto a gurney by the paramedics.

'How's me mate?' he had asked.

'Your mate was dead before he hit the floor,' the ambo replied.

Much later on and Wrout still doesn't know why he called Lewis his mate that day. It burns him each time he is mentioned in the media as 'Lewis Moran's mate' or a 'Moran family associate'. Wrout's rancour has grown more toxic and self-destructive with time.

'Me *mate*?. . . He wasn't my *mate*!' he says almost cringing with shame. Maybe it's the dreams, he says. Every night he is back in the Brunswick Club, reliving the gunfire, the sirens, the screams of onlookers and Lewis's pitiful cry. Or he is in a shoot-out with the dog-man who's barking and slavering at him. And just when he tries to pull the trigger, his gun turns into a hammer or some other builder's tool, he says.

The dreams bring the regrets flooding back. He is usually with Lewis again, running from a formless enemy through the streets of inner Melbourne. They are swallowed up by a tunnel made of rusty corrugated iron collapsing around them as they plunge into darkness.

Or they're back in the Brunswick Club replaying Lewis's death in endless variations. Rendered helpless, he is consumed by the predator, the bullets ripping his flesh apart. He dies over and over in his dreams for his loyalty to Lewis. In life, he had put himself in the crossfire of Carl's war with the Morans. He had taken a bullet for Lewis, someone who couldn't give a fuck for him.

All he has left now is his integrity. He has scruples, principles. He can be trusted and relied on. He has never given up anyone in his entire life. Yet he will forever be linked to the Morans, a family of rats, shitmen and informers, he says. He has been asked so many times why he had stayed faithful to the Morans. It's the greatest paradox of his life, he says.

And the best answer Wrout can come up with is that it had 'suited him', and at the time he had enjoyed his line of work. But for a short stint in the book trade, Bert had been a crook all his life.

Back in the old days there were only a few hundred crooks nationwide and everyone knew each other, who was a shitman or a dog, who could be trusted. The gold standard was a bloke you could bury a body with, and he was rare. Mostly people came together for specific jobs or commodities. These alliances shifted depending on what was required to achieve the goal.

Wrout had been cursed with enough intelligence to know he was too smart for everyday work. His family had one of the first telephones in West Melbourne and as a kid every Saturday he would run the prices down to the SP bookies in the laneways and pubs. His mother made three quid a week off it. You took advantage of your upbringing and whatever opportunities it offered.

Bert and Lewis had come together because of guns, which were a speciality of Bert's. The two had become especially close when, in the 1980s, the Morans had moved into drugs, supplying the ecstasy party scene that was booming in Melbourne. Lewis had always been tight with money, mean even. You even had to watch your change on the bar when Lewis was around. But sometimes that change might turn into twenty or thirty grand. And there were other attractions. It was flattering for a man of fifty to have a nineteen-year-old groupie stroking his cock at the bar of the Laurel Hotel. It was amazing what a nineteen-year-old would do for a line of speed or a pill.

The Morans sat at the top of the tree, their prosperity built on guns, drugs and stolen property. They were connected to, and respected by, all who mattered in the underworld. Lewis's closest friend was Graham 'the Munster' Kinniburgh, universally regarded as one of the best crims of all time. If there were a Mister Big of Australia, it was the Munster, an old-style crook who commanded respect not through fear but common sense – he could be trusted. The Munster's network included gangsters, old and new, lawyers, police, politicians and more than a few gunmen. Lewis was lucky to have him onside, Wrout says, given Moran's many failings.

As for Bert, he was convenient to the Morans, an associate used to run errands, to carry their firearms and to take a fall if needed. He had no illusions about how this was going to end. Everyone who grew up in West Melbourne, including Bert, knew how the Morans had got to where they were.

In the 1950s, Lewis's mother, Belle, carried out illegal abortions in partnership with a crooked police inspector. The story went that the policeman would leave a key under the mat at home when he and the family left for the day. Belle and her assistants would take the kitchen table into the garage, where they would perform their grisly operations. At night, the cop's family would come home and eat dinner off the same table.

Later, in the 1960s, Belle brazenly operated out of premises next to the County Court on La Trobe Street in the city. Nice girls from middle-class families could find 'good' doctors to fix their mistakes.

Poor ones went to butchers like Moran. God knows how many women were mutilated and how many more died after visiting Belle Moran's 'clinic'. But Belle made more than a comfortable living from it, as did her police protectors. It was enough to make old-time crims turn in their graves, says Wrout. According to fair dinkum knockabouts, in those days you couldn't find a lower occupation than backyard abortionist.

Lewis's father, Desmond, gave the family a touch of respectability as an SP bookmaker, based at the Pastoral Hotel in Flemington. But he was also a low thief, according to Wrout: 'He was a cheap miserable thing, who was renowned for stealing the tills off bar counters.' And stealing from a publican was considered a cardinal sin.

While the Williamses and Denmans were battling for survival in the squalor of Camp Pell, the Morans were living a comfortable existence in Ascot Vale. Dessie had two sons: Lewis, born in 1941, and Desmond 'Tuppence', born eight years later. His father had so nicknamed Des because he wasn't worth a tuppence to anyone.

Lewis and Tuppence would never know the feeling of going hungry, as Barbara and George had in their early days. Things came easily to the Morans, they always had. They had started out as slaughtermen in the abattoirs of Newmarket in the northern suburbs. According to Wrout, this was where Lewis had learnt to 'go in for the kill without conscience'.

Soon both Moran brothers found their way to the racetrack, where the work was less demanding and their father was a leading personality. Dessie's contemporaries included William 'Wee Jimmy' Lloyd, one of the best trackside thieves that Melbourne ever produced, and Mickie Mutch. Mutch was the prince of pickpockets, or 'takes' as they were known back then. Every race day you would find Mutch and his team mingling with the punters in the betting ring, or on the trams and trains home from the track, where they would follow any bloke with a smile on his face and relieve him of his winnings. For years, young police officers at the training depot were shown a mugshot of Mutch as part of their instruction.

Lewis had been one of Mutch's most-promising apprentices in the 1960s, and the master thief taught him how to plunder without mercy. It didn't matter if the victim was a workingman; if he didn't watch his wallet, he was fair game. Lewis's young mate Graham Kinniburgh tried his hand at the trade too, but found it wasn't to his liking: there was something about robbing ordinary blokes that offended him.

From his mentor, Mickie Mutch, Lewis also learnt that you needed a copper or two in your pocket if you were going to be a successful crook. Fortunately, Lewis had grown up in the same street as the boy destined to be one of the most senior officers in Carlton. Belle had virtually brought up the future cop in her own home, and the strong ties between the two families reportedly served Lewis well in later years. As well as his SP activities, Lewis was a major fence for stolen goods in the Flemington and Moonee Ponds areas. He was prepared to dabble in whatever criminal enterprise was going.

Lewis's future wife, Judith Brooks, had also grown up in the relative comfort of Northcote in Melbourne's north. The family of Judy's mother, Olive McShanag, had owned a couple of pubs in Carlton and was rather well-to-do.

Her father, Leo Brooks, was a knockabout who'd gained a reputation as a fixer in his thirty years of working as a general assistant at the Carlton Football Club. Known as 'the Godfather of Drummond Street', Brooks would billet young Carlton footballers from the bush or interstate in his home, while doing a brisk trade selling them stolen goods. His house became known as 'Leo's Emporium'. Leo's brother 'Boysie' Brooks was a leading SP bookmaker and a contemporary of Dessie Moran.

But Judy grew up away from all that. She liked to paint herself as a genteel young woman with a passion for ballroom dancing. Even so, criminal connections never seemed to be far away. She had known the budding Melbourne gangster Alphonse Gangitano from when he was sixteen because their fathers both loved the Carlton footy club.

Although she was ten years older than Gangitano, Judy thought of him as a younger brother, another member of the family.

Judy had a short stint working as a department-store shop assistant, during which time she acquired a taste for life's finer things. But she quickly ditched work when she found it was easier to steal whatever she wanted. She became one of the champion shoplifters of her day, but to her this was just a pastime while she looked for a man to make her dreams of luxury come true.

Wrout says her father Leo had regarded Judy from the age of five as the worst liar he had ever come across. 'He said to me when she was about twenty-one: "She is the greatest cunt that God has ever put breath into and always will be." ' Judy's choice of men confirmed her preference for the louche criminal lifestyle. Leslie 'Johnny' Cole was a highly popular crook in Melbourne. He had made his name around the Melbourne docks as an enforcer and hired gun. He was good-looking and dashing and Judy fell hard for him.

They were married in March 1963 and a year later she gave birth to a son, Mark. But the marriage didn't last and five months later Judy left Cole. He didn't mourn her departure.

Cole didn't play much of a role in his son's life. Cole later left Melbourne for Sydney, to work for Frederick 'Paddles' Anderson, then the undisputed boss of crime in the harbourside capital. By 1965, Judy had taken up with her new partner, Lewis Moran.

Like many former Melbourne gunnies, Johnny Cole liked to keep his hand in down south, and remained an occasional player in the dock wars that raged through the 1970s.

But Cole was making enemies in Sydney too. In October 1982, there had been an unsuccessful attempt on his life. A month later, he was arriving home after a physiotherapy session when two gunmen, thought to be Christopher Dale 'Rent-a-kill' Flannery and

Mick Sayers, opened fire on him. His house in Kyle Bay was fortified but he never made it inside. Cole was said to be the first victim of a Sydney gangland war that would go on to claim the lives of eight of Sydney's finest hoods. The reality may be less glamorous: other sources suggest that someone ordered the hit on Cole because they didn't like the way he treated women.

Whatever the case, in taking up with Lewis, Judy had swapped one abusive thug for another. In September 1967, Judy gave birth to Lewis's son, Jason, and the criminal brood was complete. With vicious killers as fathers and a lazy shoplifter with delusions of grandeur for a mother, the boys never had a chance.

5

THE PRINCES OF DARKNESS

Mark and Jason Moran grew up in what looked like a middle-class household. They lived in a nice house and always had lots of money, though they were careful not to talk about what their father did to get it. The steady stream of criminals running in and out of the Moran's Ascot Vale home would have convinced any visitor that this was not the abode of a workingman.

Though they were three years apart in age, the half-brothers were very close. They had both witnessed Lewis's brutality towards their mother. In his early days, Lewis had been a tough guy feared by all, but as he aged he reserved his best punches for women and other defenceless targets. Judy copped regular savage beatings from Lewis, especially when he was drunk. Judy had a smart mouth and a way of pushing Lewis's buttons but nothing could justify the abuse she suffered. There were times when Jason and Mark were terrified that Lewis was going to kill her.

The boys copped their fair share of violence too, yet as Jason grew, he could see that his father treated Mark differently from him. Lewis resented having to look after Johnny Cole's kid and took it out on Mark. Bert Wrout says Lewis's treatment of Mark amounted to torture and obscene cruelty, behaviour that would scar the boy for life. Lewis once bragged of suspending Mark from a fence and beating him senseless. And for what? Nothing in particular. Wrout long suspected that Lewis was a sadist or a closet homosexual, or both. This was confirmed when they were together in prison on drug charges in 2003. Bert came to the view that Lewis was a dog, a coward and a sexual predator of the lowest order. He tells a story of a young man forced to share a cell with Lewis. The next day the kid begged the warders not to make him stay another night with Moran, who had raped him brutally all night.

The dysfunction in the family brought the two boys closer together. Jason idolised his older brother and in return Mark protected Jason, who from an early age found it difficult to back down from a fight, especially when he had a bigger older brother to step in for him. One classmate from Ascot Vale West Primary School remembers Mark standing over another kid at school because Jason was short twenty cents for lunch: 'The kid's first refusal got him a punch in the guts, the second a kick when he was down. Finally, he coughed up the twenty cents. All of this happened in the blink of an eye, like no thought had to go into it. It was learnt behaviour. Even back then you could see the debt of protection and brotherhood that existed between Mark and Jason.'

Despite a brutal home life, Mark grew up to be the shining light of the family. To his friends, he was a rock star, a Hollywood leading man. According to Bert Wrout, Mark was big, strong and handsome with 'more dash than Errol Flynn and Clark Gable put together'. He was fearless but tortured by self-doubt and depression that lived with him his whole life. The contrast between Mark and Carl could not have been more marked. Carl had grown up with very little except the love of his family, while Mark had everything but.

Mark was a gifted athlete and could have been a top-flight Australian Rules footballer had a career in organised crime not prevailed. In addition to this talent, Mark had a nasty streak that made him a feared adversary. Once Mark got over the top of a rival, there was no mercy.

Jason wanted to emulate his brother's prowess in footy but he lacked his talent so he compensated with intense physicality. He made himself into a scrapper who would be at the centre of every fight, at the bottom of every pack. Finally when his lack of pace was exposed, Jason took to king-hitting opponents in back play and was eventually banned from local footy.

By contrast, Mark was graceful and athletic, the consummate schoolyard player and a bright, good-looking kid. He was a natural leader among his peers who could charm the pants off teachers and get away with the playground equivalent of murder.

Mark had dash from an early age. In Year 6, he was best mates with another kid from the Kensington Community School, Jedd Houghton. They'd later commit armed hold-ups together. Through Houghton, Moran would be introduced to Melbourne's hardest men, while Houghton would go on to be involved in a plot to murder two police constables in Walsh Street, South Yarra. Houghton was shot down in a Bendigo caravan park later that year as the Special Operations Group tried to bring him in over Walsh Street.

Lewis was raising little gangsters, there's no doubt about it. From their late teens, his sons were used as muscle to enforce Lewis's will over lesser beings in the local area. For example, one night Lewis was drinking at his favourite hotel, the Laurel in Ascot Vale, with Bert Wrout. Lewis regarded the Laurel as his turf, a place where anybody misbehaving could expect summary justice from him. That night a well-known villain and his friend were drinking at the bar. The friend decided it would be a lark to pour himself a beer while the barman's back was turned. Lewis was incensed. He took a poker from the fireplace and crept up behind the bloke and let him have it on the back of the head. The victim was dazed but not out. Blood streaming from his head, he flogged Lewis with a bar stool.

Lewis, his dignity crushed, ordered Mark and Jason to hunt down his attacker or any of his friends and deal with them. Three men were shot in the legs or shoulders that night, but no one ran to the cops. People understood the power of the Morans.

Jason's only ambition in life was to become a gangster, like he'd seen in the movies. At fourteen, he had his own handgun, which he showed off at football practice. The following year, 1982, he met Trisha Kane – daughter of the notorious Les Kane – whom he later married.

It was a good marriage for the Morans in terms of underworld prestige. The Kanes and Morans had been on the same side in the most recent underworld stoush. In 1976, armed robber Raymond 'Chuck' Bennett had pulled off a mammoth heist on the Victoria Racing Club, which became known as 'the great bookie robbery'. The Kanes had wanted their cut of the loot, thought to be $16 million in cash, even though they hadn't been involved. This set off a murderous chain of events.

In October 1978, Bennett and his gang killed Les Kane in his bathroom while his wife and two young children were held at gunpoint in other rooms of their unit. Four years later Kane's brother, Brian, was shot dead in the bar of a Brunswick hotel. It wasn't entirely unexpected. Brian had been the prime suspect when Bennett had been murdered inside the Melbourne Magistrates Court in 1979.

Jason was feared but not respected among Melbourne crooks. After leaving school, he worked as a slaughterman like his father and later on the docks: he had the pedigree but most believed he was a violent loon. One minute Jason was all friendliness and charm, the next he would be breaking a bottle over your head. This unpredictability only worsened when he began hitting the cocaine hard from his twenties onwards.

Mark was the Moran whom everyone wanted to be near. Jason came with the package. From the early 1990s Mark began building an empire selling cocaine and cannabis. Carl's brother, Shane, had bought his smoke from a house in Broadmeadows that Mark Moran had used as a base. Shane disliked the Moran brothers, though he was their regular customer. They had treated him with contempt even as they took his money, the same way they dealt with the rest of their clientele. If people didn't like it, they could fuck off. There were plenty of others who would humble themselves for the chance to buy their gear.

Like Carl, Mark and Jason grew up with an unshakeable sense of entitlement. They weren't bound by the same rules as others. The Morans behaved like princes of the Melbourne underworld, set to inherit the kingdom. This would prove their undoing. And it would eventually bring their entire family down.

6

SHANE AND DEANA

The first time Deana Falcone saw Shane Williams outside of a jail or a courtroom, he was standing at her parents' front door, on the run from the law. It was 1990 and Shane had just been paroled after twelve months in jail for theft. Shane's bail conditions required that he complete a twelve-month live-in rehabilitation program at Odyssey House for his heroin addiction. He lasted two days before staff had ordered him to clean a floor with a toothbrush. He wasn't about to lower himself like that for anyone so he absconded and went straight to Deana.

For her, it was the start of a destructive and turbulent six-year relationship with Shane and a lifelong bond with the Williams family.

A few months earlier, Carl Williams had turned up at a house Deana was sharing with a young girlfriend, Misty. He was sitting on her couch, a chubby, self-conscious kid in his Ralph Lauren streetwear, his runners immaculate, as though they were straight from the box. With his dimples and rosy cheeks, he looked like a big, plump baby dressed up by Mum for a trip to the mall.

Carl had met Misty at a nightclub and he had begun taking her out shopping and spoiling her, but they never slept together. Carl was twenty and to Deana he seemed polite, shy and even a bit immature. Or maybe he was just aloof. Even though Carl would happily talk about himself, or at least his clothing and appearance, he was insecure about his weight and needed reassurance, she could tell.

Deana had never met a kid who loved going shopping more than Carl. Every other week, he would be down at the factory seconds shops on Smith Street, Collingwood, buying up the latest Adidas leisurewear. He was also building a collection of Ralph Lauren gear that he reserved for formal occasions. Everything was always spotless and perfectly ironed by his mother. Later, Barb would confide to Deana that growing up Carl had been so neat and fastidious that she had worried there was something wrong with him.

As a kid Carl had played footy and soccer, but he would always come home with his uniform perfectly clean. He just hated getting dirty, unlike the other boys. She once threatened to stop Carl playing unless he got stuck in like the rest. He made a token effort. After all, he had already found a way to make money from junior sport. His coach, Dennis Reardon, reported that Carl had been charging the parents money to park their cars at the ground.

Carl was certainly self-centred, but not in a malicious way. He just didn't know how to engage in conversation that wasn't about him. He would just tune people out. His greatest fear was being drawn into a lengthy conversation about someone else's problems. He could not even feign sympathy; he would just remove himself from the situation. From the earliest age, he had come to believe that the world revolved around him.

Yet there was still something attractive about Carl, and Deana had taken an immediate liking to him. Carl was gentle and respectful, not in any way tough. For one thing, he was terrified of spiders; just the mere mention of one and he would flee in terror.

There was even something a bit feminine about Carl, something his friends could never quite put a finger on. 'He was just that little bit feminine,' she says, laughing.

Carl would often turn up at Deana's place with his Broadie crew, the twin brothers Travis and Heath Day, Wes, Buzza, Terry Tolra and a revolving selection of associates. They were just ordinary young blokes with no greater desire than getting on the piss and chasing girls. None of them even remotely looked like they were headed for a life of crime.

Carl was the leader of the group, no question. He was good company in a group, constantly 'shit-stirring' and 'taking the piss'. That was his mode of communication, he entertained himself and others by needling his mates. He wasn't the smartest, the funniest, the best-looking or most athletic, but he was the most generous, by far. He had been like that since all the lads had met at school. His generosity drew people to him, even bullies who had once stood over him became his friends. Carl had learnt that everyone has their price.

Carl had left school in Year 11 despite his parents' objections. They had hoped he might go on to tertiary education, which would have been a first for either of their broods. But there had been a scandal over an alleged sexual assault of a girl in the school toilets. Nothing ever came of it, most probably because Carl had abruptly left the school soon after. He wasn't interested in education anyway. His favourite subject had been maths and he had learnt all he needed to know – just enough to count his money.

After school, Carl had stacked shelves at the local supermarket for a while. His parents had organised a glazing apprenticeship for him, but he showed no enthusiasm for it. Then they had arranged a position for him with a gardening business, but he had showed no skill or interest in that either: he mowed down the prize roses of one client and poisoned the lawn of another before he gave up. By the time he met Deana, Carl was supporting himself by selling a little marijuana, or maybe it was quite a bit, judging from the wad of bank notes he always carried.

Whenever the crew went out on the town, it was always Carl paying. He didn't have a car or a driver's licence, so Wes used to drive him around all day. He seemed to resent being driven around in Wes's battered Toyota Corolla but he had no choice. He used to say he wasn't going to buy a car until he could afford a Merc or a Beemer.

During one night out, Carl talked to Deana about his brother, Shane, who was in Beechworth jail. Deana had grown up in a working-class family as square as a butter box, as criminals describe citizens, but when Carl asked if she would write to Shane in jail, she thought, 'Why not? It might be something different.' As they corresponded, Deana found herself falling for Shane. 'Pear', as he was known by all, was funny and self-deprecating and seemed a little bit dangerous.

Deana thought she could change Shane, the fatal mistake made by so many women who hook up with prisoners. He had been in jail for each of the past five Christmases, punctuated by short interludes of freedom. She began writing to him each week.

Deana went along to Shane's court hearings and met his family. She could see something in Shane beyond the heroin, the tattoos and the complete lack of ambition. There was evidence of a strong bond among the Williams family, which Deana admired. She had given birth to Benjamin when she was just seventeen; the father hadn't wanted a bar of the kid from the beginning. She felt alone in the world and the Williams welcomed her and Benjamin into their circle.

All except one of Barb's ten siblings had children struggling with drug or alcohol addiction. It was like a family curse. Several, like Shane, got on heroin while others hit the grog hard and went off the rails. When the kids came out of rehab, they would stay with their nan, Mary Denman, for a while; her place became a kind of halfway house, according to Deana.

Mary lived alone in a filthy one-bedroom unit in Richmond with her Jack Russell terriers. The dogs relieved themselves wherever they pleased and the place was coated in dog hair and stunk of piss. Many of Mary's children were dealing with their own issues: gambling, grog and domestic violence. They had escaped the abject poverty of their childhood but substance abuse created fault lines in the family.

While everyone in the Williams family agreed that Deana was good for Shane, no one considered whether the reverse was true. Her devotion to Shane would cause Deana the greatest pain and suffering. She would lose herself entirely to the abusive, destructive relationship.

At the beginning, Shane kept his drug use away from Deana, but over time he relaxed and began shooting up in front of her. She saw the full ugly truth of his heroin habit. Deana never succumbed to the drug – otherwise they both might have died. Not only did she keep him alive for years, she also kept him out of prison for the longest period of his adult life. And, in return, he kicked the shit out of her.

Domestic violence was rife in the suburbs back then. Women expected, even tolerated, an occasional clip on the ear from their men, but what Deana copped from Shane was something else.

'A few clips would have been all right,' Deana says.

'I got a broken jaw, I got king hit. I got beaten in front of my kid till I was out cold. I got choked, battered, kicked in the face. I got dragged across the floor by my hair. I got smashed in the face with a club lock,' she remembers.

There were many violent moments with Shane but the club-lock attack had been the worst. Deana was driving Shane down the Tullamarine Freeway in search of heroin. Shane was hanging out but couldn't locate his dealer. Deana made the mistake of asking whether they should take the Brunswick Road exit. In response, he hit her flush on the jaw with the club lock.

Shane Williams began his fatal love affair with heroin in his mid-teens. An imposing figure at 188 cm and 125 kilos, he was intelligent and humorous, universally popular. Unlike his shy little brother, Shane was an outgoing, gregarious character. But heroin hooked him hard and didn't let him go till it killed him fifteen years later. To feed his habit he became involved in the usual petty crime of the heroin addict: shop break-ins and the occasional burglary. Substance abuse had touched almost all the families in the Denman and Williams clans, but Shane's criminal history set him apart.

Shane was never invited to functions with the extended family for fear he would nick something or cause some other drama.

However, Shane firmly believed he had some honour, even if he was a hopeless junkie. He never stole from his family to finance his habit, as most of his peers did. That was weak, Shane believed. 'Why pick on your family when there are all those shops out there to choose from?' he used to say.

Early on, Carl had tagged along on some of Shane's adventures, though he had little enthusiasm for his brother's kind of crime. As he grew older, Carl considered stealing beneath him. Murder was acceptable but not theft – that was an act of desperation.

Back when Carl was fifteen, Shane's prolific thieving brought him to the attention of the local cops. The police saw the big, soft kid as an easy mark: a little roughing up would persuade him to lag his brother. But throughout the ordeal Carl kept quiet even though he was deathly afraid. Barb was called to Broadie police station to pick up Carl. She found him sobbing in the waiting room. Through his tears, he said a sergeant had bashed him around the head with a telephone book. He had pissed his pants in terror.

It changed him, Barb said. Until then, Carl had been set on becoming a policeman when he grew up. The idea had gone out the window that day.

Like Carl, Shane was generous and felt he had to buy his friends. Shane was forever scoring heroin for other people. Someone would ring up, hanging out for a fix, and Shane would race off to shoplift enough stuff to buy a cap. If he got caught hoisting, he'd do the jail time, no dramas. He would even put his hand up for things he hadn't done to save his friends from jail. He earnt a reputation for being staunch, for all the good it did him, but it was something he clung to dearly. In Shane's world, you didn't tell on people, not anyone, not even your enemies, not even coppers when they belted you. There was precious little else in his life that meant much – just his family, his relationship with Deana and the motley crew of fawning junkies.

Of course, these hopeless parasites loved Shane. Deana thought if she could just get Pear away from them, he'd have a better chance of getting clean. He would get a job and make something of his life. She was kidding herself. Shane craved the popularity as much as the smack. Without it, he feared that he had nothing to offer people.

George and Barb had already done everything they could to get him clean, paying for numerous stints in rehab. Finally, his father had to conclude that Shane didn't want to be saved.

Against her family's wishes, Deana immersed herself in the Williamses' household and was soon staying there four or five nights a week.

'These people need to get out of the seventies,' Deana thought to herself the first time she walked into the Williamses' house. The decor was in tones of brown and tan from the cheap wall veneers to the rocker recliners in the lounge.

On any given day, Deana would find the family in more or less the same position, doing much the same thing: Shane, George and Barb would be on the couch in the living room, reading the form guide with the races on the telly; Carl would be lying on his bed, reading the form guide with the races on the telly, a pudgy Pomeranian dog named Ozzie by his side. Carl's TV was inside a built-in wardrobe with a shelf above, on which he kept his numerous bottles of aftershave and cologne like others might display sporting trophies.

To break the monotony, the family would occasionally gather around the Nintendo console in Shane's room to play Super

Mario Bros. Carl rarely played for long. He wasn't much good and would soon retire to his room, mocking the others as he went.

The rest of the day, the family could be found lying on their beds, watching the same program on different televisions. Carl might call out that one of his mates was coming to pick him up to get McDonald's. The walls were so thin they could communicate with each other from one end of the house to the other in normal speaking voices. It was always the same routine.

'Would anyone like anything?' Carl would say.

'What have they got there, son?' George would ask.

'Burgers and stuff, Dad.'

'Oh, well, get me some of what you're having, Carl.'

'No worries, Dad,' Carl would say, halfway out the door, but he would invariably come home hours later with nothing.

Other nights, Carl was too lazy to get off his bed and would pay Shane to run errands for him.

'Hey, Pear, go up to the shop and get me an Eskimo Pie, wouldja?' Carl would call out. 'I'll put fifty bucks in your TAB account.' And Shane, broke as usual, would always do his little brother's bidding.

Carl's friends usually came to him. The door was always open and the house frequently full. That's how Barb liked it too, running around after Carl and his mates. Watching from the kitchen window as they splashed in the pool; she used to think nothing was ever too much trouble. She was pleased Carl was popular. The world held fears for wimpy little boys like Carl. With a strong group of mates around him, he could achieve whatever he wanted to.

Barb kept the house running. In fact, she was the only one who ever did anything. Even Ozzie the dog was as slothful as his owners. On the odd occasion Ozzie would be taken for a walk to the shop, he would refuse to walk at about the halfway point and have to be carried home. Barb would buy a roast chicken, take off the skin, and cut it into bite-sized chunks for Ozzie. If Carl was the golden child, then Ozzie wasn't far behind.

George had long since stopped working. He had hurt his back on the job and got a healthy worker's compensation payment. Then he had heart problems, which required three bypass operations.

By his mid-forties, George was done with any work beyond tending his cypress hedges, mowing the lawn and keeping the pool functioning. He had coached local juniors' footy at Oak Park Football Club for years, but that had gone by the wayside too when his health had declined. Barb continued to work at the TAB on Dorset Road, Pascoe Vale, but she was the only one in the household earning an honest dollar. Carl used to go down to help Barb out at work but that was rare. Barb didn't mind being the only worker, though: it gave her a sense of purpose.

Every night there would be a meal on the table or at least on a tray in the bedroom. And every night at ten o'clock, Barb would get up to bring George tea and toast in bed.

A big family outing was a night at Moonee Valley Raceway. They would play the pokies, place small bets on every race, and enjoy a meal in air-conditioned comfort. Shane and Deana always stayed with Barb and George, but not Carl. He was always off with the SP bookies by the course. He didn't want to be seen with his family around these guys.

His nan, Barb's mother, Mary, would often be there, now looking like Mrs McGillicuddy, a toothless old hag from the variety show *Hey Hey It's Saturday*. Her foul mouth and appetite for the punt were undiminished even in her eighties. One night, after feeding a poker machine all her money, she lost her cool.

'If you're that fuckin' hungry,' Nan screeched, raising her pie above her head, 'then eat this, ya cunt!' She dashed the pie in the blinking face of the machine and ground it to pieces.

Shane and Deana had to shuffle Nan away from the machine.

Such were the priceless family memories. Once a year, the family would make a trip to Yarrawonga, a resort town on the Murray River where they would rent a cabin and do much the same as they did at home, watch television, punt and drink. They filled family albums with years of the same images over and over.

Although the day-to-day lives of the Williamses were mundane, there was a lot going on below the surface that no one ever talked about. There was no family discussion beyond who was going to win at Flemington that weekend or how many goals the star full-forward was going to kick in the match of the day. Barb made sure that everything was kept superficial, especially when it came to her marital issues. She had forbidden, for instance, all talk of George's affair with her sister Kath. Everyone was to pretend the illegitimate son produced by the union did not exist. To make sure of this Kath was ostracised from the extended family, as if she had somehow been the sole villain.

As a teenager, Shane had found out that his cousin was really his half-brother, and it had shattered him. Barb and George had made Shane promise never to tell Carl this shocking secret. Despite their best efforts, one night, in the early 1990s, it had spilled out in front of Carl. One of Barb's sisters and her husband were around, getting stuck into the piss with the family. Out of the blue, Carl's uncle had brought up the kid's name, taunting George about his other son. Everyone was thunderstruck. This was an unimaginable disaster. Barb and Shane had quickly shuffled Carl out of the room, but the genie was out of the bottle.

Carl was devastated that his father had cheated on his beloved mum with his Auntie Kath. To him, it was as if his family was inbred or something. It just ruined everything for Carl.

Carl already believed it was unfair that he had been born into poverty. He was better than his upbringing, so he thought, and

George's sleazy, grubby affair with Kath reflected badly on him. It was too awful to deal with, so no one ever mentioned it again, at least not as a family. Things were easier that way.

Carl never went to functions with his cousins after that. He was ashamed of what his father had done and he hated that everyone knew about it. The scandal seemed to weigh heavily on Carl and Shane. The night that Shane told Deana about his half-brother he had burst into tears. It was the worst shock of his life, he told her, one that was gradually undermining his family.

To the outsider, it appeared there was no moral core to this family, just a veneer of manners and cheerfulness. Underneath there was a coarse and cruel self-interest at play. It's tempting to suggest that Camp Pell, 'the breeding ground of spiritual and physical disease', had left its mark on the families that emerged. Not all those families were affected, but maybe in the Williams clan and others there was a bad gene at work. Maybe the Camp Pell chickens were coming home to roost, as *The Argus* in 1953 had warned they would.

While Barb and George were determined to stay together, this infidelity was corroding their relationship. It affected the family dynamic profoundly. Barb had gradually redirected her affection from George to Carl, and in the process Shane had missed out. Barb had always loved Carl more than Shane. It was a source of bitterness for her eldest son. He couldn't help that he was different to Carl. He couldn't make money like his brother did to buy his mum presents; he had to steal them. He wasn't a flash dresser like Carl in his designer gear. He was just as happy in stuff he had hoisted from KMart.

Barb admired Carl for his style and his ambition. If anyone was going to take the family places it was Carl. It didn't matter how he made his money as long as she didn't have to see it. Whatever Carl did was right by Barb.

Shane, on the other hand, was a disappointment to his mother. She never leapt to Shane's defence when Carl bagged him for being a loser and a junkie. 'Hey, Pear, how's your mate Sharky? Looks like all his teeth are falling out,' Carl would say to Shane.

Carl loved Shane, and they were close, but at the same time he despised him for his weakness. Over time, Shane's bond with his father became tighter.

Carl drew his mother ever closer. Occasionally, Deana would see Barb sitting on his bed, Carl lying beside her; the two talking quietly together. About what, she couldn't tell, but these were intimate conversations, stuff that Carl shared only with his mother. She was his confidante and sounding-board.

Barb tried hard to paper over the cracks in her family. At Christmas time, she would deck out the house with masses of decorations and lights. Carols and other festive music would play night and day, and she would make a huge fuss with presents and Christmas dinner. She would also always make a special chocolate cake for the boys' birthdays. These little things were signs of optimism. She would overcome the poverty of her upbringing that she regarded as a stain. Money would make up for the moral weakness slowly eating away at her marriage. Carl, with a little help from George, was going to make it all right. Barb deserved to get something back.

7

HEADING UPTOWN

Most of the important moments in Carl's life happened in the double lock-up garage at home in Broadie. George had taught his sons to play eight-ball and table tennis there. Shane had grown a small crop of marijuana in there. The cops had raided them and George had taken the fall for Shane. Later Carl and George would use the garage as a base for their amphetamine operation until the business outgrew the space.

But in October 1991, long before greed and the viciousness took over their lives, the garage was the venue for Carl's twenty-first birthday party. It was a big occasion for Barb too.

Shane had spent his twenty-first and several other birthdays in jail so Barb was determined to put on a memorable night for Carl. He was the golden child and this was the night she would show it. The garage was cleared out and a tarpaulin erected for the occasion; a huge spread of food and alcohol was laid on. Barb had made Carl his customary chocolate cake, complete with twenty-one candles.

Eighty people turned up and it began as an idyllic evening. Barb was hoeing into the champagne and got a bit weepy when Carl gave a short, awkward speech to thank his family for all they had done for him, especially his mum. He even thanked Deana for helping to organise the night. It touched Deana's heart – Carl wasn't one to express gratitude too freely.

The DJ turned up Bryan Adams' hit '(Everything I Do) I Do It For You', and the guests got back to getting shitfaced. There was no dancing at this sort of party just a steady consumption of alcohol.

Barb, in particular, was busy getting hammered. She loved being around Carl and his mates. On these nights when all these fit, rowdy young men were around her, Barb came alive.

There had been talk previously that Barb was a little too friendly with one of Carl's mates, Terry Tolra. Terry was a champion footballer with North Melbourne juniors. He was good-looking, charismatic, full of mischief and he had a thing for older women. If there was one kid who was destined to go off the rails, it was Terry. He'd been the first one to get into drugs and to get a tattoo. People used to say that Terry walked into the Williamses' house like he owned the joint, especially when George was not around.

The rumours burst into the open after Carl's party. One of the female guests had strayed down the back of the house and walked around a corner only to find Terry, his pants halfway down his thighs, vigorously humping Barb. What made matters worse was this girl had also been rooting Terry. She was outraged and in the days after the party, everyone found out about it.

From there, things fell apart quickly. Shane was feeling jealous of the attention that Carl was getting, and he got nasty. He had a drunken argument with a friend over a gold chain, which erupted into a brawl. Suddenly, there were plastic chairs flying, people crashing across tables, glass shattering and the nice white shirt that Barb had ironed for Shane was ripped open, exposing his belly.

Carl had stood back while this was all going on, even as he saw Shane getting a flogging. He wasn't a fighter and he certainly wouldn't have risked messing up his party outfit defending his brother. Even Ozzie did better than Carl, yapping and growling at the combatants' heels. The party broke up quickly, before the cops arrived, leaving Barb and Deana to clean up the wreckage. Shane was full of remorse for getting into a blue on Carl's special night.

The next morning, or maybe it was mid-afternoon, Barb put on one of her Sunday cooked breakfasts for the survivors. She acted as if nothing was amiss. She must have thought no one had noticed her quickie with Terry. Anyway, this infidelity was minor compared to George's dalliance with Kath. As long as she was there for the family, especially Carl, nothing else mattered.

During this time, George started hosting epic poker nights. They started out around the kitchen table, but grew so big that they had to take the games out to the garage, even building a special table to accommodate the numbers.

As the games got bigger, George expanded to include a circuit of six or so home venues, and every six weeks a different family hosted a night at their place. These were lucrative events for George; it wasn't uncommon to pull in five or ten grand if the players had enough dash, or got drunk enough, to bet big.

It was a family enterprise: Barb and Deana would organise the drinks and sandwiches for the players while George would act as dealer and banker. Shane would also be a dealer but was always begging George to be allowed to play. The whingeing would start the day before, but George never let him. Why should Shane occupy a seat a mug could use?

Carl would rarely show his face at these games, much less help run them. It was too much like hard work, the like of which he considered beneath him. He would stay in his room with Ozzie or head out with his mates. The card games seemed trivial; he was already thinking how he could make serious money. But, nevertheless, the poker nights did provide him with his big break, getting into drugs.

One of the regulars at the game was a small-time drug dealer named 'Kiwi' Joe Moran (no relation to Lewis Moran). Kiwi Joe had made a name for himself as a supplier of pseudoephedrine, a precursor for the production of speed; he was also active in distributing cocaine around the country. Kiwi Joe had a pretty young daughter called Priscilla, who would become Carl's first serious girlfriend. Priscilla was petite and gorgeous. Always immaculately dressed, she lived in a luxury high-rise apartment in the city. She didn't have to work and was always flush with cash, which she carried around in the latest Louis Vuitton handbags.

Carl was infatuated – with Priscilla but even more with the lifestyle that she led. This was the destiny that Carl craved but he was never going to attain it selling pot in Broadie. He needed to go uptown to mingle in the circles where the big money was. In Carl's simplistic view of life, he saw a chance to make up for the failure of his parents to make enough money. They had tried their best, but from here it was up to him. This all seemed to vindicate his earlier conclusion that working was for mugs.

Kiwi Joe welcomed him into his operation and soon Carl was doing runs to Perth carrying product. Carl was dependable and businesslike, which is not so common in the drug world. He understood money and its power. Even Kiwi Joe himself wasn't as professional. Carl complained that Moran had accompanied him to Perth on one occasion and lost the entire proceeds of the trip gambling at Burswood Casino.

Carl had begun to see less of his old mates from Broadie. They didn't fit with the new circles he was moving in. The old crowd still came around to the house and hung out, but they had less and less in common. While Carl was finding his way into the underworld, they were thinking of jobs, mortgages and saving up for weddings. Of Carl's mates, only Terry Tolra seemed set on a similar path but his life was cut short in a street fight. He was accidentally stabbed through the heart and died. It was a shock to everyone and a sure sign that life was changing.

Carl's world was changing too. One day Barb was sunbaking in a quiet corner of the back garden when one of Carl's new friends came outside and, oblivious to her presence, produced a handgun from his trousers. Barb was terrified; she had never seen a gun before. The man fired a few shots into the back fence before he noticed Barb there, cowering.

'Sorry,' he said. It was just a little target practice, he said sheepishly. Barb's whole body was shaking in terror. But in later interviews, I got the impression that there was a part of Barb that found Carl's new friends racy and exciting. She intimated that she had tried a pill or two and found the effect highly agreeable. There seemed to be no losers in this transaction. In a way, Carl was spreading happiness, she said.

Still, Carl couldn't risk letting people know what he was up to. He was becoming more circumspect, like most of the drug dealers he was meeting. Business was booming for him. He was branching out into speed and ecstasy, helping his new partners with the manufacturing process. Carl was on his way.

8

CLANDESTINE COPS

In the late 1990s, as it is today, a kilo bag of speed was worth $1 million on the street. And it was relatively easy to make.

Underground chemists in the US and Europe were posting their recipes on the internet. It opened up a new world of opportunity for a generation of DIY drug lords. Previously, the big money had been made from importing heroin and coke but now a fortune could be made with stuff they could buy at the local chemists, if they were able to access enough. All they needed was a reliable supply of chemicals, a remote location for the cook-up and a good network of dealers and heavies to take care of the business.

The beauty of this cottage industry was that if you were smart and disciplined, you could stay below the radar in the local drug scene. In this small gossipy milieu, word passed around quickly. If it became known a new player had a supply of chemicals, the dealers would soon be crawling all over them, trying to be their friends. But the people who confused friendship with business generally came unstuck.

If you avoided the big crews in the purchase of key ingredients like pseudoephedrine and red phosphorous, it was unlikely you would come to the notice of police. They focused their efforts on the big-noters who hung out in nightclubs, bragging of their success to anyone who would listen. When these sorts paraded themselves in nightclubs, it was a simple job for undercover police to work out the networks. But the penalties for getting caught with speed were relatively light. Back in the early nineties, a heroin trafficker might get sixteen to eighteen years' jail for a decent commercial quantity, whereas the same quantity of speed might see someone only receive four to five years.

In this period, seizures of amphetamines were outstripping heroin three to one. Speed didn't have the stigma that was attached to smack either. There was no sticking a dirty needle in your arm and seemingly no addiction issues, though it was certainly habit-forming. It was becoming Australia's drug of choice, the must-have accessory for the go-set. Ecstasy was a natural progression from this. It was a party in a pill, its destructive properties disguised in a colourful tablet stamped with a fashionable logo.

In 1991, Victoria Police had begun to use undercover agents and informers to ensnare the budding speed kings of Melbourne. Back then, citizens could buy all the precursor chemicals for amphetamine production at wholesale prices from chemical companies.

'It was ridiculously lax. The only legal requirement was that the buyer signed a form declaring they were using the chemicals for good not evil,' says one former drug squad officer. But the chemical companies did report large or suspicious buys to the drug squad. With supplies of speed and other party drugs starting to increase on the street, Victoria Police decided it was time for some innovative tactics. The very first job they called 'Operation Chances', named for a raunchy television show of the day, which focused on an ordinary family who'd won $3 million in a lottery. For the crooks, the easy availability of chemicals had been as good as winning the lottery but that was about to change.

A highly respected officer, Detective Senior Sergeant Wayne Strawhorn, posed as a staff member when the target arrived to pick up his supplies from the warehouse. Other cops were hiding, snapping pictures of the target and noting registration plates of vehicles. The crooks were then followed and photographed handing over the booty to a group of outlaw bikies, who were duly arrested.

Operation Chances was a spectacular success. Unlike its TV

counterpart, which was axed after just two years of offending public decency, the principle behind Operation Chances continued in one form or another for most of the 1990s. It turned Wayne Strawhorn into the poster boy of the drug squad. Strawhorn studied similar responses to the burgeoning amphetamine problem overseas and pushed for the creation of what became known as the 'Chemical Diversion Desk'. It involved finding crooks willing to sell precursor chemicals to the clandestine lab operators. Using listening devices and vehicle trackers, it was a simple matter of following the trails back to the labs. Most of the crooks were careless with their telephone use and the company they kept.

It worked so well for the cops that it became the preferred method of catching these crooks for a number of years. The police destabilised the drug elites almost at will, according to a former drug squad officer, Lachlan McCulloch.

'When the plan first came out, it was that successful we went from [busting] three or four labs to twelve to fifteen in twelve months – and these are major labs making speed,' he says. 'The only part where it fell down was the possible lack of checks and balances on the actual physical side of delivering the chemicals, because we were in a situation where we were making a profit.'

As regulation of precursor chemicals tightened from 1992 onwards, the street price of these vital ingredients skyrocketed. Chemicals previously bought at cost now fetched at least five times their value.

'Basically, the crooks would pay almost any price to get their hands on the chemicals. It was a long time before it dawned on the bosses that Victoria Police was now in the drug business too,' says another former officer.

Not surprisingly, the Clandestine Laboratories program turned a number of cops into villains, even its mastermind Wayne Strawhorn.

Drug squad officers on $75 000 a year were suddenly exposed to a business where the villains were making that kind of money in a weekend. They had access to the chemicals and the buyers, and virtually a free hand from the bosses, a sure-fire recipe for temptation.

By 2002, the Clandestine Laboratories program had collapsed, and many of the key officers who had run it, including Strawhorn, had been prosecuted or incarcerated. Even though the program had failed catastrophically, shaking the foundations of the police service, there was no denying it had successful elements. It had spread mistrust and suspicion throughout the underworld.

It was now even harder to distinguish friend from foe, as rumours circulated as to who was on the payroll of the drug squad.

Mark Moran's relationship with Strawhorn and a few other select members of the drug squad had made his family very powerful. Strawhorn had planned to take the Morans' operation down with the controlled deliveries of chemicals, but instead he became an illicit supplier to them. With the cops on their side, the Morans rose to a new level. And Jason let everyone know it, with the violence and attitude of someone untouchable.

By the mid-1990s, Carl had made a fateful decision to swap one Moran family for another. The partnership with Kiwi Joe had been profitable but Carl had greater ambitions. He had tired of Priscilla, whose youthful bloom was starting to fade from her heavy drug use.

He was ready to move on to a new crew. After his introduction to Mark Moran, his life changed profoundly. At this time, Bert Wrout was living next door to Suzanne Kane, the sister of Jason's girlfriend, Trish. Lewis regarded Suzanne as the daughter he'd never had and showered her with money and gifts. It's not clear how Carl came into the orbit of Suzanne, who was several years older than him, but one day Wrout was introduced to him at Suzanne's house.

'Who is this young fat fool?' Wrout thought. Carl would be chewed up and spat out before long, Wrout concluded, but somehow he had found himself a place in the Moran organisation. He was no more than a gopher to Jason and Mark, rather like Wrout was to Lewis. Carl didn't seem cut out for life with the Morans. He was too soft and weak, like a puppy dog. Soon enough, there would be a rude awakening for the gormless tubby kid.

Still, Carl seemed to have a little entrepreneurial flair about him. While he was running up and down for the Morans, Carl had also been working with another crew, cooking up speed in the northern suburbs.

Mark Moran was impressed with the quality of the gear they were producing and asked to be hooked up with them. Here was the chance to graduate from gopher to equal partner in the Moran organisation, or so Carl believed. Carl introduced Mark Moran to some people who could supply large amounts of chemicals. Mark agreed he would share the profits from processing the precursors fifty–fifty with Carl.

Carl believed he and Mark were becoming close friends. He was part of the crew, not just the hired help. There were parties and nights on the town. He also formed a friendship with a Moran associate, Dean Stephens, who was married to an attractive feisty woman named Roberta Mercieca.

Carl and Roberta had clicked straightaway. Her relationship with Dean was abusive and turbulent. By contrast, Carl seemed funny and gentle, if a little soft. He seemed to understand what she was going through. She claimed that Dean was breaking her down physically and mentally. Roberta had begun to believe that she deserved the cruelty she had suffered her whole life. Carl was the first man who had listened to her problems and encouraged her to hold her head up. One day she would walk away from this, he told her. She could have a life where a man didn't stand over her.

Carl's rude awakening came in the form of a jail sentence in 1995. Carl was arrested and charged in a big sweep of crooks involved in pseudoephedrine and speed trafficking. He was booked for a commercial quantity but as it was his first offence he only copped a six-month lagging. That sentence was overturned on appeal and he was released.

Carl's first stint in jail was an important part of his education. He quickly worked out that you needed protection to survive in that jungle. Just like in the schoolyard, everyone had their price. He made solid connections in there with thugs, hit men and drug dealers, all of whom would prove very useful. They weren't friends by any stretch of the imagination, but Carl was losing sight of the distinction between friendship and business. Carl in his naivety had always confused popularity with true friendship.

When he emerged from jail, Carl believed all was well with the world, that his future was secure. By his reckoning, Mark Moran owed him $1 million from their joint venture. There was no reason to think that Mark wouldn't pay. He was a friend after all.

As Carl was to learn soon, there was a lot of viciousness and greed in this business. A promise was worth nothing at all. Only cash in hand meant anything. And with the money came suspicion, fear and paranoia.

9

THE BETRAYAL

For much of the 1990s, Antonios Sajih 'Fat Tony' Mokbel had run a money-making machine tucked away in a nondescript house in Brunswick. The speed lab hidden inside reportedly churned out up to $80 million in product before it mysteriously blew up in February 1997, the resulting fire consuming the property and almost incinerating the head chef Paul Edward Howden. Police later caught up with Howden, in the hospital with serious burns to 30 per cent of his body. But Howden stayed staunch; even when he was sentenced to four years' jail, he never lagged his boss.

On the surface, it appeared to be a grievous loss: Mokbel had manufactured speed at the Brunswick lab for a range of partners, including the Moran clan. They had trusted Mokbel to store their precursor chemicals on the premises. Mokbel told his partners that four 25-kilo tubs of pseudoephedrine, worth $300 000, had gone up in the blaze. But they hadn't. In reality, Mokbel had moved the chemicals out of the lab before the fire. And Mokbel with his new partner, Carl Williams, helped themselves to a multimillion-dollar windfall.

It was through the Morans that Carl had met Mokbel. And the fire was an opportunity for Carl to get one back. The $1 million that Mark had promised would await Carl when he was released from jail turned out to be just $4000. Mark had kept putting Carl off, telling him he should be patient, he would get his money. The proceeds of the joint venture had been invested in another bigger deal and they would soon all enjoy a bonanza, Mark had told Carl. After more than a year of this, Carl concluded he was being taken for a mug. It was a humiliating slap in the face. He had believed he was on an equal footing with the Morans, but this told him he would always be a gopher to them, a dogsbody there to do their bidding.

Now Carl was making serious money for the first time, courtesy of the deception over the Brunswick lab fire. He and Mokbel were soon churning out pills made from the chemicals of their erstwhile partners. A number of dealers worked for them; one remembers moving 40 000 pills in a single six-week period. Mokbel and Carl were getting fatter and greedier by the day.

The Kuwaiti-born Mokbel had begun his career as the proprietor of a suburban milk bar before graduating to confidence trickster. Yet drugs had been the making of him. Drugs had given him a foothold in polite society. He was investing his cash in buying nightclubs, clothing boutiques and a string of thoroughbreds. He was making millions buying and selling apartments in the property boom that was then reaching its zenith.

A few years earlier, Mokbel had been the leader of the Tracksuit Gang, a group of big-spending punters who would turn up to city race meetings dressed in garish designer tracksuits. Police suspected the crew of being involved in daylight robberies of trackside bookmakers. Members of the gang had simply reefed handfuls of cash from the bags of the bookies, who were too terrified to say anything.

By the late 1990s, it was said, Mokbel was literally moving money around on pallet trucks. He was importing large amounts of ecstasy and cocaine hidden in shipping containers. He reportedly had corrupt officials in shipping companies and the customs service helping him. He was on his way to building a $100-million fortune from drugs. And Carl was right alongside him, helping to distribute the product. Meanwhile, Carl was working up his own ventures.

His big break came when he found a cheap way to make ecstasy, or at least a substitute that met the needs of the market. The key ingredient was ketamine, a powerful battlefield anaesthetic that had been used up until the 1970s for stabilising wounded troops. It was effective but crude, and had a range of side-effects, from hallucinations to convulsions, which caused most western forces to abandon its use.

Carl was able to produce a fairly exotic pill by combining ketamine and speed.

A long-time mate of George, Dennis Reardon, had once been Carl's junior soccer coach. Now he agreed to be a crash-test dummy for Carl's new go-fast product. The first batches were a little too potent, sending Reardon into paralysis, fits and semi-comatose states for hours. So they altered the dose, reasoning that their customers would not regard paralysis followed by convulsions as a good night.

To make 1000 pills they needed 28 grams of speed and 110 grams of ketamine, with 142 grams of glucose to hold the pills together. They sold each pill wholesale for $15. Later, they diluted the recipe further, getting an extra 10 per cent more out of each batch. Having had great feedback from the market, they were eager to get as much product out there as possible. Their wholesale price dropped to about $8 to $10 – a far cheaper pill than the competition could produce.

People were paying $20–30 a pill in clubs and up to $50 later in the night. It was an unbelievably good business.

Carl's pills, stamped FUBU or UFO, began to dominate the market. At first, he was doing a batch of 1000 pills each week out of the garage in Broadie. Later, after teaming up with Mokbel, they trebled production. Carl and George were getting rich. They started moving coke and pills from Melbourne to the Gold Coast and Perth. Carl's advantage was that he had access to large amounts of precursor chemicals. He could either make his own product or on-sell the precursor chemicals for a mighty profit.

Carl wanted to channel his money into legitimate investments, and began buying property and planning his own developments.

He had actually completed one project in inner-city Fitzroy, a pair of warehouse apartments. He always hid his wealth by taking out mortgages, though he could have paid cash straight up.

The Morans were starting to look at him differently. No longer was he just the harmless fat bloke helping them make money. He was now looming as a commercial threat in a market that was getting too crowded. And the Morans never liked to see anyone getting ahead, even people they called mates.

By late 1997, Carl was flying, making more money than he could have ever imagined, even if Mark Moran had ripped him off for nearly a million bucks. There was talk that Carl had managed to secure a container load of pseudoephedrine; it was supposed to be enough chemicals to make him a billionaire. It was most probably bullshit but he didn't discourage the talk; he liked the prestige that went with his growing notoriety. There was no more queuing up at nightclubs: when bouncers saw him coming they waved him inside straight into the VIP area. With a gram or two of coke in his pocket, he was the most popular man in the club. Celebrities and AFL footballers hung off him, hoping for a line or two. Everybody wanted to be Carl's friend.

In late 1997, Deana Falcone was away at Beechworth in central Victoria when she got the call from Carl. She had finally broken away from Shane a year earlier, buying a house far away from him and making sure he didn't know the address. She would always love Shane but she couldn't save him. He was pulling her under and she had to get away. As soon as Deana heard Carl's voice on the phone, she knew he was calling to tell her Shane had died.

The Vietnamese dealers were distributing a new stronger batch of heroin in Broadie. Long-time users like Shane were used to 10 per cent purity, but what hit the streets in the late 1990s was up to 80 per cent pure. It was killing even experienced junkies. They would shoot up and as soon as the drug hit their bloodstream they would keel over, before they'd even drawn back the blood into the syringe. Broadie police were being called to fatal overdoses almost every day. They would find the deceased on the couch, still with the needle in their arm. Shooting up this powerful gear alone was a fatal error for many, including Shane. The following year deaths from heroin overdoses would outstrip Victoria's road toll.

Deana went straight to Broadie and embraced a sobbing Carl. For the first couple of days, he was inconsolable but soon he took control. Someone had to. Barb and George were devastated, although they had both known this day was coming. Once Shane had protected his little brother from bullies, but Carl had long since taken over looking after his accident-prone brother. He organised Shane's funeral, even down to selecting the coffin and hymns for the service. He wouldn't let his parents do a thing. Through her sorrow, Barb was proud of Carl and she wondered where the new hardness she saw in him had come from. He was growing up. He had answered the call of his family in its time of need.

Shane's funeral was a dismal affair. Only one of his friends, 'Sharky', had bothered to turn up, and that was only because Shane had died in his flat. The rest of them, all those who had sponged off Shane for years, were nowhere to be seen. Shane had thought they were his mates for life. He had done time for them, hooked them up with gear countless times, and they had forgotten him, or died before him. Most would end up the same way as Shane, members of a dead-end generation, consumed by the only thing that created any passion in them. Things had turned ugly at the wake, held in a suburban pub, and a fight had broken out. George was getting a hiding, his glasses were broken and there was blood everywhere. Carl had stepped in and defended his father, though it cost him a punch or two in the head. This had surprised Deana. Perhaps Mummy's Boy had some balls after all, she thought.

10

KEEPSAKES

On the morning of 13 October 1999, Barb made a chocolate cake for Carl's twenty-ninth birthday, just as she had every birthday for the kids since they were babies. She was only making one cake a year these days. Since Shane had died birthdays were all the more special, so this time she put extra effort into getting Carl's cake just as he liked it. It was the last one she would ever make.

Life was changing rapidly. Carl was a huge success in Barb's eyes. She didn't like to dwell on how he made his money but she certainly enjoyed its benefits. Carl and George were building a townhouse for her in Essendon that she would soon move into. She would have her freedom at last. She had stayed in the marriage because she had to, but she and George were living together like brother and sister, just as they had growing up in Richmond all those years ago.

Since Shane's death, Barb had found it harder and harder to pretend. The townhouse was modest but it was going to be all Barb's, a sanctuary.

Carl may have been running a pill press in the family garage, but he always respected his parents. Barb couldn't remember more than three occasions in twenty-nine years when her beautiful boy had answered her back. They loved a laugh together or a chat over Carl's favourite homemade dish: baked beans, eggs and chips. As she iced the cake, she was looking forward to Carl coming home early that morning. But Carl was late, and he hadn't called.

When Carl eventually did arrive home at midday, he was pale and drawn. He barely looked at his cake and hurried past to the bedroom she still kept for him. Barb was disappointed; she had been looking forward to lighting the candles.

'What's wrong with you?' she asked, following him to the bedroom.

'Nothing. Just going to have a lie-down,' said Carl, closing the door behind him. A few minutes later Carl called out to his father to come in and have a quick chat. He still didn't want Mum, just Dad.

Since Shane's death, George had become much closer to his second son. Barb was now getting the message that this would be no ordinary birthday.

When she was finally allowed into Carl's room, she saw George examining a small hole in the left side of Carl's abdomen – a gunshot wound. Carl wondered whether he could just do nothing. He didn't feel too bad. Maybe they could just forget about it and let the wound heal.

Barb was sent to a doctor to ask a hypothetical question: what if someone, no one in particular of course, had a bullet in him? If he was feeling okay, could he just leave it and get on with life?

Crooks learn that if you can staunch the bleeding from a gunshot wound, surgery is not always necessary. Especially if the bullet goes right through you, without hitting any major pieces of anatomy. However, a .22 slug, as this was, tends to ricochet around inside, destroying soft tissue and organs until it stops deep inside the body. Infection was the biggest worry for Carl.

The GP recommended a trip to hospital, and nearly five hours after the shooting Carl reluctantly agreed. The bullet had hit a layer of fat and muscle and travelled straight downwards, lodging inside Carl's pelvis behind his genitals. The surgery was straightforward but for the large, ugly incision they made to get at the bullet. Carl wanted to keep the bullet to put in a frame behind the bar with his Muhammad Ali gloves and *Scarface* portraits, but when he came to after the operation, he was disappointed to learn that the cops had taken his souvenir away as evidence.

When police interviewed Carl, he stuck to a simple if implausible story. He had been walking along the road and out of the blue he had been knocked out by somebody he hadn't seen. When he woke up, he'd found a hole in his guts. He had no idea how it had happened or who had done it. End of interview.

But the police quickly worked out the story. In the hours after the incident, the Moran brothers had been picked up on listening devices bragging that they had taught the fat boy a lesson he wouldn't forget in a hurry.

The Morans had also dispatched a friend, Lee Pascu, to the hospital to ensure that Carl wasn't talking to the jacks. Carl knew what this meant. If he gave evidence against the Morans, he and his family were in mortal danger. Later, Jason followed up with a menacing phone call. He told Carl that he wanted his .22 slug back and he would be coming to get it. Oh, yes, Carl thought to himself. You'll be getting it back with interest, you dog.

Just how the shooting, the seminal moment in Carl's rise and fall, occurred is the subject of many conflicting stories and theories.

According to George Williams, the falling-out had begun months earlier over a piano, believe it or not.

Jason was all hot and bothered looking for a piano that he'd stored with a friend of Carl who had made himself scarce. Jason bumped into Carl on Union Street, Ascot Vale, and demanded he hand over a number for the alleged piano thief. According to George, Carl refused, saying he would get the bloke to call Jason. That did not please Moran who pursued Carl up the street, haranguing him. It turned into a minor scuffle on the street. Carl gave a good account of himself, according to George. Despite having his right arm in a sling from recent shoulder surgery, he still got in a couple of good lefts to the head when Jason swung at him.

Jason, never liking a fair fight or one he couldn't win, backed off. He eventually got his piano back, but not his dignity after coming off second in a fight with a one-armed fat man.

Carl had also offended Jason Moran by taking up with Roberta, the wife of their associate Dean Stephens, with whom she had two children. Roberta stoutly denies that she cheated on Dean with Carl, saying that they got together only after her marriage broke down. Carl had been a confidant and a friend, not a lover. Yet Moran associates say that Roberta had taunted her then-husband, showing off expensive gifts Carl had given her. They deny her stories of abuse at the hands of Dean Stephens. 'She gave as good as she got,' Bert Wrout says. 'She made him out to be something he wasn't.'

Barb was disappointed that Carl had got together with Roberta. She wasn't at all the type of girl that Barb had hoped that Carl would end up with. Roberta was rough and tough and already had kids with two other men. Barb thought he was making a big mistake.

Carl had been with a local girl, Nicole Mottram, whose twin brother was a cop. They had been in love but Nicole backed away after Carl went deep into the drug scene. Nicole was from a good family; she had nice manners and a future. She was blonde and pretty, and respectful to Barb, while Roberta was coarse and loud, and every second word from her mouth was an expletive.

Carl admired Roberta's toughness, her ability to survive. He learnt a lot from her and she definitely stiffened his resolve to take on the Morans. She was an ally as much as a lover.

Roberta was one of seven children born to a Maltese immigrant truck driver named Emmanuel and his Australian wife, Dorothy Hughes. She grew up on the streets of Frankston, one of the most down-at-heel suburbs in bayside Melbourne. The kids looked after each other, even if their parents couldn't, but it all fell apart after Manny's death. When Roberta was just eight months old, he was involved in a collision in his truck near Wagga Wagga in southern New South Wales, and was trapped in the cabin as the rig went up in flames. Manny was virtually incinerated, but survived for another six days.

After that, Dorothy went from one abusive relationship to the next, and at age eleven Roberta was made a ward of the state and packed off to foster homes and orphanages. There, she learnt to fight for whatever she had, and ended up in the juvenile justice system. It was always her fists that got her into trouble. Hard and wiry, she was a ball of fury when she went off.

To Barb, Carl and Roberta seemed more like mates than lovers. There was lots of piss-taking and play fighting between them. They also shared a hatred for the Morans.

Roberta especially loathed Trisha and Antonella, who were married to Jason and Mark respectively. They had looked down on her as trash. The wives of thugs and drug dealers, they had put on airs and graces as if their dirty money had elevated them to a higher class. They had shunned Roberta and never lifted a finger to help her on the several occasions when Dean had almost bashed her to death.

'They were just fakes through and through, with their silicone tits and expensive fake teeth and dyed hair. They shunned me from the beginning because they thought they were better than me. They didn't give a fuck if Dean killed me and the kids. All they cared about was money and living like fucking royalty. But their husbands made their money just like we did, from drugs,' she says.

Judy Moran was even worse, in Roberta's eyes, a common shoplifter parading around as though she were a member of the aristocracy. Their whole show of family unity was a charade.

Roberta says Mark and Jason never gave their mother more than a few dollars here and there from their villainous activities over the years. In fact, Roberta claims that Jason, whom she idolised, had once bashed Judy in the bar of a hotel.

It was a measure of how little class the Morans really had, what terrible hypocrites they were. They had tried to lord it over her and Dean when they were married too. Roberta alleges that Jason and Mark had set up their mate Dean with a large amount of hash. He had done a year's jail over it and when he got out, the Morans had made him pay them back $15 000 for the drugs that he had 'lost'.

Dean was no high-rolling crook, just a slaughterman at the local abattoir, but Jason and Mark had decided to keep him down too. Dean had just copped it all without complaint, but she was going to make sure Carl stood up for himself. In fact, Roberta couldn't care less if Carl killed the lot of them.

The simmering tensions spilled over in July 1998. Carl was already moving around with a bodyguard he had hired, fearing that Jason Moran was out to get him, on behalf of Dean Stephens. The bodyguard, Rocco Arico, was just nineteen, a gangster wannabe from Brunswick, but he claimed he had the dash for the job. Others had already knocked it back.

Carl was offering big money – $1 million – to keep him alive, such was his fear of Jason. Through his Moran connections, he had met a man well-regarded in Carlton. Though this man had been an associate of Jason for years, Carl summoned him to his Fitzroy apartment to offer him the job. There, on the kitchen table, Carl had laid out a small arsenal.

'There was an Uzi machine gun, an assault rifle, a shotgun, Glock 9-mms, a .45; every type of weapon you could imagine,' says the Carlton man.

'He was just smiling, saying, "These are all yours if you take the job." I didn't want it, not for any amount of money. This was all going to end in a mess. Carl was a good bloke, he was well liked. But he wouldn't have a chance against the Morans. They were ruthless – much harder than we thought Carl ever was. He was a good organiser, he knew how to set up and manage a cashflow, but he was no tough guy.'

In July 1998, Carl, George and Arico were at a fight night at the Melbourne Aquatic Centre, the main event being a gimmick bout between former footballers Rene Kink and Mark 'Jacko' Jackson. As the would-be pugilists filed in and the houselights went down, Jason Moran and seven of his followers walked in and without warning attacked Carl. The Carlton man saw what was going on and dived over the seats to help Carl but his assailants had the benefit of surprise. Carl got, what they call in the trade, a good kicking. Arico was powerless to stop it. Carl was pistol-whipped with a .45-calibre handgun, leaving him with a nasty gash on his scalp.

Arico, George and Carl, with blood streaming from his head, made for the exits. Arico told the Carlton man that he was scared Jason would shoot them in the car park. He asked to be escorted to the car, rather than risk another confrontation. Carl had been seriously embarrassed by this rout. Meanwhile, Jason and his crew were laughing.

'The Morans had never taken him seriously. When he was working with them, they used to make fun of him all the time, belittling him constantly, kicking him up the arse, slapping him on the back of the head. It was supposed to be all in fun but it was always Carl who copped it. He put up with it, because he was making money. They never imagined that he could turn on them,' says the Carlton man. 'When he started to make serious money, that's when they began to look at him differently. They didn't like competition of any kind.'

In early 1999, there was a drama over the ownership of the pill press Carl was using. It was said to be the property of Danielle McGuire, Carl's friend, who grew up nearby in Broadie. Though he was married to Antonella, Mark Moran was also in a relationship with Danielle. This gave him some kind of proprietary right to the pill press, he believed. But he was prepared to give Carl full ownership of the press for the bargain price of $400 000.

In Carl's view, he owed the Morans nothing. On the contrary, they owed him $996 000, the balance of the deal Mark had reneged on. He wasn't going to chase it. Carl was now making enough money to let that old debt go, as long as the Morans left him alone. There was enough demand in the party drugs business for all the crooks to become rich beyond their wildest dreams. Why worry over $1 million? Carl reasoned. Still, he wasn't going to pay them a cent while that debt was outstanding.

Despite all these issues swirling around, Mark and Carl continued to do business together. Mark was still buying chemicals from Carl, but now Carl was ripping him off, inflating the prices and foisting substandard merchandise on him. Mark had continued to buy the chemicals and Carl, though he no longer trusted Mark, was prepared to continue taking his money.

On Carl's birthday, Mark had arranged to meet him in the car park of Gladstone Park shopping centre in Melbourne's northern suburbs. When Carl arrived in a hire car, he was concerned to see that Mark had brought his brother along. The enmity between Carl and Jason was well-known after the incident at the Melbourne Aquatic Centre, but Carl was blinded by greed. He had a loaded Glock 9-mm in his bumbag if anything went wrong.

Mark and Jason were concerned they might be under police surveillance (they were right), so they all got in Carl's car and drove through the backstreets till they found a small reserve where they could talk in private. They moved away from the car, out of the range of any listening devices the cops might have planted. It was a hire car, but everyone was getting paranoid. Both sides had police in their pockets so the game was getting more complicated. The two groups of corrupt cops were waging their own struggles through their villain proxies. Anything was possible, given the big money at stake.

Mark asked Carl if he could get some more chemicals to produce a new batch of ecstasy. Carl agreed but reminded Mark he still owed him $60 000 from an earlier deal. Mark accused Carl of ripping him off, saying he had heard he was buying the chemicals for just $5000.

'Carl just said it was tough shit. No one was forcing them to buy his chemicals and if he had made a good profit, then that was his good luck. The Morans would do exactly the same. Carl said Mark's face went dark red in anger. He was filthy on him,' says Roberta.

Mark became highly agitated, accusing Carl of being involved in a plot to run through his house to steal cash and drugs. Carl denied this. Then, without warning, Mark pulled a wooden baton from his jacket and clubbed Carl over the head, knocking him down. Though he was dazed, Carl launched himself at Mark, tackling him to the ground and the pair began wrestling. Carl then heard a gunshot. He looked up to see Jason Moran pointing a snub-nosed .22 handgun at him. For all his strength and prowess as a footballer, Mark couldn't shift Carl off him. He was shouting at Jason to kill Carl.

'Shoot him in the head, Jason, put one in his head,' Mark screamed. But strangely Jason couldn't do it. Carl said later that Jason's hand was shaking so badly he couldn't shoot straight. It was like Jason had Parkinson's disease, he said. He fired three or four shots that all missed. Finally, he put the muzzle against the left side of Carl's belly and pulled the trigger.

Carl didn't feel a thing, he said later, on account of the adrenaline flowing through him but it took all the fight out of him. Mark and Jason found the Glock in his bumbag: with a hole in his guts and no gun, he was defenceless. The Morans cursed and swore at him. They said they had done this many times before. They had protection from the cops so if Carl lagged them they would know immediately; they would kill his entire family and his friends too.

Remarkably, they all got back in Carl's car and returned to the shopping centre, their business concluded.

The first shot in a gangland war that would claim more than thirty lives had been fired. Some of the killings were directly related to this moment in Gladstone Park, some had nothing to do with Carl.

They were a by-product of the fear and paranoia that hung over the city then. As complex relationships unravelled, threatening to expose the seedy underbelly of Melbourne's party drug scene, killing became the best and cleanest option. Yet the violence only begot more violence. Like a raging bush fire, the malevolent forces driving the conflict eventually took on a life of their own.

11

A TATTSLOTTO MOMENT

As his bullet wound healed, Carl was on the move. He had checked himself out of the hospital only a few days after surgery. Jason's threatening phone call to Carl was enough to get him out of bed. He wasn't going to just lie there waiting for someone to finish the job that Jason had stuffed up. He wasn't going to fall into another trap. He was going to make them regret that they hadn't killed him when they had the chance.

For six weeks, he didn't sleep more than a couple of nights in a row in the same bed, alternating between his place in Fitzroy, Broadie and his auntie's place in Doncaster.

Unable to find Carl, Mark and Jason had already had a crack at George. George and Barb were at the Earl of Lincoln in Richmond having a few drinks one Friday night when the Morans turned up. With fake friendliness, Jason asked George to come outside for a chat, but George could see Moran had a handgun in his pocket and refused to go with him. Jason had then lost it and told George he would have them all knocked. Even Nan, Barb's mum, was apparently included in this.

Barb was terrified, but she wanted to throw pool balls at Jason. How dare that thug Jason threaten her family, especially when Carl had made so much money for the Morans, she thought.

Carl was livid when he found out about this incident. With each passing day, his resentment of the Morans deepened and his resolve to square the ledger hardened. The Morans were equally determined to neutralise the commercial threat that Carl represented.

Six weeks after Carl's wounding, police attended a two-storey townhouse in Broadie to serve a warrant for a minor fraud matter on a man who was registered at the address. Carl had also been using the place to lie low since the shooting, while catching up on lost production. It was his latest manufacturing base, which he had kept a closely guarded secret.

The officers heard a strange whirring sound from upstairs, like someone was operating an industrial washing machine in an upstairs room. Gaining entry to the premises, they found Carl and George hiding in the bedrooms. Carl claimed he was just there having a nap: he hadn't heard the pill press and he had no idea what it was. But he was dressed in a Mambo T-shirt dusted with fine white powder.

Police call these pinches 'Tattslotto moments'. Cops serve a minor warrant and stumble on a major drug lab. Broadie was dotted with such backyard 'clan labs'. Carl had a different perspective. He gets shot and then six weeks later, out of the blue, he and George get busted. This had to be another set-up by the Morans and their corrupt police mates, a convenient means of eliminating the competition.

Roberta claims that Mark Moran tipped off the cops about the pill press. She says that Mark had even been carrying out surveillance on the place, waiting for Carl to turn up. When Carl did front, Mark called in the cops he had been paying for protection, according to Roberta. Senior police have denied this version of events, but there was something highly coincidental about the bust.

Police found 30 000 ecstasy tablets and nearly 7 kilos of various powders, including methamphetamine, ketamine and pseudoephedrine, with a potential street value of $20 million – which explained the need for the loaded pistol also found at the scene.

There was indeed corrupt police involved, as it turned out. The drug squad detective who took over the investigation, Detective Sergeant Malcolm Rosenes, was later arrested and charged with trafficking cocaine, hashish and ecstasy. In October 2003, he was sentenced to a minimum of three and a half years in jail.

Carl became convinced that the whole thing was a set-up. It was clear to him that the Morans would never let him get ahead. In fact, if he didn't leave the marketplace to them, they would have him killed without a pang of conscience.

Carl was bailed on 21 January 2000 on the drugs charges and was free to lay his own plans for revenge against the Morans. He had assembled his own team now. The Carlton man hadn't taken on the job as Carl's bodyguard, but he had introduced him to a number of people he had grown up with in the western suburbs.

The Sunshine Boys had been a fearsome crew but they were in the process of a messy, bloody break-up, their bonds of trust destroyed by paranoia and greed. Their leader Paul Kallipolitis had predicted it a few years before.

One afternoon in 1998, 'PK' had told them they were all marked for death. The only unknown was which of them would cop it first.

'We've done so many bad things to so many bad people that something is bound to come back to us sooner or later,' he'd told them solemnly. They had all passed the point of no return. Perhaps PK already knew that their enemies were standing among them.

Within four years all but one of them would be dead, all of them murdered by people they'd known and trusted. As young street hoodlums, they had sworn they would become the toughest team of crooks in Australia, but ultimately they posed the most deadly threat to each other. They had been drawn into a lethal cycle that none had the power to break.

When Carl came on the scene, the tensions were just about to boil over. And perhaps his money, or the thirst for it, was the catalyst. He needed the muscle for his war with the Morans, but it came with a whole lot of baggage, rivalries and an almost insatiable blood lust. Carl would be a player in almost every one of the intrigues that unfolded. Some of the Sunshine crew lined up behind Carl, others chose the Morans and some alternated between the two.

At twenty-three, Dino Dibra was a young, flashy punk from Sunshine, a man who had only one ambition – to be a gangster like the movie characters he saw on television. He had a liking for cocaine and violence that would eventually prove his undoing.

Dino's criminal record was paltry considering the lofty criminal status he aspired to. His greatest thrill in life was to lead the jacks on high-speed pursuits. He had a friend with a car-rental business who was foolhardy enough to let him hire exotic rides such as Lamborghinis and Ferraris. The cars invariably came back with smoking gearboxes and thrashed engines. With a head full of coke, Dino would take to the highway or just throw donuts in the car park of the Glengala Hotel for the enjoyment of his associates.

At the age of nineteen, he was charged with threatening to kill, threatening to inflict serious injury and unlawful drug possession. He was jailed for a year and fined for these offences. In October 1996, Dibra was locked up again; this time for eighteen months for serious reckless driving offences. During the sentencing, the judge noted that Dibra had 'the worst driving record I have ever seen'.

Now, he was Carl's new best friend. And for years Carl would keep a picture of him and Dino by his bed. For Carl, he was a welcome addition to the team. As a bodyguard, Rocco Arico was next to useless, according to Roberta.

Arico had grown up in his parents' pool hall – the infamous Johnny's Green Room, where many budding gangsters hung out. Rocco had the swagger but he wasn't yet in the same class as Dino, whom he idolised. Roberta had nothing but scorn for Arico, and was always telling Carl to get rid of him. She suspected Carl only kept Rocco around because he was having an affair with Arico's sister.

'It was typical Carl, just fuckin' typical,' laughs Roberta. 'It was always about him.'

His most faithful lieutenant was undoubtedly 'Little' Tommy Ivanovic, who grew up with Rocco.

Tommy was raised in Brunswick West, the son of a Croatian–Macedonian marriage. It had been a conventional upbringing: his father worked and his mother ran the house. As a child, he had played in his mum's vegetable garden at home with his three siblings. It was a close-knit family.

Some of the local families were wealthier than theirs but didn't seem to work. It never occurred to Tommy to ask why. It wouldn't be right, in any case, to be too nosy. Tommy always tried hard to be accepted.

Tommy was a follower; he gravitated towards strong, assertive leaders. Life at home was stifling under a dictatorial father who did not want Tommy to mingle with Australian kids, even though he was born here. The streets provided a sense of freedom and adventure. He had fallen under the spell of Rocco Arico in his teens. A group of them, led by Rocco, would get around the clubs like characters from *Scarface*, in oversized gangster suits with their hair slicked back.

Some of them were destined for the underworld but Tommy was a simple, easygoing kid with no history of violence. He was just coming along for the ride. The destination didn't matter, as long as he had his mates.

He completed an apprenticeship as a chef and was working at a popular Brunswick restaurant, Bolero. In Bolero, he had met Roberta and Carl. Roberta took a shine to the pleasant, yet naive young man and soon they were close friends.

Carl liked the fact that Tommy came from a solid family background with proper values. Above all, he was trustworthy and would do whatever Carl wanted, short of murder. But there were other people for that.

Around this time, Carl made another important inner-city connection: a cop he had met around the Brunswick area, Paul Dale.

The two got on pretty well, and certainly from Carl's point of view, it was a relationship that was enhanced by Dale's day job at the drug squad.

Carl knew the old adage that a successful crook always has a copper in his pocket, no matter what they say. You had to trade information with the police to buy a blind eye to your activities. You needed a copper to fix the blues of your mates and your kids. And the copper needed something in return: the names, addresses and recent activities of villains, which he could serve up to his superiors. But the association came with risks, as Carl was later to learn.

If any of Dino Dibra's childhood mates – PK, Andrew 'Benji' Veniamin, Mark Mallia and John Auciello – had mingled with cops, he would have been kneecapped. Out in Sunshine, a dog was a dog, no matter how much money was involved. It was a much tougher school than Johnny's Green Room.

In the 1950s and '60s, Sunshine had been a dormitory suburb for immigrant families looking for a dream of employment and home ownership. Police used to joke they needed translators in sixty different languages just to walk the beat in Sunshine back then.

By the early 1990s, the employment prospects of Sunshine kids were all but dashed: factories closed down by the dozen as Australia's manufacturing sector wound down. The local hoodlums were finding much easier ways of making money than having to work for it.

The Sunshine Boys were all from different ethnic and religious backgrounds: Johnny's family were from Naples, Dino's were Muslims from Albania, Benji's were Greek Cypriots, and Mallia was Maltese. They became renowned as playground bullies at Ardeer High School, honing the violence and lack of mercy that would mark their short, pitiless lives.

The lads found a mentor in a Greek boy, Paul Kallipolitis, who was four years their senior. PK would later help them to become the most feared crew in Sunshine.

Striding down to Glengala Road shops in his favourite snakeskin boots, there was no one in Sunshine who could touch PK. Beefed up on steroids or human growth hormone, no one dared take him on. When crossed, or simply in a bad mood, PK was a raging force of nature. PK and his two brothers had all attained black belts in martial arts and PK loved showing off his skills.

In Greek, *kallipolitis* means 'good citizen', but PK knew his future was in the ganglands. He loved the power that drugs and money held over the poor kids of his neighbourhood. He quickly organised the younger boys into a gang that did his bidding unquestioningly, anything from running drugs and guns to stealing cars for the rebirthing trade. He expected loyalty, and taught them the rules.

You 'chopped out' your mates no matter what, whether it was money, drugs, a woman you had just met, or a rival that needed a bashing or even a burial. You chopped them out, or you couldn't call yourself a mate.

Sunshine police identified the threat the Sunshine crew posed and tried unsuccessfully to beat it out of them. Crime, however, was an adventure, and getting caught was part of the fun.

As minors, the Sunshine Boys could rack up lots of convictions before they would ever be locked up. They worked the juvenile justice system, which mistakenly put faith in their rehabilitation. The only justice they feared was from their associates, not the police.

They learnt early on that the jacks could hurt them, but they couldn't kill them. Whereas your mates could, and would. They also learnt that torture was fun too.

The favoured method was to handcuff the victim to the top rail of a garage roller door and go to work on him with a baseball bat, soldering iron or pair of boltcutters.

The methods were their own, but the cruelty they had learnt inside the Sunshine Police Station. Many of the troublemakers found themselves shackled to an old gas heater and being given a flogging. Before officers ripped into them with batons, the boys would be forced to shove a telephone directory up their T-shirts so the bruising would be internal. If they lagged the cops, no one would believe them. And anyway, it was a sign of character if you didn't squeal. The worst crime was to be a dog.

Yet 'red-lighting' – showing off – was almost as great a threat to the enterprise. One night in 1994, Benji and Dino were cruising around Port Melbourne, looking for a VN Holden Calais to steal to fill an order. It was a regular earner for Dino and Benji: they would supply late-model stolen cars for about $1500 each to the rebirthers. The rebirthers would buy wrecks from auctions and combine them with parts from stolen cars of the same make and model to create a new vehicle.

But this time, Dino and Benji had stolen a cop's private car, which had a laptop computer in the boot. The computer had the details of a number of police informers and the home addresses of officers.

Rather than deliver the car, they decided it would be more fun to make a statement by burning it instead.

Then on the stolen laptop they found the home address of a hated local cop. The next day Benji and Dino drove past the cop's home with music blaring full bore. The officer was out mowing his front lawn. They slowed to a crawl and gave him the royal wave.

Not surprisingly, Dino and Benji were hauled in and thrown into a police holding cell. Dino always liked a chat and began to mouth off to the heavily tattooed man with long hair who was in the holding cell with them.

Benji tried to shut him up but Dino was off, and before long he had begun boasting that they had stolen the jack's car. Having burnt the car, there was nothing to link them to the crime, except of course Dino's confession. The cellmate turned out to be a police informer who had been put in the cells to catch them out. Benji and Dino were then separated and interrogated. Benji said nothing and was eventually sentenced to twelve months' jail and fined $2574, but Dino got off with a lot less, only a few months' jail.

Benji was convinced that Dino had sold him out, and thrown a number of others into the bargain. He discovered that at the same time he was being questioned Dino was making suspicious calls to several associates. The following day, sixteen homes around Sunshine were raided. To top it off, the cop's insurance company sued Benji for burning the car.

The trust between Benji and Dino was broken. This moment would have far-reaching consequences.

In March 1996, after being released from jail, Benji publicly declared Dino a dog and set about enforcing some summary justice.

Benji convened what he called a 'kangaroo court' on his back verandah. He accused Dino of lagging his crew and other treachery. Dibra pleaded his innocence but this was ignored. Then he swore he would exact revenge on Benji if he didn't let this go. It had gone past that already, as far as Benji was concerned.

Then Dibra made the mistake of accusing Benji of being a dog, because he was hanging round with the likes of Carlton boss Alphonse Gangitano. Benji had plans to ingratiate himself with the Carlton Crew, and didn't need Dino running his big mouth, criticising his new friends.

Dino had been making a fool of himself around Carlton, seeking out the heavies and hassling them to be his mate. He had also made it known that he was taking a fancy to some of their women. One night he had pulled a wad of nearly $20 000 from his pants and waved it around a nightclub, claiming he could buy every one of 'their bitches'.

Benji's friends, like Johnny, believed they had no choice but to kill Dino. Shooting him in the leg would not be enough. These kids had never been good students but they understood the danger of a wounded animal. It was like Niccoló Machiavelli had written in the sixteenth century: 'If an injury has to be done to a man, it should be so severe that his vengeance need not be feared'. It didn't take a genius to work out what Dino would do if he were left alive.

The next day, Benji reconvened his kangaroo court, but this time with a gun pointed at Dibra's head.

Johnny and Benji pushed Dibra into the back of a car, driven by another man. They sat, flanking him, in the back seat as they drove out of the Glengala Road shops. Their adventures had begun on this little strip when they used to play-act as gangsters, quoting lines from crime flicks. This was no longer a game, but real life. They were driving out of Sunshine with Dino's life in their hands.

Benji was torn between friendship and what he knew was right. He wasn't sure whether he could kill Dino. His childhood friend was begging for his life, asking that Benji shoot him in the legs in a location where he could get help. If they shot him out in the farmlands beyond the city limits, he was certain he would die before anyone found him.

Benji relented and decided to give Dino a second chance. He ordered the car to be turned around and they headed back into town. They took Dino to Footscray across the road from the Western Hospital. Benji and Johnny dragged Dino out of the car and put two shots into his left leg.

Johnny said he knew this would not be the end of it. He knew that he and Benji would be looking over their shoulders for years to come. They weren't even sure that Dino would keep his mouth shut, so they visited him in the hospital a couple of days later to make sure.

Benji drew the curtains around the bed and warned Dibra that if he lagged them for the shooting, he would make sure that he fixed him once and for all. Benji grabbed Dino's badly broken leg and twisted it powerfully to reinforce the message.

Four days later, Dino was out of hospital and already looking for revenge, just as Johnny had warned Benji. But Dino was after Johnny, who had counselled Benji to shoot him. Dino forced a friend of Johnny's to set him up, inviting him over to partake in some drugs.

When Johnny was nice and relaxed after a few bongs, Dino and an associate walked in and proceeded to beat him savagely with the butt of a pistol, then tossed him in the boot of their car.

They took him out to a remote location on a dirt road far from town, the precise place that Johnny had suggested as the ideal place to kill Dino. Johnny told them that they should get on with what they had planned, fully expecting to die.

But Dino was reluctant, even though Johnny had shown him no mercy. The other gunman became impatient, threatening to shoot Dino if he didn't let Johnny have it.

With an apologetic shrug, Dino blasted Johnny's right leg with his magnum, knocking him on his backside. The second shooter pushed a sawn-off shotgun to Johnny's other leg and shredded the limb with one barrel. The two gunmen left him where he lay and took off in their vehicle.

Fortunately for Johnny, there was a bushfire in the area. Fire crews were descending on the scene and almost literally ran over Johnny. Without their help, he would probably have bled to death within an hour or so.

Johnny kept quiet about what really happened, claiming that he had fallen foul of an Asian gang, which had brought him out here. He kept to the same story when talking to police, which meant they had nowhere to go with their investigation. Not that the law had much interest in shitheads like these taking pot shots at one another.

The *Herald Sun* newspaper would later describe the tit-for-tat shooting as part of an underworld power struggle between Asian and Australian gangs. There was no link made between the shooting and Dino and Benji's theft of the undercover police car and the computer disk, even though the fall-out from that theft would yet claim several lives.

In a striking coincidence, Johnny found himself in the very same bed at the Western Hospital that Dino had occupied four days earlier. Johnny couldn't wait to get out of hospital, just in case Dino had changed his mind and now wanted to kill him. It was obvious to all that two non-fatal woundings had settled nothing; in fact, they had made matters much worse. The next time there would be no warning shots, or woundings. Only a corpse would do, maybe several before matters were resolved.

In the meantime, they would make sure they knew what their enemies were up to. A few weeks after shooting Dino, Benji was seen in the company of his old friend, carrying on as if all was sweet between them.

When asked why he had accepted Dino back after declaring him a dog and shooting him, Benji was defensive. Benji claimed that he had wanted to make an example of Dino but now it was all over. Johnny suspected this was all about money. Dino was flush with cash and was doubtless sharing some with Benji so he was prepared to tolerate the earlier transgressions.

But the peace between them was uneasy. Johnny knew that Benji could change his mind at any time, such was his volatile personality. Meanwhile, there was talk around Sunshine that Dino still harboured a thirst for revenge against Benji. When the time was right, he would pop the little cunt, Johnny had heard.

This two-faced treachery was all too common in the western suburbs at this stage.

Dino was in conflict with a number of people, but he still did business with them, providing credit on drugs and lending them money so he could act like a big shot. His cousin Rezza was a good example.

Rezza had once ripped Dino off on a pound of weed and then absconded to Queensland. Dino and Benji had retrieved him and tortured the hapless thief for days before they let him go, his debt seemingly extinguished. Dino even later hired Rezza as his driver. But Rezza was faint-hearted. Whenever they ran across a police car, Rezza would stop the car and bail out, leaving his employer to explain what the hell they were up to.

Under the influence of cocaine, Dino Dibra was the loudest and most obnoxious man in Melbourne. His crew was renowned for turning up at flash nightclubs, like the Dome at the old Chevron Hotel in Prahran, dressed in their Kappa tracksuits and runners and demanding to be admitted. The Dome had been a haunt of the Morans and their associates for years, and management was under instructions to keep the 'upstart wogs' like Dibra out, according to a bouncer who worked the door in that era.

'We looked after the Morans because they stayed below the radar. We knew they were doing some drug business in the club, but it was all low-key. Occasionally Jason would make a fuss, but Mark made sure everything went nice and smooth while they were in the house. There was too much riding on that, considering how much money they were making and their relationships with the cops,' he says.

'Dibra and his mates would turn up in their tracksuits and their gold chains, without any girls, and demand entry. And we would keep them out, or face the wrath of the Morans. Knowing that "old school" people like the Morans had the run of the place and that they couldn't get in the door drove guys like Dibra crazy. He thought his money entitled him to entry,' says the ex-bouncer.

In December 1998, Dibra's resentment boiled over. He shot two bouncers outside the Dome. The press speculated that the shooting had been related to extortion or drug business in the club, but in fact it was all to do with respect. Dibra had shot the pair, one in the arm and the other in the guts, because the bouncers had belittled him and his crew. It was one thing to refuse them entry but another to rub it in their faces. People close to Dino say it was an entirely spontaneous action. He believed he was a law unto himself at such moments. In his own mind, Dino was now bigger than the movie villains he had modelled himself on.

When he wasn't on drugs, Dibra was much the same kid Johnny had grown up with. He wasn't a natural-born killer, otherwise he would have killed Johnny back in 1996. He just liked to talk big. As Dino told one newspaper, 'I've seen *Reservoir Dogs* too many times, mate.'

By 2000, Johnny hadn't spoken to Dino in nearly three years, except for the occasional verbal encounter at a nightclub. Dino would challenge Johnny to come out for a fight and then back down, making big noises about how he planned to kill Johnny and his family.

Senior men in Carlton had attempted a mediation and there was an uneasy truce between them. This was never going to last, both sides knew it. So it was better to avoid each other until what they imagined would be a final confrontation.

Meanwhile, Benji continued to hang around Dino, doing jobs for him for cash, picking up debts and threatening rivals. Everyone, except Dino, seemed to realise that this arrangement could not last. People were starting to talk behind Benji's back.

Then one day Dino made a fatal error. He ordered Benji to choose between him and Johnny. He told Benji that he could no longer play both sides of the street. He didn't want to hear Johnny's name again.

That was the end of any kind of friendship Benji and Dino might have had. Benji was headed onto bigger and better things in Carlton. Dino was ancient history to him now.

12

BENJI

Benji liked to say that he had many associates but only a handful of friends – and most of those died young. The rest of his relationships were strictly business. But, in the end, it was Benji's friends who had the most to fear from him.

A part of Benji's character was always rooted in his upbringing as a good Greek boy. Even as he became a bigger figure in the underworld, he kept his criminal life away from his family. He told them there were things about his life they should never know. It was just better that way, he said, safer for everyone.

According to Johnny Auciello, Benji boasted that his father had registered his second-born son with two different surnames. One birth certificate bore the name 'Andrew Veniamin' and the other 'Andrew Benjamin'. From day one, the boy had two identities. 'They must have known he was going to be a crim,' one former policeman had said. Though his father never explained why he had done it, Benji was thankful for the dual identities. He had driver's licences in each name – until he racked up enough fines and demerits to lose both of them. He didn't bother with a licence at all after that.

By his early teens, Benji was running amok in Sunshine. One day, he was in the milk bar at the Glengala shops in Sunshine when the owner accused him of shoplifting, slapped him hard across the face and threw him out of the shop. Benji went straight home to get a baseball bat, then returned to the shop and set about smashing everything he could. Benji's father, Apollo, had emigrated from Cyprus in 1970 and for years worked as a welder at the Sunshine

Harvester Works. Like his son, Veniamin senior had found it hard to turn the other cheek to bullies. He was a hard worker and a quiet man but gained a reputation as someone who could not be pushed around. Apollo and his wife, Marianna, had tried hard to raise their three children in the Australian way, but Greek culture and tradition ruled at home. The kids went to Greek school every Saturday to learn the language and customs of their heritage. Andrew and his brother, Steve, both did their time as altar boys at St Andrew's Greek Orthodox Church near the Glengala shops – the same church where Benji's funeral would be held in March 2004.

From his teens onwards, Benji complained that he was being picked on by the local police. He resented that his small stature made him a target. PK called him 'Weed' because he was so slight; no one else could get away with that. This inferiority complex contributed to a deep loathing for anyone who pushed him around, especially the police.

Benji made his name synonymous with loyalty and crazy bravery. When he and several older men hijacked a truckload of cigarettes, Benji had been the only one not to disguise his face. He had allowed the gang to park the truck at his house and the contraband was concealed under his house, ready for distribution.

When he was arrested, Benji refused to finger his confederates, despite copping a hiding in custody. He was offered a suspended sentence or a bond if he cooperated, but he refused to budge. In the end, only he was convicted, landing a sentence in a juvenile detention centre. The conviction cost him the chance to go to the 1994 Commonwealth Games as a boxer, but it won him huge credit in Sunshine.

Though he weighed just 52.5 kilos in his boxing days, Andrew 'the Vice' Veniamin had more dash than men twice his size. As a flyweight kickboxer 'Benji' would take on all comers. Outside of the ring, he was just the same, even more so after he began taking steroids to beef himself up.

A local boxing trainer, Johnny Schida, who had a history of producing champions, said he'd take Benji on if he promised to leave his gangster business at the door. Schida believed he had the potential to be a champ but a reckless ride on the motorbike in 1998 left him with a smashed knee, and ended any hopes of a legitimate career.

There was rage growing in Benji throughout his twenties. He wanted to show everyone he was just as staunch as the rest, that the police couldn't break him. He was out to prove their cruelty had inspired him, and many others just like him.

Until the last few years of his life, Benji didn't take recreational drugs and hardly ever took a drink. He despised what he saw as the weakness in people who needed drugs to get by, even if he made his living from them. He believed in keeping business and pleasure separate. He had learnt from his favourite film, *Scarface*, that a wise man never 'got high on his own supply'. Benji would threaten to shoot anyone who used the company products for recreational purposes.

As he grew, so too did his penchant for cruelty and capricious violence. One time he slept with the girlfriend of an associate who was minding a cannabis crop for him. A few weeks later, the sitter had complained in company that Benji rooting his girlfriend had been a 'doggish act'. Benji went hunting for the man, promising to shoot him. Benji also demanded the man's parents hand over $20 000 in compensation or he would kill their son. The family took out a mortgage on their house to make the payment, but that wasn't enough for Benji. He demanded another $20 000, but they said their credit was exhausted. Benji then shot up the parents' house and motor vehicle. Finally, he located the offender and shot him in the legs and buttocks as a lesson to others who might dare cross him.

Benji came to regard himself as a kind of vigilante. People would come to him with problems for him to solve. The sister of an associate once complained that another motorist had collided with her vehicle and drove away without exchanging details. A fortnight later Benji picked up the girl and went to the house of the offending driver whom he had somehow located. He burst into the man's house and dragged him out at gunpoint. He shot him right there in the street. Police were made aware of the attack but were powerless to act because the victim dared not assist: any other course of action and he would never be safe from Benji's wrath.

Benji had ambitions way beyond Sunshine. He was headed for the big-time crime scene in the city, he told friends. By 2000, he was regularly in the company of Dominic 'Mick' Gatto, renowned as the head of the Carlton Crew. Years earlier, Benji vowed that he would be at Mick's right hand before he was finished. His mates had laughed at this: what would Mick do with an angry little shitkicker from Sunshine like him? But Benji was determined. It was his one chance to be someone, even if that someone was a criminal. He explained that one of the reasons he had taken up kickboxing was because all the top gangsters in town were into the sport. A fight night was where you got to meet the city's leading men of honour, men like Mick Gatto and his mate Mario Condello, a disbarred lawyer who allegedly ran things in Carlton.

This was the arena Benji aspired to be in, where the great and powerful gathered. He promised that one day he would be among them, right alongside Mick. Everything he did was about achieving that goal. Even if Mick had no idea who Benji was back then.

Benji's break came when he met the cousin of a leading figure in Carlton who ran a small factory in Sunshine, making curios for two-dollar shops. For nearly a year, Benji worked in the factory, putting together cheap souvenirs, taking his chances to meet the most powerful men in town.

Mick admired the front and boldness of this little man from Sunshine and welcomed him into his circle. Benji was now meeting Mick's mates, including big business people who employed him to do certain delicate jobs for them. Benji quickly fitted into the organisation, doing odd jobs for Mick, like repossessing the motor vehicles of recalcitrant debtors. He would move around with a pink slip in his car so he could quickly transfer ownership of the vehicles.

By the late 1990s, Benji was on top of the world. He idolised Mick and his stylish gangster ways. In return, Mick treated Benji like a surrogate son.

One night, Benji wanted to take in a show at the Men's Gallery strip club, even if he didn't meet the dress code, attired as usual in jeans and a body-hugging T-shirt. The bouncer refused him entry but Benji just marched past him. Two or three bouncers then grabbed him and ejected him onto the street, giving him a few to go on with. Benji was straight on the phone to Mick, who happened to be dining a few blocks away.

Within five minutes, Mick and some heavy mates were on the scene to give the bouncers a severe hiding. Gatto struck one so forcefully he sailed through the air and crashed into a table, fracturing his leg. Later, the club owner made an abject apology to Benji for what he said was a misunderstanding.

From that moment, Benji felt like he had the key to Melbourne. No one would fuck with him if he had the backing of the Carlton Crew. No longer could bouncers get away with pushing Benji around like he was just some punk from the suburbs.

Benji's father, Apollo, warned that nothing good would come from these new friendships. He was certain his son would end up in hell for all the sins he was committing. Benji was becoming a loose cannon even within his own family.

He had got into an argument with his father over some trivial matter. In a psychotic eruption, Benji had jammed a handgun between his father's lips and threatened to spray his brains all over the family home. Benji's mum had to call the police to quell the rage of his son, but Apollo refused to give evidence against his own flesh and blood. And yet he saw only disaster ahead for his wayward boy.

By 2000, the Sunshine crew were headed in different directions. Benji was with the Carlton Crew. Dino was best pals with Carl. Mark Mallia had hooked up with Nikolai 'the Russian' Radev, a vicious psychopath from Eastern Europe. Carl had been doing business with Radev for some time in drug precursors and they had formed a friendship.

Only PK was doing his own thing in West Sunshine with dope grow-houses and coke; he didn't need anybody else. Johnny Auciello had found God, who did indeed deliver him from evil. By the end he was the only one left standing.

13

TURNCOATS AND LIONHEARTS

Carl took a certain pleasure in staying on top of all the infighting and dramas going on between his new pals. It became something of a game for him, working out who was with him and who was not. It was also key to his survival. The Morans were plotting against him, he knew that. They had even approached members of Carl's own crew to do the job; they had come straight back to Carl and told him.

The Morans were cheap; that was a big plus for Carl. They were offering just half the going rate of $100 000 a hit. There was no certainty they would pay up either. It was just as easy to have someone else kill the shooter. You could always find someone desperate who would work for less, but nobody who was any good. Their only top-notch killer was Andrew Veniamin, but he was just stepping up for work in 2000. And by then he already had his doubts about the Morans.

Carl had some of the best gunnies in town on his side now. He had bought them just like he had his schoolmates in Broadie. It also helped that the Moran family was deeply unpopular, and there were lots of people with scores to settle with them. To get paid for it would be a welcome bonus. It was pitiful how little it took to buy someone's loyalty. There would be cash for punting on a promise of big money later, a regular supply of drugs, some new clothes, maybe a car. But Carl knew that if he could manipulate people, then others could too.

Carl fancied himself as an astute judge of character, especially under the influence of crack cocaine, which he was smoking plenty of at that time. He was, in fact, a terrible judge of character, according to Roberta, prone to snap judgements based on gut feeling and dodgy references from the idiots he trusted. He even found something to like about Greg Domaszewicz, who in 1998 had beaten the rap for the murder of his girlfriend's infant son, Jaidyn Leskie. Domaszewicz's cousin had lived next door to Carl and Roberta in Hillside. Domaszewicz fell in love with Roberta and tried to persuade her to leave Carl for him.

Carl thought he was assembling the greatest team ever known. In reality, he was gathering a group of misfits, halfwits and freaks, all of whom shared his delusions of grandeur when in the grip of one narcotic or another.

Carl's paranoid suspicions on the crack had a way of coming true: it was enough for someone to say the wrong thing, to hold something back, to be seen talking to the wrong girl. Like a card player, he was constantly searching the faces of his associates for 'tells', tiny intimations of deception, fear and treachery. Carl resolved to keep them around till there was proof of their double-dealing, believing he would know when that was. In the meantime, he could console himself with the fact there was safety in numbers.

Carl had met career criminal Richard Mladenich in jail back in 1995. Mladenich had twenty-four aliases but preferred to go by 'King Richard' or 'Richard the Lionheart'. He had grown up in Roberta's social circle in Frankston and so came into Carl's circle with her recommendation. Carl had needed Richard's protection in jail. Without it, Carl would have fallen prey to any thug, thief or sodomite; Barb's little boy would not have lasted a week inside on his own. His generosity, and the perhaps-apocryphal container of pseudoephedrine he had stashed away somewhere, had made him extremely vulnerable. His lack of physical prowess meant he quickly became a hostage to his protectors.

According to Roberta, Carl loved Richard. She says after getting out of jail he spent every day with him, no doubt supplying Richard's voracious drug habit in return for his dubious services as a bodyguard. Richard was wild and dishevelled, forever high on something, often raving and incoherent. At least his craziness was some kind of asset to Carl.

That oddness perhaps came as a result of an altercation with legendary standover man turned star of stage and screen Mark Brandon 'Chopper' Read in Pentridge Prison in the 1980s.

Read says one night, after lockdown, Mladenich consumed a sheet of Rohypnol tablets and when he was well off his head, began denouncing every prisoner in the division as a dog, cell by cell, demanding they acknowledge his charge. When Read refused, Mladenich promised to beat him up in the exercise yard the following day.

Next morning, when Read saw Mladenich coming, he motioned to an associate to catch him by the coat to distract him, whereupon a friendly screw handed Read a garden spade.

Read called out cheerily, 'Hi, Richard.'

When Mladenich turned, Read hit him full force with the edge of the spade across the forehead, opening up his skull. It was like cracking a boiled egg with a teaspoon, Read recalls. It was amazing that the blow didn't kill him. There were no hard feelings though. Mladenich told the screws he had fallen down and hit his head on a rock. Soon he was botting smokes off Read as if nothing had ever happened. After the incident, he came to be known by all as 'Spade Brain'.

Richard recovered but he was never quite the same again. For one, he abandoned any semblance of a personal-hygiene regimen. According to Read, he would fail to shower for weeks on end, 'and even wiping his arse was beyond him'. How Carl, with his fastidious, almost compulsive, attitude to cleanliness, could have sat in a hot car all day with this defies explanation. Certainly, King Richard's reign over Carl didn't last long.

Mladenich fell out with Arico and Dibra amid talk that he was also hanging around with Mark Moran. In August 1999, Arico and Dibra took Mladenich hostage in broad daylight, throwing him into the boot of the car. At one stage, Mladenich managed to pop the boot from the inside and made off into traffic. Onlookers were treated to the spectacle of the kidnappers chasing their hostage down the road and marching him at gunpoint back to the car and into the boot once more. Eventually, Mladenich's brother paid a ransom for his hapless sibling's freedom. Carl had done nothing to assist; indeed, the exercise surely must have been carried out with his knowledge, such was his close relationship with Arico and Dibra at that time.

'Spade Brain' might not have realised it, but he was living on borrowed time. On 16 May 2000 it ran out.

Mladenich was visiting a drug dealer who was using Room 18 of the seedy Esquire Motel in St Kilda as his base. There were three others present at the time in various states of intoxication. At 3.30 a.m., there was a knock at the door. The visitor walked in, produced a gun, shot Mladenich in the back of the head and then calmly left the premises. None of the witnesses could assist police.

Carl's associate Rocco Arico was named by police as the prime suspect in the murder. Later, in jail, Arico boasted that he had killed Mladenich on Carl's behalf. The story went that Mladenich had taken a down payment to kill one of the Morans, and then reneged, so Carl had contracted Arico to do the job on him. Others say he was killed simply for being a dill – people had become tired of Richard, he was annoying. Not much of a motive. All it took were a few conversations, an exchange of money and someone's life was ended. He was just a problem swept out of the way.

By this time, Mark Moran was becoming increasingly unhinged. After the incident with Carl the year before at Gladstone Park, he had suffered bouts of severe depression, which had required hospitalisation. There had been several attempts at suicide, says Bert Wrout.

'I still remember the phone calls, Lewis saying, "Quick, get over here, Markie's tried to kill himself again,"' says Wrout. On one occasion, Mark had stuffed a large quantity of ecstasy tablets up his arse, he recalls. These were perhaps cries for help, not serious attempts at suicide. Wrout says Mark's mental illness was connected to the abuse he had suffered at the hands of Lewis. Mark had real dash like his father, Johnny Cole, says Wrout. Not like 'the weak dog' Lewis who had raised him.

No matter how much he worked out, or how finely he dressed, it seemed that Mark could not fill the emptiness within. Part of him wanted to be the prosperous pastry chef that he pretended to be to outsiders.

A schoolfriend encountered Mark in 1999 after a long time apart.

'Mark talked of his journey into trade school and chef work, and lots of other "good stuff" he had going on. He seemed happy and proud of his two kids and wife, Antonella, but was frustrated with Jason,' he says. The elapse of ten years had not changed Mark's nervous habits. His old classmate couldn't remember a time when Mark wasn't chewing his nails out of anxiety, and he was still doing it.

Meanwhile, though, there was business to transact. Without Mark, the family empire would quickly fall into chaos.

At this time, Jason was in jail on serious assault charges. He and Alphonse Gangitano had run amok at the Sports Bar on King Street in December 1995, attacking innocent bystanders with pool cues. It was believed that the owner of the club had refused to pay protection money to Gangitano so he had taken it out on the patrons.

In January 1998, Gangitano had been murdered at his home in Templestowe. It was thought the Morans had eliminated him after he had decided to plead guilty over the Sports Bar assault. If Gangitano nodded to this charge, then Jason would go to jail as well, and Lewis wasn't having that. Bert Wrout believes that Lewis dispatched Mark and long-time friend Graham 'the Munster' Kinniburgh to kill Gangitano. The coroner concluded that Jason was in on the kill but he was never charged for it.

Wrout alleges that it was the Munster who pulled the trigger on Gangitano but that is hotly disputed. What is agreed on is that Jason didn't do it. Mark Moran had the cruel, ruthless streak to get the job done, no matter what it was. Jason was just a poseur.

It's unclear whether Mark knew that Carl was plotting against him. He didn't seem overly concerned. Wrout says it made sense that Mark was the first Moran to be hit.

He was the biggest threat.

'Mark was the smartest and bravest of the crew. He had been Lewis's attack dog from an early age. Now he was running the show. He was just too loyal or greedy to get away from his family that was about to come to a sticky end,' says Wrout.

It seemed that 15 June 2000 was a normal day for Mark Moran. He took the kids to school, then went shopping with his mother. Later, he met his wife, Antonella, for lunch. Then his working day began. At 7.10 p.m. he went to Gladstone Park shopping centre to meet an associate, Darren Hafner, to transact some business. He handed over the ecstasy tabs as promised, but had forgotten the cannabis. Mark said he would bring it the following day. Hafner later told the coroner he had been concerned about Moran, saying he seemed distracted, not quite himself. As always, Mark's fingernails were bitten down to the quick. He arrived back home at 7.45 p.m. but was soon off again, this time to deliver some football tickets to another friend.

This was Moran's life – a mundane series of errands and meetings. The years of armed robbery and drug manufacture with the Ascot Vale crew had been very good to him. He told police he was a qualified pastry chef and part-time personal trainer, yet he lived in a million-dollar home in a yuppie enclave, with no mortgage, and his kids attended private school. The men he had run with on the streets of Melbourne's north had become the hardest in Melbourne. Armed robbers and gunmen Jedd Houghton, Graeme Jensen, Gary Abdallah and Mark Militano had all died at the hands of police during the wars of the 1980s, while Victor Peirce would live another two years before he met his executioner.

Mark Moran's brains had taken his family to the top, yet he seemed unaware that things had now taken a turn for the worse. Roberta says he was probably too self-absorbed to notice. There was definitely a feud on after Jason had shot Carl. Both Mark and Roberta's kids went to Penleigh and Essendon Grammar School. There had been several ugly confrontations between Roberta and Mark in the school drop-off zone. She says Mark told her it was kill or be killed between him and Carl, but many doubt this. Bert Wrout is adamant that Mark had no fear of Carl. He was too arrogant for that.

He had been under police surveillance at different times in the recent past, or perhaps for a long period, under what police were calling 'Operation Via'. However, just four days before his death the dog squad was called off.

Moran was opening the door of his car when his killer strode up from behind and opened fire. Residents heard two big explosions followed by two smaller ones. The gunman, later described by a witness simply as a man in dark clothes, had fired a shotgun twice into Mark's chest and face, blasting him back into his vehicle. He then delivered the coup de grâce, two more shots from a .32-calibre handgun, before fleeing. One witness reported seeing Mark still moving feebly at this point but he had no chance of survival. He was dead seconds later when residents went to lend assistance. Police photographs showed a pair of slender long legs shod in white runners sticking out of the open driver's-side door.

Bert Wrout had been drinking with Lewis at the Laurel but someone else was driving Moran home that night. Bert was on his way home when he got the call.

All the remaining senior men in Lewis's faction gathered at an apartment owned by a friend in Essendon. There was the Munster, Lewis, Wrout, Lou Cozzo and Mick Gatto. It was described as a council of war in the media but it was closer to a council of despair, according to Wrout. No one seemed to have any idea who had killed Mark. Certainly no one suspected Carl, says Wrout. He didn't have the balls for it, or so they thought. 'The opposition had relied on a shock-and-awe tactic when they killed Mark and they sure succeeded,' says Wrout.

What shocked Wrout was that nobody was taking control. There were no threats of revenge or movements towards making any sort of plan. Lewis Moran simply stared into his glass and let out the occasional groan, almost as if he were gasping for breath. Munster was like a statue at Lewis's side, saying nothing but occasionally pounding his fist on the table.

But talk of Carl's involvement spread quickly from the moment Rocco Arico stormed into a city club later that night loudly boasting, 'We got Mark tonight!'

Police were later told by two of Carl's associates that he had been the assassin in the murder of Mark Moran, but that would have been close to physically impossible. At 7.21 p.m. Carl, with Dennis Reardon, had picked up a rental car at Melbourne airport. Reardon had driven his own car to Carl's residence in Taylors Lakes, where he waited for Carl. At 7.48 p.m., phone records show that Carl made a call from the Tullamarine Freeway on his way home.

He claimed that when he got home, Reardon and his son, Shane, were there. At 7.55 p.m., Carl made a call from home, nearly 16 kilometres away from Mark Moran's house or twenty-one minutes' drive if Carl were travelling within the speed limits. Reardon and his son set off for Melton, as they had to pick up methadone for Shane by 8.30 p.m.

Soon after, Carl then left home to drive to Reardon's place at Melton South, a distance of 23 kilometres. At 8.36 p.m. when Mark Moran was lying riddled with bullets and shotgun pellets, Carl was on the telephone in the Taylors Lakes area.

At 8.49 p.m., Carl was caught on a CCTV camera buying a bottle of water at a service station just a few minutes' drive away from Reardon's home.

Police later drove from Taylors Lakes to Melton South, observing all road rules, and found it took twenty-four minutes. They cut the time to just eighteen minutes in a second attempt but still for Carl to shoot Mark Moran and then make it to Reardon's house without his driving attracting attention seems unlikely.

Soon after Mark was shot, Carl rang Roberta to ask her to heat up his frozen diet meal for the night, as he was trying to lose weight. He wouldn't microwave his own food; why would he kill a person when someone else could be paid to do it?

Veteran homicide investigator Detective Senior Sergeant Ron Iddles had led a raid on Carl's home at 5.30 a.m. the next morning. He had found the clothes Carl had been wearing the previous evening thrown on the floor near his bed. There were no bloodstains or gunshot residues and there was no evidence to be found in Carl's car either. Carl had been completely cool, despite being dragged from bed before dawn. He knew there was nothing linking him to the murder. That was the beauty of ordering a hit; the shooter bore all the risk.

Iddles knew almost immediately that Carl hadn't been the shooter but was up to his neck in Mark Moran's murder. Despite this, police did later charge Carl over the killing, after orders from on high, but investigators were never able to plug the gaping holes in their case.

Many believe the shooter, paid by Carl, was an old family friend.

The man had been a regular player at George's card games, and already had a reputation for extreme brutality, a blood lust even. He had pedigree. He can't be named for legal reasons so let's call him 'the Savage'. He would accumulate more than sixty convictions in his long and bloody career, including several for murder. The Savage was like a second father to Carl. In fact, the Savage would go on to carry out several hits on Carl's behalf. An informer later told police that the shotgun used in the killing of Mark Moran was one of a pair bought by an associate of Carl from Dino Dibra.

This associate, let's call him 'Snalfy', was a jack-of-all-trades for Carl. He had helped set up the pill press at the family's garage in Broadmeadows and had been a major distributor of pills, cocaine and pot for Tony Mokbel and the Williamses. A trained fitter and turner, Snalfy knew how to cut down long rifles into easily concealed weapons. Snalfy kept one shotgun for himself and gave the older one, a 12-gauge under-and-over, to Carl. It had an inscription on the breech that read: 'Mitch on your 21st. From . . . The Boy's 23/4/56'.

Dibra was so pleased to be involved in the deal, he never asked to be paid for the shotguns, and even took to claiming Mark Moran's hit for himself.

Mark was buried two days later, after a service at St Therese's Church in Essendon. Jason managed to obtain permission from prison authorities to attend. He sat in the church with his head buried in his hands.

Forbidden by authorities to speak to his father at the funeral, Jason had sought out Lewis's eyes several times during the service.

Jason wanted a sign from Lewis that something was being done to square up for Mark. Blood had to be spilled. If Jason had been free that day there would have been a bloodbath.

Jason expressed that blood lust in a death notice for Mark: 'Words could never, ever express the way I am feeling. This is only the beginning. It will never end. Remember, I will never forget.'

But anyone who knew Jason didn't think he was up to the task of killing Carl. He had gained the nickname 'Billy the Kid', but his friends knew he didn't have it in him. He was a bully who was used to people backing down when he threatened them. Carl had called his bluff.

Carl seemed relaxed and happy after Mark's death. His biggest threat now six feet under, he and Mokbel could take over Mark Moran's business. There was a fortune to be made. The balance of power changed the night Mark Moran died and everyone knew it.

Wrout couldn't believe that the Morans and Mark's mates, whom he had enriched through his dash and criminal acumen, were going to do nothing to avenge his murder.

'Integrity and honour died that night. It wasn't only Mark that perished, but with him went those simpering, spineless arseholes with hearts as big as peas; his so-called friends. They vaporised from our world virtually overnight,' Wrout says.

Roberta, in contrast, was over the moon that Mark was gone. She rang the *Herald Sun* and tried to place a death notice for Mark, just to mock them.

She asked that it read 'from the dog squad, "Thanks for all your help, Mark, we'll really miss you – St Kilda Road Police Station."' But the newspaper wouldn't accept it.

14

LEAD RAIN

On the evening of 14 October 2000, Dino Dibra was leaving his dope shack in West Sunshine. It was just a place where he grew his hydroponic cash crops; besides the lights and other equipment there was just a sofa, fridge and a TV there. He had been to a barbecue with his family that afternoon and had dropped by the shack to hook up with a few of his crew before heading out for a night on the town.

Dino was making enemies all over town; he didn't seem to care who he offended. In 1998, he had declared Alphonse Gangitano a dog. You didn't fuck with Alphonse unless you wanted a war. Nightclub owners paid him thousands of dollars just to stay away from their places, and any rival dealers who stepped onto Al's Lygon Street turf were dealt with personally. Though he was not connected with the major Italian families, Al had the protection of forces much higher up the chain of the Honoured Society. He was a rarity among the Carlton Crew, in that he was involved in drugs as well as the traditional standover and illegal gaming businesses. Al was arrogant and unpredictable, with a very broad sphere of influence. He wasn't going to take shit from some loudmouth kid from Sunshine, and anybody who sat around idly listening to such braggadocio would be presumed an enemy too.

For the next two years, Al waited for his chance to get Dino, but it never came. Whenever Dino was out of prison Al was going in, and vice versa, and two weeks before Dino was due for release from his last stint in jail, someone from the Moran camp popped Alphonse at his home in Templestowe. Even in death Al couldn't get near Dino. They are buried five minutes' walk apart in the Fawkner Cemetery.

Dino was getting very paranoid at that time, a consequence of his cocaine use and the very real possibility that people were out to get him. Johnny Auciello says one night in July 2000, Dino believed that an innocent motorist with whom he had clashed was, in fact, a rival out to get him. Dibra and Arico were racing another carload of hoons through the back streets of Taylors Lakes. They sped through a roundabout at high speed, causing a car driven by twenty-nine-year-old Vincent Godino to spin 180 degrees.

Unwisely, Godino chased the two cars. He drove past them while they were parked whereupon one of the vehicles, carrying Arico, followed him. After the car stopped alongside, Godino recognised Arico and the pair began arguing over the traffic incident. According to Godino's evidence, he complained that one of Arico's friends had almost run him off the road.

Arico replied, 'So what do you want to do about it?'

Godino responded, 'Well, I want to put his head through the windscreen.'

Arico had then pulled out a handgun and started to fire. Godino, trapped by his seatbelt, was helpless as Arico emptied his gun into the car. Godino was hit five times, in his forearms, abdomen, right elbow and shoulder, and feared at any moment he would die.

Supreme Court Justice Coldrey gave Arico a seven-year minimum term after he was found guilty of attempting to murder Godino.

This was the mentality of the people around Dibra. Already Arico had drawn the ire of the Moran clan by claiming to have been in on the murder of Mark Moran. Rather than trying to quell the talk, Dino had also taken to claiming he was responsible for Mark's death. In reality, he had done nothing more than supply the shotgun.

By this time, Andrew Veniamin was firmly entrenched in the Moran camp. While he and Dibra had grown up together, they were now on opposite sides of a war. And Veniamin's career as a hit man was well underway.

The dawn of the new millennium had been tumultuous for Francesco Benvenuto, long reputed to be the Godfather of Melbourne.

Early in 2000, Benvenuto had made the acquaintance of Andrew Veniamin. Frank had fallen out with a business associate at the Queen Victoria wholesale fruit-and-vegetable market and relations had become tense. Benji had accosted Frank on behalf of this rival and pushed him into the back of a car at gunpoint for a chat.

Benji had passed on the message that Frank should stay away from his competitor and leave well enough alone. Frank had taken this badly. At the age of fifty-two, Frank had come out on top of a long and bloody power struggle for control of Melbourne's Mafia. This little arsehole from Sunshine couldn't be telling him what to do. Benji would get his right whack when Frank was good and ready.

On 8 May 2000, Benji, reportedly with the assistance of Mark Moran, got in first. It was perhaps Benji's first kill and he opened his account with an easy one. It's not known whether Mark or Benji pulled the trigger but the shooter appeared to have fired from inside Benvenuto's car before escaping.

But the killer hadn't killed Benvenuto outright. Frank lingered long enough to make a phone call to his bodyguard, Victor Peirce, the legendary gunman who had graduated from stick-up man to cop killer after being involved in the murder of policemen Steven Tynan and Damian Eyre at Walsh Street, South Yarra, in 1988. Those killings had been a random act of savagery, payback for the death of Peirce's mate Graeme Jensen days earlier. By 2000, Peirce was looking after Benvenuto, but in reality he would work for the highest bidder.

Victor was certain that Benji had knocked Frank. Robbery hadn't been the motive: $60 000 cash was left untouched in the boot of Frank's car when he died. And Victor was equally sure that this bloodletting would not end with Frank. Benji would be expecting some blowback and as Frank's bodyguard it would logically come from Victor.

While Benvenuto's murder was unrelated to Carl's feud with the Morans, it showed the temperature in Melbourne's underworld was rising rapidly. If someone as well connected and respected as Benvenuto could be knocked, then no one was safe.

The killing of Mark Moran just five weeks later set the scene for a bloodbath. With Benji on the team, Jason now had a willing assassin who was a genuine killer, not just a gangster wannabe playing dress-ups. Benji was the real deal, as Dino Dibra was about to find out.

As he walked to his rented Fairlane parked out the front, a car pulled up alongside. Three gunmen in balaclavas jumped out and opened fire on Dino. In the first volley he took at least five shots to the upper body. He sank to his knees in the driveway, but the shooters continued to blaze away, one even going back to their vehicle to reload.

Dino had been shot more than a dozen times, but remarkably he survived for several more hours in hospital. There was little clue as to the identity of the killers. A witness said they thought one of the shooters had a Russian accent. Strangely, when the bystanders tried to take shelter in the house during the shooting, they couldn't open the door. When they forced it open, they found that Dino's cousin Rezza had been bracing his legs against it to keep it shut. One of the witnesses remembered Rezza taking a call earlier that evening during which he clearly said, 'He's here' and 'There's five of them'.

Carl had been one of the first to call Dino's parents, about half an hour after the shooting. Ramiz and Violetta Dibra had been employed by Carl as house cleaners and they had become friendly.

Carl asked Ramiz whether it was true that Dino had been shot outside his shack earlier that night. That was impossible, replied Ramiz. They had left Dino a couple of hours before. Surely this was a joke, asked Ramiz, his concern growing.

'Uh huh. So it must be lies then,' Carl said, before hanging up abruptly. It took the Dibras another three hours to confirm that their son was dead. It wasn't long before Carl discovered that he was next on Benji's hit list: the Morans' associates were saying of Dino's death: 'One down, one to go.'

Maybe that's why Carl didn't attend Dino's funeral. Or maybe he was just moving on. The survival and prosperity of his family came before all else. Dino had outlived his usefulness.

Meanwhile, police could do little more than chalk the outlines on the pavement where the gangsters fell. No one was talking, at least not in statements homicide detectives could use. The joke going around VicPol was that this was a self-cleaning oven: if they waited long enough the shooters would become the victims, and open cases would be solved without investigators having to lift a finger.

15

A WHOLE LOTTA LOVE

All this death and treachery had a strange effect on Carl. He wanted to become a father, or perhaps, more accurately, he gave in to Roberta's determination to make him one.

Up until then, Roberta had found him to be a most unusual partner. He was more like a friend, someone she rumbled and play fought with, rather than a lover. The relationship between Carlos the Jackal and Bert, as they called each other, was not overtly sexual, and that suited her. Looking after the three children was her first priority; she had little interest in having a mad, passionate sexual relationship. It seemed that Carl loved her not because of sex but because she was a great mum. Here was a surrogate mother for Carl, someone who would look after his every need, just as Barb had, but she would also be available to sleep with him occasionally. Roberta even used to say being with Carl was like having another kid. It was all very convenient for Carl, another benefit of having money.

And, in return, Carl had had been incredibly generous. He had fed, clothed and educated Roberta's kids. He had paid for Roberta to travel to Europe and Asia. With her divorce settlement from Dean, Roberta had bought a luxury home in Hillside, which she had decked out in fine style using Carl's drug money. He could come and go as he pleased, knowing that all would be in order at home. He could live his emotionally remote lifestyle, spending all day driving around with his mates, drinking and doing drugs. He could have his girls on the side too. Carl was still seeing Nicole Mottram, though it's unclear whether she knew about Roberta.

When things got hot at home, or with Nicole, Carl would disappear for days on end with other women. And then there was always Barb's house in Essendon where he could retreat to, for a bit of home cooking and mollycoddling.

Barb would always take his side, even after he began knocking off his rivals. Carl was blameless in her eyes. Barb had stopped work at the TAB by this time, and Carl met all her financial needs. Most days Barb could be found down at the Moonee Valley Tabaret, playing the pokies or betting on horses. She was proud that Carl would drop by to give her money to keep her happy. He was a good son who looked after his mother. The Morans could rot in hell for all she cared. They had started this thing.

Despite the obvious risks to his self-centred, adolescent approach to life, Carl agreed it was time to have a child. But Roberta had suffered complications from earlier births, which meant she could not conceive easily. So around the time that Mark Moran was dispatched, Roberta was undergoing IVF.

They conceived by way of the procedure, but long before that moment, Roberta had gone to Europe to buy baby clothes and every accessory available to deck out the nursery. Both Roberta and Carl were determined that their child would have everything they never had. Pouring love into children seemed to be an antidote to the ugly realities of their lives. Perhaps there could be some redemption for all the deadly sins Carl was committing and from which Roberta was benefitting.

Besides that, there was fierce competition between the wives and girlfriends of Carl's circle. It was the subtext of Carl's feud with the Moran men. The Moran women had scorned Roberta. They had looked down on her fashion sense, the way she spoke, her manners, as if they were something better. 'We all played the game but some people's husbands played it better than others . . . Some people made more than others and some people stayed alive longer,' she says.

Having perfect, well-groomed and polished children who wanted for nothing was a kind of achievement in the lives they were leading.

Carl wanted a boy and was going to name him Castor Troy after the villain in *Face/Off*, the 1997 blockbuster from 'gun fu' director John Woo. It shows Carl's mindset that he would want to name his kid after a murderous terrorist who had killed an FBI agent's baby son in the film.

Yet life in the Williams home was often far from idyllic. As Roberta's pregnancy went on, she found Carl's absences and suspected infidelities almost unbearable. It all came to a head on Christmas Day 2000. Roberta had prepared lunch for numerous members of Carl's family and entourage. After eating and drinking their fill, they all promptly departed the scene, leaving Roberta to clean up. After she sorted out the mess, Roberta tracked down Carl to Rocco Arico's family home in Brunswick West. Roberta suspected that Carl was sleeping with Rocco's sister, and went over there to confront them.

At first Carl had refused to come out, but it was clear that Roberta was not going to leave quietly. She was making him look stupid in front of his mistress and that was more than his crack-enlarged ego could stand. Roberta was actually leaving when he finally emerged. Far from being apologetic, Carl was furious, shouting at her to fuck off and leave him alone. He had his .38 calibre pistol in hand and to Roberta's amazement he pointed it at her and pulled the trigger. This was perhaps the only time when Carl actually pulled the trigger in anger, and the target was the mother of his unborn child.

To Roberta it showed what an arsehole he really was. And what a bad shot. He missed her and the car with four bullets.

Carl was never going to change and Roberta had to accept that fact. Just weeks before she was due to deliver, she found a text message on Carl's phone from Nicole Mottram, declaring her love for him. This had led to an almost comical stand-up brawl in a Port Melbourne street. Roberta kicked him out but when he begged to return she relented. She needed a father for her baby and Carl needed to be looked after.

Out of all this chaos and conflict, Carl decided the best course of action was to marry Roberta. Roberta says she was in the bath one evening when Carl just walked in and handed her a one-and-a-half-carat diamond ring. It was all very matter of fact. Apparently, he wouldn't allow his daughter to be born out of wedlock.

16

WIFE AND BABY

Just days before his planned lavish wedding ceremony, Carl decided he didn't want to get married after all. He confided to his mother that he was going to call the whole thing off. Barb was rather pleased. Maybe there was time to pull out and get back with Nicole, who was much more to her liking. Still, it was a shame that there would be no party; Barb loved a good knees-up.

Roberta was in the thick of organising the huge event: hundreds of guests had been invited, a wedding dress from one of Australia's leading designers bought, live music booked, and a dazzling spread of food and drink arranged. It was all too much for Carl. He would be expected to speak and that terrified him as well. It had been hard enough getting up in front of a few dozen friends at his twenty-first.

All this fuss was way over the top for him. He was a simple bloke, he liked to say. When he wasn't planning the demise of the Morans or dealing drugs, Carl wanted a quiet life: his choice of fast food, a comfortable ensemble of trackie daks, Ralph Lauren polo shirts and moccasins. So he decided he wasn't going ahead with the wedding – he just had to tell Roberta, who he feared might punch his head in for ruining everything.

Instead, Roberta was understanding and told him he didn't have to go through with it. She thanked him for his honesty. He felt so bad that he had let her down. A few days later he came back to apologise to her and the underworld wedding of the year was back on track.

The bridal party entered the reception centre to the strains of Shania Twain's 'You're Still the One'. One hundred and ten guests were on hand for the party and cheered loudly as the couple, with Roberta eight months pregnant, cut an enormous multi-tiered wedding cake.

One guest, Victor Peirce, was thinking to himself that their wedded bliss would be short-lived. The next gathering was going to be a funeral. He had come with Roberta's sister Sharon but he wasn't there to toast the happy couple's health, wealth and prosperity. He was there on a mission from Lewis and Jason Moran to kill Carl, and Roberta too if she got in the way. The plan was to assess the strength that Carl had at hand. If Victor thought Carl was vulnerable, he was to order two hired gunmen to run through the event and shoot him down in front of his family and friends.

Roberta says that on the day Victor was acting oddly and Carl, hyper-vigilant since being shot, picked up on it. Victor had called earlier in the day to say he had been up all night and wouldn't be attending. Then he just turned up all the same.

Roberta says Carl had anticipated that the Morans might have planned a foul deed and so he stationed armed goons on the doors to keep watch.

Victor obviously decided he would bide his time or the wedding would have turned into the most spectacular shoot-out of the entire gangland war. It turned out to be a quieter affair than Carl's twenty-first, and the happy couple, with Roberta just weeks away from giving birth, retired to the bridal suite at Crown Towers that night.

When Carl discovered from associates that Peirce was working for the Morans, he resolved to have him killed. But Peirce was no pushover; Carl would need a top-notch professional to hit him. There would be time for that later but first there was a child to be born.

Tears rolled down Carl's cheeks the first time he held his baby daughter. It was a moment when the tough gangster image he cultivated fell away to reveal the soft, vulnerable underbelly. Roberta felt close to Carl again, or perhaps for the first time.

That feeling was shattered only a few weeks later when Carl took Roberta and baby Dhakota to Yarrawonga, where he had spent his childhood holidays. It was all going beautifully until Roberta discovered that Nicole Mottram was staying in the same motel. Carl's two worlds collided.

Apparently, Carl hadn't told Nicole that Roberta was even pregnant, let alone that baby Dhakota was on the same holiday. It hurt Roberta deeply that Carl kept Nicole in his heart. Why did he stay with her and agree to have a child together? At the end of the day, Carl would do whatever suited Carl. And Roberta had to admit that she could have walked out on him any time, and she didn't have to go through IVF. It was how his mother had raised him: to believe he was special and that the normal rules did not apply to him.

Roberta's answer to this was to throw another party. If life could be like a fairytale, then Carl's infidelities and indifference wouldn't hurt so much. The wedding was to be nothing compared to Dhakota's christening, which would take place in May 2001. It would be held at the same Keilor reception centre as the wedding and Roberta planned to go all out, spending $150 000.

Meanwhile, the Morans were not being as passive. Police learnt, through listening devices, that Lewis and Jason had hired two men to assassinate Carl at Dhakota's christening. They had to intervene to avert an embarrassing public killing. Police weren't concerned if the bad guys killed each other in private but to let it happen at a busy reception centre with plenty of innocent bystanders would have been a very bad look.

At the time, Carl was on bail, awaiting trial for a charge as a result of the November 1999 drugs bust. Any arrest would see him returned to custody, safely beyond the reach of the Morans' hired killers.

Just days prior to the christening, police set up a sting operation. An undercover officer would buy $100 000 worth of ecstasy (8000 pills) from an associate of Carl, Walter Foletti.

In telephone intercepts, police heard Carl and Foletti discussing the supply of 'soccer balls', a codename for ounces of cocaine. Carl had been suspicious about doing business with Foletti from the start, but this was Roberta's deal. She had met Foletti and his wife, Libby, because their daughter was at school with her daughter. They were less than accomplished drug dealers, though, just a mum and dad who saw a way out of their financial problems through drug dealing. Carl was sceptical of the buyer that Foletti had lined up. Who bought 8000 pills without even seeing a sample? But Roberta told him he was just being paranoid. By now, all of Carl and Roberta's phones were bugged, and the cops were listening to every word.

The day before the police swooped, the undercover operative ordered ten 'soccer balls' from Foletti. He was also asked to supply 27 500 ecstasy tablets. Carl, whom Foletti called 'my boss', stood to make $10 per tablet, while Foletti would make just $3. After the officer gave Foletti $100 000 in exchange for the ecstasy tablets, Roberta drove to Foletti's home in her BMW coupé and left three minutes later with a shopping bag.

She then drove to Watergardens Shopping Centre, where she was arrested along with Carl, who was found looking inside the bag at the money.

Roberta got bail within forty-eight hours, but Carl remained inside for sixteen months. The christening was rescheduled for December 2003.

There hadn't even been time to tell the guests that the christening was off. According to Roberta, guests still turned up on the day to find an empty reception centre. Worse was to come. The police raided the Hillside home that Roberta had decorated and furnished from scratch, taking most of the furniture. The house was sold soon after and Carl and Roberta rented a series of homes over the next few years. They were going to need the $300 000 the sale raised to pay lawyers and school fees while Carl was inside.

The police sting saved Carl's life that day, but just delayed the inevitable conflict.

Carl's partner Tony Mokbel, meanwhile, was having troubles of his own.

On 24 August 2001, Victorian and federal police launched Victoria's biggest-ever series of drug raids, codenamed 'Operation Kayak'. They would lay charges against a range of villains, including Mokbel, for trafficking in speed, ecstasy, precursor chemicals, cocaine, hashish and LSD. In a shipping container holding ceramic toilets at a Coburg factory, police had found enough pseudoephedrine to produce $2 billion's worth of drugs. Mokbel was described in court as the principal player in the scheme. A senior police officer suggested that the ephedrine seized would have serviced the state's ecstasy market for six months. The cops also seized $15 million in assets, including Mokbel's Ferrari, a penthouse and his jetski.

Two men had given up Mokbel to police, sharing intimate details of his operations. Now Mokbel could see a $2-billion empire crumbling before his eyes. It had been quite a journey from humble beginnings for Mokbel, who had arrived in Australia from Kuwait as an eight-year-old without a word of English. His illiterate parents had worked in factories until his father's death from a heart attack on his son's fifteenth birthday. Young Tony worked a range of jobs, including managing a restaurant at a young age, but his growing love of gambling meant that he would not live within his means for long.

In 2012, a psychologist suggested that Mokbel had struggled to adjust to his father's death, becoming 'an angry, oppositionally defiant young man with antisocial traits and poor emotional regulation at times'. Nonetheless, over two decades in the criminal world he had earnt a reputation for professionalism and having great attention to detail, which was recognised even by a Supreme Court judge. In 2012, while sentencing Mokbel to a minimum of twenty-three years' jail, Justice Simon Whelan said that Mokbel had conducted himself as a manager.

'You delegated. You gave advice. You encouraged cooperation. You sought to maintain morale . . . [T]hose who . . . dealt directly with you displayed respect for you, and loyalty to you. It was your capacity to manage and coordinate, and to command respect and loyalty, which enabled these criminal activities to succeed, for a time,' Whelan said.

Despite his proprietorial attitude to business, his two associates had given him up.

The traitors had been working with Mokbel to organise the importation from Mexico of 2.9 kilos of cocaine, hidden in candles and statues, in November 2000. After everyone was arrested, it got back to one of the men that Mokbel had been overheard in telephone intercepts suggesting that his former associates could rot in prison for all he cared. One of them received a discounted sentence of two-and-a-half years' jail after agreeing to help police bring down Mokbel. When he found out, Mokbel apparently responded by putting a contract on the man's life.

Meanwhile, Lewis and Jason Moran, and Bert Wrout were also arrested, over a relatively small haul of ecstasy, and remanded in custody as part of the same operation. It seemed that police were determined to keep the warring factions apart, even if they couldn't stop the feud.

On remand in Port Phillip Prison, Mokbel linked up with Carl, who was using his enforced time off to build his network.

In particular, Carl had made friends with a career criminal whom I shall call 'the Raptor'. Fit and strong, he was renowned as an armed robber who would literally run from the scene of his jobs. He once escaped custody by jumping out of a police car and tearing off through traffic. He was regarded as staunch and loyal, a man for whom brutality was simply a way of making money. Those who knew him say that he had not a shred of compassion for anyone, except his ageing mother. The two criminals formed a practical relationship, as are most in jail or the underworld.

The Raptor later told police that after a period of time, Tony became part of their crew. They would together occasionally drink alcohol that had been smuggled into the prison. The Raptor was working in the kitchen at the time and 'used to smuggle food out for Tony, as he loved his food'. Mokbel warmed to the Raptor not just for his catering but because of his ability to get anything into the prison: from drugs and alcohol to mobile phones and guns.

By the time the Raptor was transferred to Beechworth Prison in Victoria's north later that year, the three had developed a firm friendship. When all three men were back on the streets in late 2002, the feud with the Morans resumed in earnest.

At this time, Victoria Police was busy dealing with its own problems. The drug squad's brazen involvement in the narcotics trade was now coming to light. It was remarkable how little scrutiny had been brought to bear on its operations, either from force command or the media. The squad was fighting a pointless war against drugs, so it was given a free hand. It was told to get results and the bosses didn't want to know how they were achieved. In fact, many reporters had lauded the squad's achievements. It was only years later the deep corruption was acknowledged.

'It was once considered the best in Australia, then came a series of poor management decisions, unwise appointments and slack leadership that allowed a fermentation of corruption to brew a series of scandals,' *The Age*'s John Silvester wrote in May 2012.

In July 2002, more than twenty-five Victorian detectives were named in a secret report on corruption delivered to Chief Commissioner Christine Nixon. The report, by the police internal investigators, identified more than a hundred allegations, many against former members of the drug squad.

The report detailed the widespread criminal culture that was operating inside the squad. Members had planted evidence and cash on suspects, stolen and resold drugs and given a green light to selected dealers, including the Morans and Mokbel.

Police eavesdropped on Mokbel boasting in a telephone call that he was so close to the drug squad that a leading officer, Detective Senior Sergeant Wayne Strawhorn, had offered him tickets to a police function.

The Ceja Taskforce was formed to investigate the activities of the former drug squad, seizing the case notes of officers who were under suspicion of working with criminals. At first, it was suggested that villains like Mokbel and Carl could remain in custody until Ceja had dealt with the corrupt officers. However, it became clear this exercise could take up to five years to complete. It was improper for suspects to be held in custody for years on end while Ceja ran its course. 'Our society will not, and should not, tolerate what is effectively the indefinite detention awaiting trial of persons such as Tony Mokbel whilst an investigation such as that currently under way takes place,' said a judge in one hearing.

The Crown put forward testimony from police informers that underlined just how dangerous Mokbel could be if released on bail. He had plans to bribe the judge, if he could manage it, and to take out witnesses if he had to. And police knew from their informers that Carl was now very close with Mokbel. If freed, they would go flat-out to build their empire, while using every means possible to corrupt, pervert and derail the prosecutions underway against them. Their knowledge of police corruption was an ace to play when it best suited them.

Defence counsel for Mokbel tried to play down these claims as mere empty boasts, saying there was a degree of puffery in almost any conversation Mokbel had. Yet the crooks had enough on the police to destabilise the cases against them. And eventually they would cut deals to share what they knew. Already, the arresting officer in Carl's 1999 drugs bust, Malcolm Rosenes, was himself awaiting trial on trafficking charges.

In July 2002, Carl got bail after the Director of Public Prosecutions ruled the case against him could not proceed until Rosenes had been dealt with.

In September 2002 Mokbel got bail with a $1-million surety. Mokbel and Carl had been handed get-out-of-jail-free cards by Victoria Police. And they were going to have a ball while it lasted. There was money to be made and enemies to be eliminated.

Carl couldn't believe how the world was opening up for him. And the cops couldn't keep him in jail. There was a new arrogance in Mokbel too. With Mark Moran gone, he ruled the party drug market in Victoria. He was hobnobbing with the best of the Melbourne mob, while mingling with the bright young things who bought his little pills at the nightclubs he owned.

Mokbel's operation was now vertically integrated and throwing off awesome amounts of cash. Still, he was tight with paying his debts, refusing to cough up for losses of $1.8 million with bookies during a post-release betting spree at Flemington. When the credit was turned off, Mokbel switched to cash and lost millions more. It was just a tiny percentage of what he was making. One bookmaker saw him putting on bets with huge wads of cash wedged between the fingers of both hands.

'In thirty years of this, I'd never seen someone fit that much money in their hands and been so keen to spend it,' he says.

17

PLOTTING

A year before, in September 2001, Jason Moran had been released from jail full of bile and hate, and looking for vengeance. It was decided he should get out of the way for a while until Lewis worked out what to do. There was a lot at stake. The police had warned Lewis that even though Carl was in jail, he had associates carrying out surveillance. Jason had a bullseye on his head.

Lewis was pragmatic, not to mention an extreme tight-arse. Getting Carl killed would cost more than he was prepared to pay. At the end of the day, Mark wasn't even Lewis's kid. He was more concerned about getting back to business. Besides, Jason was a hothead, a trait that could see them all killed. So he was dispatched overseas while the dust settled in Moonee Ponds.

For Carl, this was a victory. Jason had scarpered off to England with his tail between his legs. It confirmed Carl's power, even from jail.

Then Jason, quite by accident, bumped into Carl's pal Snalfy on a London street. Carl thought this was hilarious. Snalfy had supplied the gun used to kill Mark. It looked like Carl's network was so extensive that he could stalk Jason anywhere on the planet.

Bert Wrout says this was arrant nonsense. Jason was concerned about Carl – he was tooled up at all times – but he wasn't fearful. Jason would not give Carl the satisfaction of letting him know he was scared.

The trip overseas had been a present from his father, says Wrout, a reward for doing his time over the Sports Bar incident. It was also a morale booster after Mark's death. Jason was itching for the chance to kill Carl. He just didn't want to spend his life in jail for it, so was biding his time. He was home within a few months and ready for conflict.

With Carl back on the street in July 2002, the temperature began to rise. The school drop-off zone at Penleigh and Essendon Grammar School in Moonee Ponds became a battle ground. Perhaps to show their indifference to the Williamses, Jason and Trisha Moran had put their kids in the same school. Parents and kids alike were regularly confronted with the spectacle of Jason and Roberta trading insults and threats. Jason ordered Roberta to pull her kids out of the school, even though her daughters had been there first.

Carl got involved in this, ringing Jason to abuse him. He wasn't going to fight Jason, of course. He would get Roberta to kick the shit out of Trisha, he told him.

Roberta didn't need much encouragement by this stage. Soon after, according to Roberta, Trish called her 'a fucking scumbag whore' in front of all the other parents outside the school. When asked to repeat it, Trish obliged and Roberta launched herself across the drop-off zone. Trisha must have instantly regretted her choice of words. She managed to swat Roberta in the face with an umbrella but to no avail. Roberta, as she puts it, smashed her head in.

Over the years, she and Carl had endured a gutful of 'the Morans' shit' and it all came spilling out at that moment. The Moran men had stolen $1 million from Carl, shot him in the guts, threatened to kill his parents and family. Now their wives had the gall to look down on her. Carl could kill every last one of them as far as she was concerned. Roberta left Trisha lying on the ground, whimpering like a dog, and got back in her car. 'Fuck you, fuck the Morans,' she thought as she drove away, shaking with rage.

Soon after that, Jason attended a function where he bumped into an old friend. Jason asked him to take a walk; he needed to talk to someone. They found a bench by the Yarra River and sat for more than an hour as Jason opened up.

Jason blamed himself for his brother's death. They had underestimated Carl and it had cost Mark his life. He could have stopped this thing right in its tracks, if he had followed his brother's order and put one in Carl's head. But his hand was shaking; it just wasn't in him. He would have died for Mark, but he couldn't kill for him.

Sitting there by the river, Jason cut a sad, bewildered figure. He had tried to run, spending nine months bumming around Europe, but had come home to face the threat. Now he was back in Ascot Vale with the kids and Trisha, still doing business but running around with a 9-mm pistol down the front of his trousers. A patient foe, as slow and inexorable as the murky river sliding by in the moonlight, was stalking him. Jason had put the entire family fortune on the line for the want of better judgement. His brother was in the cemetery and anybody else close to him could follow at any moment. As Carl Williams (and many others) would say, 'In life, you can either be part of the solution or part of the problem. It's up to you.'

Moran spoke of the late-night calls from Carl when he was drunk, abusing him, promising to send Jason to the graveyard just like his brother.

'I told him that he had to kill every last one of them,' says the friend. 'Jason brought this on himself. I told him, you try to take a bloke's business and then you shoot him in the guts. What else is he supposed to do? He's going to come back hard at you, isn't he?

'Having made this mess, he was going to have to sort it out, I told him. He started it, now he was going to have to finish it. Knock the fat cunt, the fuckin' trashy wife. The father had to go too, so he couldn't come back at Jason,' says the friend.

'They were just animals, the lowest form of crooks, someone had to put them down. But I somehow knew that Jason wouldn't get the job done, not Lewis either. Once Mark was gone, they were fucked, just running on the memories. Someone else would have to help them but it wouldn't be me. Carl was as game as fuck. And meanwhile Jason was scared, but too arrogant to admit it.'

A week later, Carl and the Raptor were headed for Red Rooster in Gladstone Park near where Jason had shot him back in 1999. When they spotted Jason driving a small hatchback with one of his girlfriends next to him, all thoughts of fried chicken were abandoned. They gave chase, Carl asking the Raptor to marshal the available weapons for a hit on Moran right there and then. All they could find was a tyre lever and a screwdriver, but that didn't deter Carl, the hardware hit man. This was the first time Carl had clapped eyes on Jason since the shooting on his twenty-ninth birthday; he wasn't going to let him get away.

They pursued Moran around a roundabout three or four times and down some back streets, before the hatch of Moran's vehicle popped open. Jason fired off a salvo of shots at the pair, but from 20 metres missed everything.

The Raptor had to shout at Carl to discontinue the pursuit, so focused on his quarry was he. He didn't want to chase someone, just to be shot at. This was pointless, he told Carl.

'Fucking bastard,' growled Carl as he swung the car around. 'We'll get him another day.'

Not that Jason was being idle. He had Andrew Veniamin on contract to kill Carl. Veniamin later confessed to Roberta that he and an associate had climbed into the roof cavity of the house in Hillside, waiting for the opportunity to kill him. It seemed an unnecessary strategy given how easy it would have been to have killed Carl. He was moving around freely: any day of the week Benji could have popped him at his choice of fast-food joints, pubs or clubs.

However dubious it sounds, Roberta swears it was all true. Benji told her he had heard her singing and rocking young Dhakota to sleep. It was then Benji decided that he couldn't kill Carl, so he told her. It was more likely that he saw a better earn in changing sides.

18

THE GODFATHER

Tommy Ivanovic was the perfect godfather for Dhakota, according to Carl. Of course, there weren't too many of his 'friends' that fitted the traditional definition of someone who would ensure that Dhakota's religious instruction was attended to.

Roberta didn't think much of the rest of Carl's crew. She believed they were parasites living off his wealth. Carl had confused business with friendship, she used to tell him. He didn't know the difference. And he would reply all hurt and offended that Roberta simply didn't want him to have friends. But Tommy was different. He was from a good family, and had a solid Orthodox upbringing. He showed respect for Roberta and the kids. A bit like Carl, Tommy was in search of friendship. He wasn't a real gangster, just a willing associate. He liked to dress as a gangster with his wardrobe full of oversized suits, but underneath he was just a skinny kid.

It had been a great lark for a while. In nightclubs, he had been treated like a VIP, as a member of Carl's court. Suddenly, loose hot women wanted to be near him, AFL footballers and other minor celebrities wanted to hang with his crew. They didn't pay for drinks and the bouncers all sucked up to them. For a poor wog kid from Brunswick, this felt like success, as though he had stepped into a Hollywood movie. The handgun he carried down his pants added inches to his stature.

Now with Mark Moran's death everything had changed. This was getting serious. People were jumpy and paranoid. They imagined informers and assassins lurked everywhere.

In September 2001, police raided the Ivanovic's family home and found a quantity of ecstasy. Tommy was charged with possession and locked up at the Melbourne Remand Centre in the city. Sergeant Paul Dale had been on the raid and later recommended they not proceed with the charges against Tommy. There was no certainty that Tommy knew the drugs were there, maybe they belonged to someone else, Dale said. He also pointed out that the quantity of ecstacy was probably not enough to sustain the charges.

While still on bail on the drug charges a year later, Tommy destroyed whatever chance he had left in life. He was on edge; he had knowledge of murders and was thought to have been on the scene when his pal Rocco Arico had allegedly popped Richard Mladenich. He was convinced someone was coming for him.

Ivan Conabere, a thirty-eight-year-old motorcyclist on L-plates, gave form to Tommy's fears when he decided to follow him home after a minor traffic incident.

Conabere and his companion on another motorcycle followed Tommy all the way home and confronted him outside his parents' house. When Conabere pushed him, Tommy drew a gun from his trousers and shot him. A few seconds later, he shot Conabere again as he lay wounded on the ground. The second shot scuttled any chance of beating the murder rap on self-defence.

A witness heard Tommy say to Conabere's companion, 'Well, what was I supposed to do?'

Tommy had tried to explain his actions: 'He grabbed me around the throat . . . I got scared . . . and so I pulled out my gun and shot him.' His defence counsel Robert Richter QC suggested that Tommy's actions had been automatic. There was no time to form the intention of murdering Conabere, but the second shot, fired several seconds later, put paid to that.

All the action had been caught on Tommy's own security camera. He had helpfully chopped down a tree in his garden that had previously obscured the camera's view of the front gate. He thought the

CCTV footage would absolve him, instead it sent him down.

Paul Dale popped up again in Tommy's defence, giving character evidence on his behalf. Dale told the court that he had been drinking at the Union Hotel in Brunswick shortly before the murder and was told by an unknown man that Little Tommy was a 'dead man walking'. Dale couldn't tell the court who had told him that Ivanovic was in danger. Nor could he remember exactly when it was that he'd heard this. Dale was deemed an unreliable witness and suspicions about his allegiances began to roar through Victoria Police.

Before he imposed the minimum fifteen-year jail term, Justice Philip Cummins told Tommy, 'Life is not cheap, nor should it ever be ... Mr Conabere was a decent, law-abiding citizen who was trying to gain his motorcycle licence but dared to remonstrate with [you] about a driving incident. [This was] a wholly gratuitous killing ... because your ego was offended.'

Others had a different view. Tommy's mother said in a statement that she had been sitting in the lounge that afternoon when she heard first the two men arguing and then the shots. Tommy had come into the house as white as a sheet and in a shaky voice asked his sister Meri to call an ambulance. If killing came easy in the underworld, then maybe Tommy didn't fit in after all.

The christening of Tommy's goddaughter, Dhakota Williams, in December 2003, was a proud moment in his life, even though he couldn't be there. Having delayed the festivities until Carl's return from prison, Roberta surpassed herself, spending an estimated $200 000 on the function. Money didn't matter: by this time they were awash with it. It was a huge affair held at Crown Casino's Palladium Room, and every leading villain and his lawyer was there to celebrate with Roberta and Carl. Singer Vanessa Amorosi gave a full concert, while Roberta had flown veteran singer Brian Cadd and his band from the Gold Coast just to sing 'A Little Ray of

Sunshine' to Dhakota.

Tommy's sister read a speech to the throng and by all reports she did him proud. A man doing life takes pleasure in the briefest of moments.

Tommy, through his association with Carl, enjoyed elevated status in jail. He was an authority on the gangland war raging outside. Inmates sought his opinion on the character and ethics of the combatants.

In a letter, Tommy wrote, 'I have most of them asking me a whole lot of questions, on how I know the sketch of friends and so on. Most of the time I do not [comment], unless I see them to be in a good way of not coming back to the college. I spend time in letting them know that everything that shines is of course not gold.'

The police were working on Tommy too, trying to get him to turn on his boss so they could bring the feud to an end. But Tommy was staunch, perhaps the only one who really was. Carl had paid his legal bills and looked after his family. Just how much loyalty that bought remained to be seen.

19

COMMON CAUSE

Benji didn't like what he saw that night. He had looked on as two men laid the boot into Tony Mokbel, right there on the floor of the restaurant. They had turned Mokbel's face into a swollen wreck.

This was nothing unusual in Benji's world. You went into a blue three or four to one because you fought to win, not to fight fair. However, to be invited to a meeting and then get the shit kicked out of you offended Benji's sense of decency. For Mick Gatto to let these West Australians have their way with Tony seemed most unfair. There had to be some rules. Or else, there could be no trust.

Mick Gatto had been the smiling host for the evening. As the others filed in, he sat at his regular table with Ronnie Bongetti, his wise old consigliore. Mario Condello, Mick's best mate, was by him, scowling and posturing. It was a Friday night in spring, but the place was closed. Big black German saloons cruised the block for parking. The delegates to the mediation filed in.

John Kizon had come from Perth in the company of two outlaw bikies from the Coffin Cheaters Motorcycle Club. Kizon was one of the West's most colourful criminal identities, with a record for heroin trafficking, assault and financial offences, but for nearly twelve years life had been low-key for the one-time star boxer. Not that he'd been idle. These days, he told everyone he'd learnt his lesson: he was a legitimate businessman, running nightclubs and promoting fight nights in Perth. But still they wouldn't leave him alone: the Western Australian media continued to link him with virtually every major crime taking place in the state. Newspaper reports indicated that as of 1997, Kizon had not held any bank accounts in Australia under his own name. His income over a six-year period had averaged only $3000, yet police intelligence suggested that he had investments worth over $3 million.

All had been nice and quiet in 2002 until he got involved in this dispute. Mokbel had a major problem with the bikies. There was some money owing, but, more importantly, one of them had declared Mokbel 'a dog'.

It had been a tough time for Mokbel. Earlier in the year two associates had 'somersaulted' him to police, sharing intimate details of his operations. To his mind, Mokbel felt he had been the victim of some very poor etiquette, to say the least. He had graciously welcomed people into his circle and they had betrayed him. Now someone was calling him a dog.

Mokbel thought of himself as a reasonable man, even civilised and intelligent. He publicly disavowed violence as bad for business. So when Mick Gatto had called to invite him to La Porcella to chat about his dispute with the bikies, he agreed. John Kizon was a close friend of Gatto and most of the Carlton Crew elders, so Mick was hardly neutral, but Gatto had a reputation as someone you could trust in a mediation.

It was Mick's responsibility to ensure his safety that afternoon, so Mokbel turned up alone. Accounts differ as to what actually occurred, but some time later Mokbel tumbled out into the street pursued by the bikies. He was punched to the ground and his head and body were kicked repeatedly as he squirmed and rolled, trying to protect himself. The only thing that saved him from death was that the men were wearing runners rather than their traditional heavy boots.

And what was Gatto the mediator doing while his guest was copping a hiding? He was standing back with his arms folded across his chest, doing absolutely nothing to intercede. Perhaps he reasoned that Mokbel had it coming, that he was too big for his boots and had ceased to respect the primacy of the Carlton Crew in Melbourne. Mick was still a Calabrian, after all. Sure, Mokbel had made money, but it was blood money – wrought from drugs that were killing kids and ruining lives. Mick had been a crook but he would never stoop to the drug trade, he said. It was ruining his city.

All of Mokbel's drug money still couldn't buy the heritage that Mick Gatto regarded as his birthright. People had been talking of Mokbel and his associates as the new team in town.

It had been quiet for a decade in Melbourne's ganglands, and that had taken a lot of killing, frankly. A number of good friends of Mick had died for the fragile peace that existed, and Gatto was not about to give this drug-dealing shitbag the respect reserved for real men.

Gatto ordered Benji to take the injured Mokbel, whose head was swollen like a pumpkin, to a friendly doctor who wouldn't ask questions.

Benji found himself warming to the quiet and charming patient. This man could buy and sell the Carlton Crew a dozen times over, and none of his success had come in standover. Mokbel had joined forces with Carl and George Williams. They were taking over. And they were paying big money, Mokbel said, so Benji should get on board. What's more, Carl couldn't have cared less that it'd been Benji who'd killed Carl's former best mate Dino Dibra. He had moved on.

It took about six weeks for Mokbel's head to return to normal after the La Porcella beating. When he next turned up at court, it looked as though he'd had a little cosmetic work done too, maybe some botox. There were faint signs of bruising around his eyes from the kicking he had taken.

He now had a new friend in Andrew Veniamin. Soon Benji would meet Carl Williams, and the trio would realise they had more in common than they could have ever imagined. To share an enemy is to find common cause. Better still, Carl was paying big money for his services. Sure, he had taken contracts to kill Carl on behalf of the Morans. But now he had both options.

Their interests had begun to align even before they'd met. Other jobs Benji had done directly benefitted Carl, even though they were done for different employers.

A month earlier, Benji's childhood pal, Paul Kallipolitis, the most powerful drug dealer in the west, had been shot dead at home. The killer had been known to PK, that was for sure. Only two people got into his house without a battering ram and one of them was Benji. PK's triple-locked security door was open, the surveillance equipment had been turned off. PK was sitting on the floor with his back against the bed. Two shots to the head had done for him. His favourite 9-mm was still tucked under his mattress. He hadn't seen this coming. And now his squalid little empire was up for grabs. The competition was thinning.

PK's death was not Carl's doing, but Benji had done Carl a favour by killing him now they could share in the spoils.

On the evening of 1 May 2002, Victor Peirce was preparing to meet up with some associates to transact business in Bay Street, Port Melbourne. He was a little early so he killed time with his wife, Wendy, and son, Vinnie, kicking a footy back and forth to the boy. He told Wendy to go home and put on the coffee machine; he'd be there soon. Victor strolled to his car, which was parked across the street in front of a Telstra shop, and got inside to wait. He was unarmed, expecting only a close family friend.

At 9.15 p.m., another vehicle pulled up alongside Peirce's car. A gunman emerged from the passenger side and calmly fired three .45 slugs in rapid succession through the driver's door window into Victor's body. The first round struck his right elbow, as he raised it defensively, and continued into his chest. The second ripped straight into his chest, passing through both lungs and his liver and exiting through his left shoulder. A third shot missed altogether and lodged in the pillar of the driver's door.

Victor didn't die at the scene and might have survived but for massive internal bleeding. He was taken to the Alfred Hospital, where he underwent emergency surgery, but he had lost too much blood; there was little the surgeons could do. Another Melbourne legend had passed into history.

A year later, Benji was bragging about the killing of Peirce to an associate, saying how difficult it had been to shoot him through the car window. He'd had to get right out of the car to make sure he hit his mark.

According to informers, Benji had his own reasons for killing Peirce, tracing back to Frank Benvenuto. Back in 2000, Benvenuto had fallen out with a senior Carlton man. Benji and Victor Peirce had been contracted to kill this man, but the target had discovered the plot and confronted Benji. When Benji confessed, he was given an ultimatum: kill Frank Benvenuto or face death himself. It was the easiest hit of them all. Benji, smiling and friendly, had climbed into Benvenuto's car and shot Melbourne's most powerful don from the passenger seat. Now Benji was concerned that Peirce would strike back at him. And that's why Victor had to die, according to informers.

Given that Peirce had planned to kill him at his wedding in 2000, Carl certainly didn't shed any tears for him. To Carl, men like Peirce were part of the old school, they were past their use-by dates. A new generation was on the rise.

20

MURDER INCORPORATED

Carl had found that murder was too easy when you didn't have to pull the trigger. On the payroll he had two kill teams for whom taking a life was no greater moral dilemma than swatting a fly. The Raptor and his mate, let's call him 'Goggles' for legal reasons, were working well together. Benji was also keen for work. Then there were a string of hangers-on, men who were begging Carl for the opportunity to pick up $100 000 or more for taking a life. They were prepared to kill their own mates for that kind of money.

By April 2003, Carl and Tony Mokbel had been doing business with Nik 'the Russian' Radev for a couple of years, but the relationship was souring, according to Snalfy, one of Carl's mates who later turned informer. The truth be told, they were ripping him off.

Radev, a Bulgarian immigrant, had made a name for himself in his two decades in Australia. In the early 1980s, he worked for eight months in a fish-and-chip shop then ran his own fast-food joint for a while before his criminal career began in earnest. Fittingly, given his aversion to work, Radev was sentenced to five years' jail in 1987 over a plot to blow up a convenience store. In a long criminal history, he was also jailed for burglary, assault, attempted arson and drug-related offences. He was an extortionist who took the utmost pleasure in torture. He was a brutal degenerate, even by criminal standards. He once savagely raped a man in front of his wife and child for the sheer thrill of it. He was connected to several murders where the victims died of hotshots of heroin but he was never charged.

Radev was also the overlord of a group of small-time drug

makers and dealers who shared suppliers and speed cooks. They were all making money but Nik wanted everything. He was greedy and unreasonable, used to getting his own way in all things.

Snalfy told police that Radev suspected Carl of cutting the speed he was supplying to him. Now he was hatching a plan to kidnap one of Carl's cooks, a crim named George Peters. He would hold Peters hostage on a remote farm and make him work 24/7, churning out ecstasy and speed. If he had to kill Carl, or anybody else close to him, then so be it, he told associates.

Carl decided, in the interests of the business, that he should get in first. Radev was pestering Carl to organise a meeting with the cook. Carl agreed to the meeting, but it was only a ruse to set Radev up for slaughter. And Radev, in his greed and arrogance, walked right into the trap.

Carl and George arranged to meet Radev at the Middle Brighton Baths Café near where Radev was renting a home. As usual, Radev was concerned about the quality of the product he had been getting from the Williamses. Carl told Radev not to worry, it was all arranged. They would go from there to Queen Street, Coburg, to meet Peters, and then he could discuss all the outstanding issues. Everything would be sorted. Radev was completely taken in.

Radev would never meet Peters. Benji and the Raptor, who had been watching the meeting from nearby, raced ahead to ambush him in Queen Street. Radev actually got there first and was already out of his black Mercedes convertible when the killers arrived. However, Radev decided he wanted a cigar and returned to his car. The silver Vectra driven by Benji drew up alongside and the Raptor jumped out and emptied his gun into Radev's back. For good measure, Veniamin also put a few into Radev's corpse. Benji and the Raptor had later joked that Radev had so many holes in him they had turned him into Swiss cheese.

Radev was buried in a $35 000 gold-plated coffin that took more than a dozen pallbearers to lift. Carl didn't go to the funeral but he liked the look of that coffin and did a little research. It was a casket befitting his status, he decided, but he had some other business to attend to first.

Roberta maintains that it was Snalfy, not Carl, who had plotted Radev's death. She claims that Snalfy had wanted Benji to kill Radev at Dhakota's third birthday party. She says Carl had forbidden it, threatening to kill them both if anything serious went down at the birthday party. However, police disagree, pointing out that Snalfy would not have made the move without getting Carl's approval.

Carl was becoming obsessed with killing Jason. It was clouding his judgement. The most outlandish, even plain silly, plans were discussed and entertained. In one imagined scenario, Carl would cram himself into Moran's garbage bin for the night, then spring out in the morning to shoot him as Jason got in his car. This required intricate planning – if they got it wrong Carl could end up in the tip. In another, Benji would lure Jason to a park for a meeting. The Raptor would be dressed up as a woman in a wig and frock and pushing a pram with an arsenal of weapons concealed.

Nothing seemed to come together. Carl was starting to think Benji was a double agent. He kept promising to deliver Jason but never seemed to get around to it. He was full of excuses. Carl suspected that Benji was even warning Jason of their plans and that was why he was being so elusive. Not that Carl would have said anything, because he knew that Benji would more than likely fly off the handle and shoot him.

Instead, Carl cut Benji out of the planning, fearing he would tip off the Morans or his friends in the Carlton Crew. Carl learnt that Jason took his kids to an Auskick football clinic at Cross Keys Reserve in Essendon every Saturday morning. Jason was never alone and always tooled up, but here was one place he was vulnerable. In this family setting he would drop his guard.

On 21 June 2003, that moment came. It was 10.40 a.m. and the session was winding up. Jason was in the passenger seat of the blue Mitsubishi people mover. His mate Pasquale Barbaro was behind the wheel. 'Paddy' was only there because Jason had insisted. Paddy was loyal to the Morans, says Bert Wrout, though they had long taken him for granted. If there was a shit job to do, Paddy was their man. In the back seats of the van were five children, including Jason's twins.

The kill team, consisting of Goggles and the Raptor, cruising through the car park in a white van, made sure that they had the right man. Googles dropped the Raptor a short distance away and moved to the rendezvous spot in a nearby street. The Raptor strode purposefully towards the blue van; Jason never saw him coming. The Raptor rolled a balaclava down over his face, pulled out a sawn-off shotgun and fired at point-blank range into Jason's face, blowing his brains all over the inside of the van. He then dropped the shotgun, and fired several more shots into the van using a handgun.

Later on, the Raptor said he had hardly noticed Barbaro sitting in the driver's seat, but he had killed him too. Barbaro, the hapless sidekick, was truly collateral damage. The Raptor sprinted away from the scene, through the terrified crowd on the oval, and across a footbridge to a back street where Goggles was waiting.

Carl had made sure he had an alibi, organising for him and Snalfy to take blood tests, checking their cholesterol. Carl had gone straight to his mother's house in Essendon after the killing to tell Barb the good news. She was elated. Barb rang Deana and told her to get over there right away.

'"We're popping the champagne," Barb told me,' says Deana. When Deana got there, Carl and Barb were already halfway through a bottle. She couldn't believe how ecstatic they both were that Jason was dead. Barb was obviously so proud of her son for doing what he had to do for his family. In her mind, this was all over now. She wasn't thinking of the consequences. An evil man who had hurt her son had now paid with his life. Now they could get on with their lives, and the world would soon return to normal.

Journalists were calling Roberta, and she told them they would be partying that night. The whole team went to one of Melbourne's most exclusive restaurants, Flower Drum, and celebrated. They made drunken toasts to Jason's demise, until they were all legless. They had laughed at news bulletins showing Judy Moran arriving grief-stricken at the scene of Jason's murder.

'I am not embarrassed or shy about saying that I was happy Jason was killed. I hated his guts and I hope he burns in hell for what he did to us,' Roberta says.

But even Roberta recoiled in horror at the manner in which Jason and Paddy had been dispatched.

'I saw the crime-scene photos of them slumped over in the van, Jason with half his face blown off, and it made me think, why didn't they just follow them home and get them later? It would have been less risky and it would not have outraged people the way it did. It was out of line to shoot them in front of the kids.'

To the citizens of Melbourne, killing Moran and Barbaro in front of children spoke of the appalling depravity of the criminal class, but to old hands like Billy 'the Texan' Longley, a survivor of the bloody Painters and Dockers Wars of the 1970s, it was something special. This was a textbook hit, he says, and it spoke of a cool professionalism.

'It shocks all the bystanders and all those not involved in that sort of thing, but bear in mind the fact that nobody got hurt, nobody got killed, only the two men the hit man was after. None of the kids were hit with a bullet or anything and I've got to say to you that they are very, very professional people.'

The mythmaking had begun.

Former Detective Inspector Jim O'Brien, who would take over the investigation into the gangland war after Carl was locked up, professed amazement at how sections of the media, me included, portrayed Carl as some kind of criminal genius, a celebrity even.

'It suited a lot of people's agendas to make him seem smarter than he was. They were turning him into the crime king of the world. My attitude was that he was just a mug from Broadmeadows with the arse out of his pants,' says O'Brien, now out of the force.

'The only thing that motivated him was money. He had no ticker. Every job he was involved in someone else pulled the trigger.'

Bert Wrout and the other Moran team members couldn't believe it had happened this way. Wrout regarded Jason as a complete raving psycho whose penchant for violence was always going to come full circle – but this just broke all the rules. It spread despondency among the remaining hangers-on. Perhaps they, like poor Paddy Barbaro, might cop it for just standing next to a Moran.

'Jason had his brains blown out in front of his six-year-old twins, a boy and a girl, [now teenagers] in the van that day. It sent a chilling message to our whole crew. Children of a fourth-generation crime family bathed in their father's blood. Poor kids,' he says.

In contrast, Carl's confidence was sky-high. He thought he was untouchable. He was the prime suspect, of course, but there was nothing linking him to the murder. The Raptor had dropped his shotgun at the scene. It was a popular Miura model Boito brand firearm imported from Brazil, which bore the faded inscription 'Mitch on your 21st. From . . . The Boy's 23/4/56'. It was the shotty that Snalfy had acquired from the now-deceased Dino Dibra.

Carl knew the firearm had passed through many hands before Dibra's, so there was no connection. While the jacks were out looking for Mitch, he would be getting on with business. What he didn't know was that the police had CCTV footage from the nearby Cross Keys Hotel and they managed to identify the white van the killers had used in Jason's murder. They were closing in on him, albeit from a long distance.

21

ON THE BALL

After Jason's murder, Carl's paranoia hit fever-pitch. He decided that he would move out of the family home in Essendon and rent a high-rise apartment in the CBD's Regency Towers. At Jason's funeral, Judy Moran had promised that 'all would be dealt with'. That was a signal to Carl that he should eliminate any of the Morans or their associates who put their heads up. In the meantime, he would set about consolidating his grip on Melbourne's party drug market. With Jason and Mark out of the picture, there was a chance to control all the action.

The move to a secure block in the middle of the city served another purpose. On the thirtieth floor, with Benji as his roomie, Carl could live his own life again, free of family responsibilities.

This didn't please Roberta in the slightest.

'He didn't give a fuck if we were safe. He just organised an apartment for himself so he and Andrew could root their sluts in peace. We got sent back to the house,' she says. Given the torrid events of the coming months, this was perhaps a wise precaution.

The deaths of small-time dealers like Willie Thompson and his business partner, Michael Marshall, meant nothing to the public. It was the manner of their deaths – gunned down in nice leafy streets – that so appalled and enthralled the good citizens of Melbourne.

The long-time friends Marshall and Thompson were nobodies,

former kickboxers and nightclub bouncers who were well known only to Melbourne's club scene. Willie made his 'honest' living selling lollipop-vending machines to nightclubs, while Mick trundled his hot-dog van around the seedy strips. Mick also had a business selling a herbal product called 'Miracle water' but this was suspected to be a front for a drug business with Willie. Mick owned an upmarket two-storey home in Joy Street, South Yarra, which he reportedly paid off in just three years. Willie was also doing well: he owned a slice of a local business worth $150 000 and held $245 000 in a Greek bank account.

Thompson had made a movie that became a cult hit. As the hero in *The Nightclubber*, Willie fought a pitched battle to save the world from an army of aliens that was using the Melbourne club scene as a base to carry out an apocalyptic vision. In reality, Willie's mortal enemies looked more like the bogans who as a bouncer he'd barred from entering nightclubs.

Willie and Mick shared a speed cook, 'Murray', and he was a very good one at that – even if he was decidedly odd as a person, perhaps from ingesting all the toxic vapours from his cook-ups. Their business thrived and there was no trouble from the law. They trusted each other.

Things fell apart for Mick and Willie in early 2003. Willie went to buy chemicals from a group of crooks in Sydney's south-west. He'd gone with $400 000 in cash and come home empty-handed, no chemicals and no money. He claimed he had been ripped off but Mick didn't believe him. There was a lot of tension between them after that. However, Mick's close friends knew he wasn't a killer.

Carl wanted Willie Thompson dead for his own reasons. Thompson had been an associate of Jason Moran and passed information back to Carl on Jason's movements. Now Carl believed that information had been false and that Willie was actually trying to position him for Jason. Even though Jason was dead, Willie was still a threat, Carl believed. Or perhaps he was just a loose end.

One night, the Raptor ran into Carl and Benji at a South Melbourne nightclub. Benji whispered in his ear that he needed help with a job: the murder of Willie Thompson. The Raptor later told police in a statement that he was incredulous.

'You're mad!' he said. 'It's too close to the other murders.' The Raptor declined the opportunity; even by his standards this was getting weird. Carl continued doing business with Thompson after Benji had taken the contract. During one meeting, Carl ordered two 25-kilo drums of pseudo from Thompson. Though it was duly supplied, Carl never paid for it.

Willie was a short, stocky man, a fanatic when it came to the sport of grappling, a form of wrestling. On the evening of 21 July 2003, he was training at the Extreme Jiu-Jitsu and Grappling gym on Warrigal Road in Chadstone, in the city's east. While Willie was coming to grips with his training partner, police believe someone made a telephone call to his killers. At 9.30 p.m. Willie left the gym, had a short conversation on the street with a friend, and then walked to his convertible Honda parked nearby.

As he pulled away from the kerb, two men in a stolen car stopped alongside, boxing him in. The two gunmen calmly got out and levelled their weapons at Willie. He was known not to carry a gun, so from there it was only a question of hitting the target.

Willie's mates would later suspect that Mick Marshall was one of the men who pulled the trigger. Carl and Benji quickly spread the rumour that Marshall had knocked Willie. The Raptor and Carl arranged to meet Thompson's business partner, Murray, at Southgate to reinforce their story. Carl sympathised with Murray for the loss of his mate. He promised to help catch Willie's killers, but first Murray had to make good on a $900 000 debt that Willie owed Carl.

Carl also wanted to know what Murray had told the police about the murder. Had his name come up in conversation? he asked. The wrong answer could have got him killed that night.

But Murray hadn't helped the police. He was already deeply paranoid and Willie's death pushed him closer to the edge. He believed that his clothes and shoes were bugged. In a later meeting, Murray handed Carl a bag containing $150 000.

In August 2003, after the killing of Thompson, Carl and Benji had another matter to sort out. Mark Mallia had been a childhood buddy of Benji, but had later become an associate of Nik Radev. It came to Carl's attention that Mallia was accusing him of knocking Radev. Mallia had wisely headed for Queensland for a while, telling his friends 'they can't kill what they can't catch', yet something drew him back.

There was talk that Mallia was looking for someone to get even.

Carl and Benji met Mallia for a chat at a seafood restaurant at Southgate. Mallia told them he was coming alone but two of his associates were secretly watching the meeting. After entrée, Carl and Benji emphatically denied they had killed Radev. They said they were committed to finding the real assassins, because Radev had been their friend. They had no drama with Mallia, said Carl. Benji played the bad cop.

'But if I hear again that you are trying to exact revenge on any of us,' said Benji slowly, leaning over the table and pointing his finger at Mallia, 'I will kill you and your family.' Mallia was in tears now; he just wanted to know who had killed his boss Radev and why. Carl assured him everything would be sweet and urged him not to worry about Benji, who was still glowering at Mallia. Later they heard again that Mallia was shopping for a shooter to kill Carl. It was enough. There was the added attraction that Mallia was said to be holding a stash of Radev's precursor chemicals.

Carl paid $50 000 to an associate, 'the Fixer', to lure Mallia over to his house in Lalor, where a group of men, including Benji, tied him to a chair in the garage and tortured him, possibly with a soldering iron. They wanted him to reveal the whereabouts of Radev's stash of drugs, chemicals and cash. They also wanted the names of dealers who owed him money. When Mallia had given all he could, he was choked to death. His body was stuffed in a wheelie bin then dumped in a West Sunshine drain. They poured petrol over his body and set it alight. A fire crew called to the blaze found part of Mallia's charred torso, which relatives identified from a tattoo.

Carl was amazed that Andrew had done the deed in such a crude way.

'They're mad for doing what they did,' he told associates. But he didn't complain too much; it was another problem solved with murder.

Mallia now dealt with, Carl and the Raptor had time for some further education. They took a three-hour jetski course, passing with flying colours. When they went to VicRoads to get their licences, the Fixer rolled up in the flash hotted-up white Commodore he had bought with the $50 000 Carl gave him for luring Mallia out. They were happy days indeed.

Carl had spread far and wide the story that Mick Marshall had killed Willie Thompson.

Marshall, though he had done nothing, had offended some very important people, including Tony Mokbel. Mokbel had been at school with Thompson and considered him a close friend.

Mokbel organised a meeting with Carl, the Raptor and various accomplices at a Red Rooster shop in Brunswick. Mokbel offered Carl and the Raptor $300 000 for the murder of Marshall.

To Carl, the businessman, murder was a commercial enterprise now. After killing Thompson, he had scooped up $150 000 of the dead man's loot, and now another $300 000 would come his way if he could kill Marshall. The Raptor was getting impatient, though: he still hadn't been paid for the murder of Jason Moran. Carl had set him up in a fully furnished apartment on Southbank and was dripfeeding him with big promises and small amounts of cash. Carl had been paying the rent, then the Raptor got an eviction notice. Now there he made another promise of a new apartment Carl was going to build in Frankston in payment for the Moran and Barbaro murders, and a manila envelope containing $50 000 turned up. Carl had to keep the Raptor sweet to get Marshall knocked before Mokbel discovered he had been cheated. The Raptor was happy enough, blowing the entire $50 000 on the horses and at the casino within a few days, leaving the rent unpaid. He was looking forward to earning another $50 000 once he did the job on Marshall.

The planning of the murder took more than a month. The Raptor and Goggles carried out surveillance on Marshall, watching his comings and goings from home with his hot-dog stand on a trailer. For the job, Goggles bought a small inconspicuous car, Mokbel supplied the guns, and all was in readiness.

But they were being watched by police. Goggles' white van – the same one as had been used in the Jason Moran hit – had been spotted at the scene of Willie Thompson's murder. Police tracked the vehicle down and now had the killers under surveillance.

Just before the hit, Goggles told the Raptor that he had found what he thought was a bug or a tracking device in their vehicle. He suggested they delay the job and find a new clean car, but the Raptor would have none of it. When the Raptor was preparing for a kill, it was like an Exocet missile locking onto a target. Nothing could distract him. He hadn't even noticed Paddy Barbaro sitting in the driver's seat when he had killed Jason at the Cross Keys Reserve, so he was hardly going to worry about a little bug.

Besides he didn't want Carl and Mokbel to think he wasn't up to the job. He was hungry for more work, as much as Carl could give him. He didn't mention the tracking device to Carl. This mistake, more than anything else, sealed the eventual fate of Carl Williams. Paranoia had got Thompson killed, greed and deception would claim Marshall, but it was stupidity that would bring Carl's whole team undone.

For nearly two weeks, police had followed their movements and listened to their conversations courtesy of that bug, reportedly concealed in one of the vehicle's indicators.

In one week, police tracked the pair travelling to the area near Marshall's home four times. The detectives were listening as they drove there again on the night of Saturday 25 October.

At 6.25 p.m. Marshall was heading out to buy bread rolls for the night's hot dogs before the shops closed. He had strapped his five-year-old son into a car seat in the back of his Hilux and was preparing to get in and drive away. He looked around to see the Raptor pointing a revolver at him. As he fired the first shot, Marshall lunged at him. The road was wet and the recoil of the weapon caused the killer to slip and fall backwards. Unsure if the first shot had hit Marshall, the Raptor jumped back up and fired three more shots into Marshall.

Marshall's wife was working on her computer in the kitchen at the time. She thought the four bangs she had heard were just a car backfiring. Then she heard her son screaming, banging on the front gate. She opened the gate and pulled her terrified son inside, then saw her husband lying face-down on the roadway. She ran over and rolled his body over but he was gone. The street was already empty.

When he got back into the getaway car, the killer noticed he had his victim's blood on his clothes and shoes – but it didn't bother him. The job was done and it was payday.

Within hours, the Raptor and Goggles would be intercepted by a team from the Special Operations Group, arrested and charged with murder.

Almost immediately, Goggles tried to do a deal with police. He told them that Benji was on a mission to kill Lewis and perhaps even Mick Gatto. If they let him go, Goggles promised to tell them much more. When between a rock and a hard place, most crooks will sell out their mates, and it was only a matter of time before Goggles spilt the beans on Carl.

Loyalty was only about money and Carl was in the red with his hired killers. The Raptor never saw the balance of his $50 000 for killing Marshall. He never got his apartment in Frankston for killing Jason Moran and Pasquale Barbaro. A few days later, Carl dropped by the Raptor's mother's house and left just $1500 in cash. Not much for the taking of three lives.

22

GRAND FINAL DAY

The 2003 AFL Grand Final was a special big day for Carl. He had been a Fitzroy supporter his entire life, all of the Denmans and Williamses had been, except George, who was a Collingwood man.

Many Fitzroy supporters had deserted the team when it had merged with the Brisbane Bears to become the Brisbane Lions in 1996, but Carl had stuck with it. With the Lions appearing in their third successive grand final, his loyalty was being rewarded. They had beaten Collingwood the previous year for a second flag in a row and Carl had been rubbing it in George's face ever since. Now they were facing off again to complete the 'three-peat' on that magical 'one day in September'.

Carl had got to know some of the Brisbane players and on the eve of the match, two Lions stars visited him at home in Regency Towers. They posed for photographs with Roberta and the kids and signed memorabilia. Carl loved these moments. He was a drug dealer steeped in blood but he could still be an ordinary bloke talking footy and racing with people he admired. He was good at pretending, or people were prepared for various reasons to overlook the obvious. Socially, Carl was a good bloke to know, he could hook you up with anything, no charge. Brisbane duly thrashed Collingwood by fifty points. Carl's mates gave him an autographed jumper. He was chuffed. They partied hard that night. It would prove to be the end of an era for the Lions, and it was Carl's last grand final as a free man.

That same night, across town, events were unfolding that would have a direct bearing on Carl's destiny. Two men were breaking into a house in Dublin Street, Oakleigh East. One was drug dealer and registered informer Terence Hodson, the other a serving police officer, Detective Senior Constable David Miechel, of the drug squad, no less.

Members of Miechel's squad were due to raid the property the following day, but he and Hodson had decided to get in first. The house was a pill factory connected to Tony Mokbel. There was 135 000 tablets and $700 000 in cash on the premises.

According to statements made by Hodson, a third man, Sergeant Paul Dale, was alleged to have been part of the plot but begged off at the last minute, claiming to have mates over at his place to watch the grand final. The statements, revealed later by the *Sunday Herald Sun*'s James Campbell, alleged that Dale and Miechel had cooked up the plan together but Dale had got cold feet, predicting that the shit would hit the fan because it was their job. The shit would still be flying nine years later in a fine spray that got into everything.

This was the moment in the gangland war when a clear nexus between the police and the underworld was established. Until this point, some police had sold drugs and turned a blind eye to dealing, but this was another level altogether.

The fall-out from this evening would cause the deaths of four people, including Carl. Many others would lose their liberty or their careers. It would resonate throughout all levels of Melbourne society. It would expose a system of government and law enforcement that was complacent and self-satisfied. It showed the war on drugs in Victoria, if it had ever been winnable, was utterly lost. The drug dealers were running the drug squad, or at least enough of it to do whatever they damn well pleased.

For Paul Dale, the nightmare began with a phone call from his colleague Dave Miechel, picked up on a telephone intercept.

Trying to stay in cop-speak, Miechel advised Dale he was in the back of an ambulance.

'There's been a bit of an incident out here,' he said.

'Out where?' Dale asked.

'Near our target address.'

'What happened?'

'I've been attacked by a police dog and hit by the handler.'

Miechel said he had been checking things out on his way past when he had seen a divvy van chasing two offenders. 'I gave chase and was attacked by a dog.'

Dale rushed to the Epworth Hospital in Richmond to meet the ambulance. En route he learnt that Miechel and Hodson had been arrested for burgling the house.

He found Miechel lying on a bed with what appeared to be severe head injuries and his face covered in blood.

They had been spotted by neighbours during the break-in and the dog squad had been called. Miechel had apparently sprayed himself with dog repellent, which proved ineffective. Fleeing the scene, he had been savaged by Silky, a police hound (and apparently assaulted by a cop). Hodson wisely gave himself up – at fifty-seven, the career drug dealer had learnt a thing or two about self-preservation.

He then proceeded to give up Dale and Miechel for the burglary and provide chapter and verse to the police on Mokbel's drug empire and a range of other topics.

That night, Dale is alleged to have rushed to his office at St Kilda Road Police Headquarters. The Victorian coroner would later find that Dale was the most likely person to have removed a confidential police information report. The IR, which was soon in the hands of Carl Williams and Tony Mokbel, outlined information that Hodson had given to police the previous year.

Hodson said that Lewis Moran had approached him in 2002 to organise a hit man to kill Carl for $40 000. Carl was outraged.

Just $40 000? It was a pittance when he was paying people (or at least promising) $150 000 a hit. That was an insult. He was worth only $400 bucks a kilo. Jokes aside, this was a serious development for Lewis. He had always been on Carl's list, but this IR had bumped him up the batting order.

Terry Hodson now had a lot to worry about too.

23

SPOTLIGHT

The Chief Commissioner of Victoria Police, Christine Nixon, wanted results and fast. By November 2003, Carl was making her look bad. Under Nixon's watch, the drug squad had gone feral, the organised crime unit had been allowed to wither, the Asian crime squad had been disbanded, allowing heroin to flood the streets, and the armed robbery squad had become a law unto itself.

However, Nixon could proudly say that she had turned the Victoria Police Force into a police *service*: she had promoted gender equality and racial tolerance, police were free to express their individuality with long hair and tattoos. She had brought in management consultants to advise how Victoria Police could be transformed from a paramilitary organisation into a corporation to better serve 'its stakeholders'.

While Nixon was promoting political correctness, some of the state's worst crooks were running wild.

Crime was falling overall, as it always does during times of prosperity. What was happening in the drug world was an indirect consequence of the good times. Drug barons with too much money were now making their own rules. They were executing their own form of justice.

In June, Assistant Commissioner (Crime) Simon Overland had begun putting together a special squad codenamed 'Purana' to investigate the spree of underworld killings. There had been seventeen unsolved gangland murders in the past five years. Not all were connected but *The Age* reported that Purana was looking at possible links between the killings of Mark Moran in 2000, Alphonse Gangitano in 1998, Dino Dibra in 2000 and Paul Kallipolitis in 2002. Curiously, the killings of Jason Moran and Pasquale Barbaro stayed with the homicide squad, as did the 2002 murder of Victor Peirce.

The Age reported that the ten-man Purana squad was 'a new push to try to force a breakthrough'.

Assistant Commissioner Noel Ashby was sceptical. When asked for help, station sergeants were always reluctant to let their best men be commandeered to taskforces like Purana. At this time, stations were being run by two or three energetic go-getters. They would never be sent to Purana. It was the plodders, the no-hopers, the dross that would end up at Purana, Ashby predicted. He was happy to sit back and watch this mess unfold. The way things were going for Nixon, Ashby was confident he would soon be the chief commissioner. And then he would put the fear of God into crooks like Williams and Mokbel.

Purana had the Raptor and Goggles in custody over the Marshall hit but they had only fallen right into their hands because of the bug in the getaway car. And, besides, they weren't saying anything helpful yet.

Meanwhile, Carl was running around the town on double bail, doing business and organising hits on Lewis Moran and Mick Gatto. It was time to get him off the street, at least for a while. Carl gave them an excuse in a series of phone calls. Carl, drunk and mischievous, had rung up Roberta at 3 a.m.

This night Carl was on his favourite topic: Detective Sergeant Stuart Bateson. Bateson, for want of any evidence to lock them up, had been riding Carl and Roberta hard. The rest of the cops had just been doing their job, but for the cocky and ambitious Bateson this appeared to be personal. Carl had nicknamed him 'Toilet Basin'. On the call, Carl had told Roberta that if Bateson came around looking for him, 'You know what to do: get the gun from under the mattress and shoot him in the head'. Roberta, knowing the call was being monitored, hung up on him.

On an earlier telephone intercept, Carl had been overheard asking the Raptor, in Barwon Prison, if he wanted him to kill Bateson's partner. It was a casual remark dropped in at the end of a general conversation.

CARL: 'Love you, mate.'

RAPTOR: 'Yeah, love you.'

CARL: 'If you want Bateson's missus . . . whatever you want me to do.'

RAPTOR: 'Yeah, get her, Toilet Basin.'

CARL: 'I will chop her up.'

Carl later claimed that his comments to the Raptor had been misheard.

'They're off their heads. You can hear it clearly on the tape. I didn't say I wanted to knock Bateson's girl. I know it's not a nice thing to say,' said Carl. 'What I really said was that I wanted to fuck her.'

On 17 November 2003, police decided to pinch Carl for making threats to kill Bateson and his girlfriend. They knew Carl would probably beat the charge in court, but it was a means of getting Carl off the street for a while.

Carl was driving down Beaconsfield Parade in Roberta's Mitsubishi Pajero, when police from Purana and the special operations group headed him off.

The SOG members had surrounded the vehicle and, with an arsenal of weapons levelled at him, begun to shout commands at Carl.

'Those dogs started screaming, "Put on the handbrake and get out of the car," ' Carl said later. He knew enough about Victoria Police to suspect it was a set-up, he said.

Carl was terrified he was about to be killed and refused to get out of the car. 'You go for the handbrake, and they shoot you and say you were going for a handgun.' A stand-off ensued until Carl crawled out of the car onto the nature strip. A passing photographer from *The Age* newspaper snapped the moment when police slammed Carl's face into the grit of the Port Melbourne nature strip as they handcuffed him. For a boy who never liked to get dirty, even when playing footy, this was an unspeakable affront.

Carl later claimed that during his arrest, a police officer had whispered softly in his ear, 'We know who you are and what you've been up to, and we're coming for you. You won't know when, but we're coming. Remember that, smartarse.'

Much to the annoyance of Purana, Carl got bail almost as soon as the judge heard the tape of his conversation with the Raptor. He wasn't going to lock up Carl for a lewd comment about Bateson's girlfriend. It was a huge relief for Roberta, who had feared that Carl would still be in custody the following Sunday when Dhakota's christening was scheduled. This was the biggest party that she had ever had and no one was going to ruin it. They were going to act like a normal family, even if they weren't.

On 2 December, when Carl emerged from the County Court a free man on three sets of bail, Judy Moran had been on hand.

Carl had been enjoying the attention of the media while cradling Dhakota in his arms. He'd thanked his legal team for their excellent work and said he just wanted to go home to have a drink and a meal. But his smile vanished when Judy Moran approached him from behind and jabbed a finger at him. She said in a low growl, 'Why don't you admit you murdered [both my] children?'

'Is this another set-up?' Carl cried as he hurried away, cutting short his media opportunity. 'It's probably why I'm here – another set-up from your family.'

For Carl, the coincidences were piling up. His shooting in 1999 and the drug bust that followed it, the arrest at Port Melbourne with *The Age* looking on, the sudden arrival of Judy on the scene this day: it all smacked of high-level conspiracy. He believed the

Morans were powerful and malevolent, with tentacles that reached everywhere in Victoria. He wouldn't feel safe until every last one of them was dead.

A few days later, Graham 'the Munster' Kinniburgh was driving an old friend home to the suburbs. The friend couldn't understand why Carl and his team were still breathing, having taken on the Morans in open warfare. Nobody, least of all the Munster and his mate, liked killing. It was always bad for business, a last resort when money or a long stretch in prison was at stake. The killing of Mark and Jason had all but destroyed the family empire and Lewis had seemingly done nothing about it. And, despite their inaction, Carl was still threatening to wipe out all of the Moran faction.

'I told him, "Graham, for Christ's sake, Carl's got to go, and the old man and the wife Roberta. They have all got to go. This thing has got to stop now,"' the old friend says. He had said the same thing to Jason and the advice had gone unheeded.

'I didn't want to lose my best friend to those animals from the western suburbs,' he says.

Munster was someone who could do what had to be done. He was always cool in a crisis, the most level-headed crook of his generation. He had been involved in, or had knowledge of, just about every rort and underworld killing for decades. He abhorred violence, but recognised that sometimes it was unavoidable. The coroner had implicated him in the January 1998 murder of Carlton crime boss Alphonse Gangitano.

Though others dispute it, Bert Wrout is convinced Munster pulled the trigger on Gangitano. Alphonse was out of control, bringing heat on them all. He had dragged Jason into his madness when the pair had run amok in the Sports Bar in King Street in 1995. To top it off, he was going to plead guilty, leaving Jason with no defence. There was also talk that Alphonse had tried to stand over Mark Moran. He was a danger to the equilibrium of life in Melbourne. It was decided he had to go.

The way Wrout tells it, the Munster got to Alphonse's place in Templestowe first, but Mark wasn't far behind. Earlier in the night at the pub, he had seen Lewis pass Mark a bundle that contained a pistol.

The Munster had left Alphonse's door ajar, as the plan called for 'Mark [Moran] to sneak in with the pistol and give it to the Munster. Perhaps the Munster caught him doing his washing. Gangitano was found shot dead by his wife in the laundry dressed in a singlet and underpants'.

No one was ever charged and the media, the coroner and a number of police concluded that Jason Moran had been Alphonse's killer. This was largely based on an informer's testimony that he had been with Jason later that night when he had thrown what the informer believed was a gun inside a paper bag off the West Gate Bridge.

The media coverage of the murder had been uncomfortable for Munster, who had made an art form of staying below the radar. In the 1990s, he and other members of the so-called Grandfather Mob had imported an estimated fifteen tonnes of hashish into Australia. The gang was reportedly caught bringing the fourth drug shipment, worth around $225 million alone, into Australia via Hervey Bay in Queensland. Kinniburgh had beaten the charge and lived quietly until the Gangitano killing. His Kew neighbours found the media coverage impossible to reconcile with the friendly senior citizen they saw walking his little white dog, carrying a plastic bag for its droppings.

Kinniburgh remained tapped into an extensive international crime network. He loved being a crook; it was his calling and he made a career from it. In his prime, he was into everything from armed robberies to safe-cutting. These days he acted mainly as a fence for stolen goods but he was still available for jobs that interested him.

'He would be into a shit sandwich without the bread,' says one former associate.

Kinniburgh always listed his occupation as 'rigger', but he hadn't worked in thirty years. If the test of a crook's success is how little jail time he does, then Munster was among the best. His family had progressed. They had gone to private schools and university on the proceeds of Munster's criminal activity. One son had married into a wealthy Melbourne family, while his daughter married the son of a former Victorian attorney-general. His other son became the professional at a prestigious Melbourne golf club, where he rubbed shoulders with celebrities and millionaires. Munster's wife, Sybil, had time to indulge her interest in Buddhism and other eastern religions in between her social pursuits and running a bead shop down at the Queen Victoria Market.

Having spent a fair chunk of his life in courts, Kinniburgh took a keen interest in legal affairs. He could often be found in the legal precinct of Melbourne finding out the latest legal gossip or researching some arcane piece of legislation. As a lawbreaker, he believed it was important that he understood the statutes.

'He would be telling his lawyers what to do. I think secretly he would have been a lawyer had he not become a villain,' his associate says. Kinniburgh spent much of his ill-gotten gains on setting up his children with property and material goods and the rest on food, drink and travel. The Munster's reputation for eating and drinking was legendary. He was reputed to be a silent partner in the city's most prestigious Chinese restaurant, having loaned its owner a large sum of money for gambling debts. So he took his interest payments in fried rice, he liked to say. Nothing could put him off a fine feed. One night, he got a chicken bone stuck in his throat and his dining companion had to perform the Heimlich manoeuvre to prevent his choking. The rather beefy friend went at it so hard, the Munster's entire lunch came up. Undaunted, Kinniburgh ordered more food and resumed his meal.

The killing of Gangitano had brought Munster into the spotlight and he hated it, but he had helped to clean up the mess for the greater good. He remained loyal to Lewis long after he ceased to be worthy of it. Munster used to say that if you were with a bloke for the sweets you had to stay with him for the sours. He believed that the Morans had brought the drama with Carl on themselves, but he was going to stick by them. As he dropped his friend off, he reassured him that all was in hand. He was carrying a high-calibre automatic handgun and he was organising someone to knock Carl, Roberta and George. He told his friend not to worry. Everything would be okay.

After midnight on 13 December, Munster was parking his old Ford sedan in the driveway of his luxury Kew home, in Melbourne's east. He had been out for dinner and had picked up a few things from the shop on the way home.

A single gunman emerged from the shadows as Munster was getting out of his car. He opened fire, hitting Munster in the chest. Though he was mortally wounded, Munster pulled out his gun and let off a single round that missed the target and lodged in the ceiling of a carport across the street. He died there outside his home.

When the Munster's friend got the news, he immediately suspected Carl and Benji. Lewis had once told him that Benji was a natural-born killer. Police suspected the same thing, though they hadn't expected Munster to be on Carl's hit list. Nonetheless with Raptor in jail, Benji was Carl's number-one shooter, and he became the prime suspect.

However, Benji was quickly eliminated as the killer. Telephone intercepts put him across town at the time of the killing. There were no cryptic phone conversations between Carl and Benji after the killing. Carl had just flatly denied everything. He hadn't ever met Kinniburgh, but on all accounts he had been a good bloke, he told the media. Rumours of Carl's involvement in Munster's murder persist to this day, though no compelling evidence has ever been produced.

Bert Wrout says Lewis told him that Carl had nothing to do with

Right: George Williams and Barbara Denman were born into grinding poverty but they were determined to make something of their life together. George was a pool shark and Barbara worked in a cigarette factory – nothing came easy.

Below: October 1970. Barbara was besotted with Carl from the day he was born. It was said that Barbara not only loved Carl but was in love with him. In her eyes, he could do no wrong.
(Photos courtesy of the Williams family)

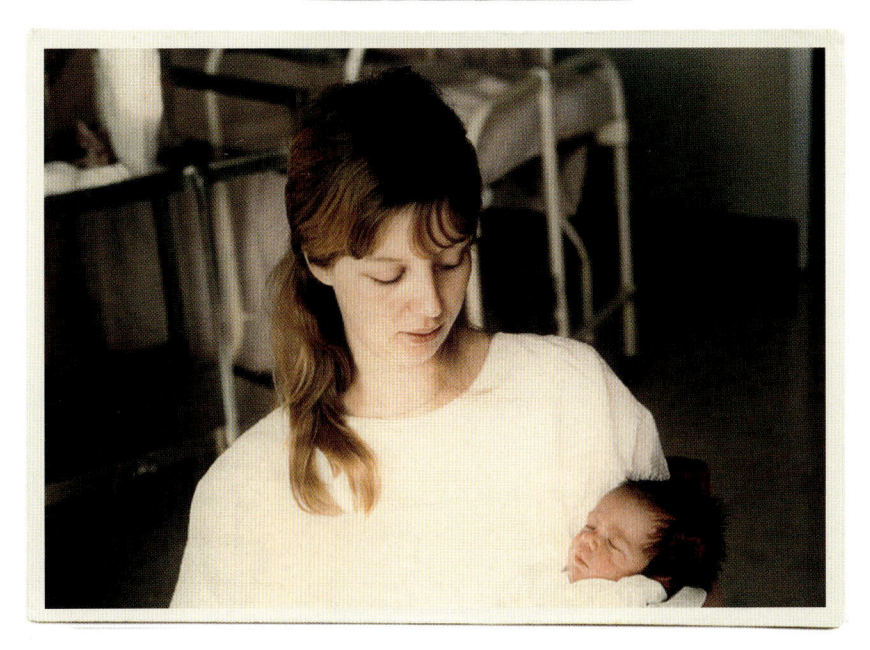

Above: Shane and Carl Williams were not tough kids growing up. They learnt that to avoid schoolyard bullies, they needed plenty of mates who could be bought.

Left: Shane (pictured) and Carl enjoyed the most conventional of childhoods revolving around school, local sport, river holidays at Yarrawonga and their big extended family. However, their home turf was a breeding ground for crime.
(Photos courtesy of the Williams family)

Below: Carl's 21st birthday party in 1991 was a great night until Shane got in a fight with someone over a gold chain. Shane found it hard to accept that Carl got more love and attention from their parents.

Below: Carl wasn't the smartest, the funniest or the most athletic kid in his social circle but his generosity made him a leader among his friends in Broadmeadows.
(Photos courtesy of the Williams family)

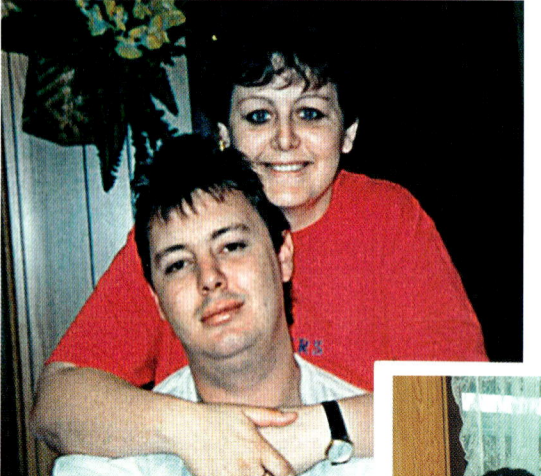

Left: Long-time girlfriend Deana Falcone believed she could save Shane if she could get him off heroin. She failed and their abusive relationship went on for six years, but at least Shane was out of jail for the longest period of his adult life.

Below: Shane with Deana mid-1990s. Shane prided himself on never dobbing on his mates, yet Deana saw those mates let him down one after another. She stayed loyal to the family even beyond Carl's death.

Below: Late 1990s. George tried everything to get Shane off heroin but in the end concluded that perhaps his son didn't want to be saved. Still, Shane's death in 1997 hit him hard.

(Photos courtesy of Deana Falcone)

Right: Carl with Roberta in the late 1990s. Carl wasn't the romantic type but struck up a strong friendship with Roberta Mercieca who was then in a violent marriage with a Moran associate Dean Stephens. He taught her to hold her head up. They both agreed later that they should probably have stayed just mates.

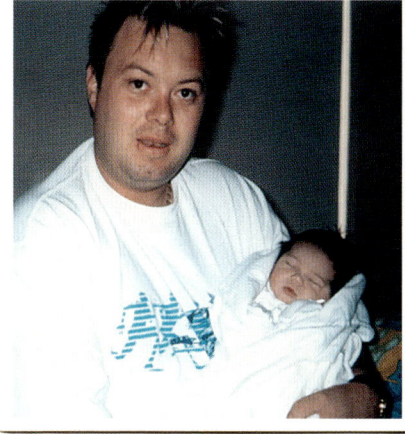

Left: Carl with newborn daughter Dhakota in 2001. Carl had been a reluctant father but Dhakota was his greatest joy. His biggest regret in spending his life in jail was that he would never see her grow up.

Below: Carl with Dhakota at their luxury home in Hillside. Like his parents had done for him, Carl resolved that his daughter would have everything that she could ever possibly want.

(Photos courtesy of the Williams family)

Above: 17 November 2003. Detectives from the Purana Taskforce arrested Carl on a Port Melbourne street and charged him with making threats to kill a police officer and his girlfriend. There were doubts the charges would stand up in court but with the bodies falling thick and fast police needed to get Carl out of circulation.
(Courtesy of Fairfax / Angela Wylie)

Left: Visiting the Magistrate's Court in February 2004. Andrew 'Benji' Veniamin (left) had once been contracted by the Morans to kill Carl but switched sides when he realised that the Williams camp was paying much bigger money for contract killings. Carl promised to share his fortune with Veniamin if the hitman helped him stay alive.
(Courtesy of Newspix / Darren McNamara)

Above: Carl hadn't been to a funeral since his brother Shane's in 1997 but in March 2004 he made an exception for Benji. His right-hand man's death rocked Carl and set off the last murderous chapter of his life on the outside.
(Courtesy of Newspix / Craig Borrow)

Above: Carl boasted that he could 'still pull chicks in jail'. Renata Laureano had been visiting Carl in Barwon Prison before his sentencing in April 2007 but had to face the wrath of ex-wife Roberta to enjoy a brief moment of fame outside court. Barbara is on the left.
(Courtesy of Newspix / Ian Currie)

Above: Right up until his sentencing in May 2007, Carl showed no remorse for his crimes, despite the urgings of his legal counsel (here, the late David Ross QC). He maintained that he had only been protecting his family from the Morans who had been in league with corrupt police.
(Courtesy of Fairfax Syndication / Jason South)

Above: The first day of shooting *Underbelly* in 2007. Carl had complained that actor Gyton Grantley (centre) had made him look like 'a brain-dead goose' in the top-rating series but those close to him knew that he was flattered by his portrayal as a hero.
(Courtesy of Newspix / Rob Baird)

Above: By April 2010, all of Carl's criminal associates and hangers-on were dead or had deserted him. There was only family and a few childhood mates on hand for his funeral, just like at Shane's in 1997. To his family, Carl would always be a hero, a small consolation for a life wasted.
(Courtesy of Newspix / Craig Borrow)

the killing. He says that Lewis told him that Munster died as a consequence of a deal gone wrong.

The killer was apparently owed up to $1.8 million by Munster and Lewis, which had made relations tense, according to Wrout. Lewis told Wrout that a fortnight before Munster was killed, he had taken $200 000 in cash around to the bloke's place and just threw it at him. Then he jumped in and beat the living crap out of him. He was getting on but he could still go.

Munster had been in a toxic rage, says Wrout, and beat the bloke severely. And that was apparently enough to get him killed, according to Wrout.

If this version is correct, then no doubt the spotlight falling on Carl and Benji was convenient for Munster's killer. But to the end Carl swore he had nothing to do with it, though he had a motive for killing Munster, even if he wasn't aware of it at the time. The Munster was plotting against him.

Dhakota's christening went ahead as planned. It was a huge affair with more than 150 guests on hand to share the family's joy. A television crew from ABC's *Four Corners* was also there to record the festivities. This was the start of a new phase for Carl. He would turn the pressure back on the police. He suggested they should look to their own before harassing a decent hardworking fellow like him. In an interview with *Four Corners*, Carl said he just wanted 'to be left alone. That's all'. He blithely told reporter Jonathan Holmes that he had not a clue what all this killing was about.

CARL WILLIAMS: 'They say it happened over money – that I was shot, everything like that. As I said, I don't know anything – who I was shot by, why I was shot.'

JONATHAN HOLMES: 'You don't know who shot you?'

CARL WILLIAMS: 'No, I don't.'

JONATHAN HOLMES: 'Did you have your eyes shut or what?'

CARL WILLIAMS: (smirking) 'Yeah, I've got no idea who shot me. It's, you know . . .'

JONATHAN HOLMES: 'It's nothing to do with you that those two men [Jason and Mark Moran] are dead now?'

CARL WILLIAMS: 'Nothing to do with me.'

Carl told Holmes it was those in the drug squad who had murder on their minds, claiming he had been threatened by a cop in May 2001.

'I'm taken from [a police station to] . . . a park, where I'm told I'm gonna be killed. "This is where you're gonna die, be killed." There was a big shipping container next to where they were pointing at,' he said.

George chimed in with allegations that police had robbed him when he and Carl were arrested on the drugs charges in 1999.

'They was invited into my house. They're supposed to be upholding the law and they can rob your house. The money was there. And when the police left, the money weren't there. Now, I don't know if Casper the Ghost came and got it, but . . . someone got it,' he said.

Carl and George knew if they kept the spotlight on the police they could make their get-out-of-jail-free card last a bit longer. More importantly, in their minds, they had done nothing wrong. They believed drugs were a victimless crime. The state could make them illegal but not unpopular. Police corruption was a far greater threat to the taxpayers of Victoria. Untangling that mess would keep the police and the state government busy for years. Carl believed that one day he would use his knowledge of corruption to wash away all his sins. And in the meantime the gentlefolk of the city would be happy that he was dealing with scum like the Morans who had worked with the bent cops.

24

BEACH BAIL

As the fall-out from Munster's death spread across the underworld, Carl decided it was time to take a break from the turbulent events unfolding in his home town. Securing a variation to his bail, Carl and Benji set off for Port Douglas in far north Queensland with two girls in tow. Remarkably, one was the daughter of a man suspected of involvement in the Munster's murder. It was, as Roberta described it later, 'a fucking week'.

Their carnal needs taken care of, Carl and Benji travelled back to Surfers Paradise, where they met the rest of the clan. Roberta brought up the kids, along with her older sister Michelle. Barb and Deana, who were by now best friends, had a separate room.

Meanwhile, Tony Mokbel was also working on his tan at Surfers, but not in the Outrigger Resort with the Williams family. He had a suite at the Palazzo Versace, where the best rooms go for $3000 a night. It had been a pleasant and quiet week for Mokbel – that was, until the arrival of the Williams clan, which signalled the resumption of the media frenzy.

The *Herald Sun* sent a reporter from Melbourne to show its readers how the criminal class was spending its holidays. He followed Carl and his family around for three days, writing that the 'unemployed property developer' was 'flaunting his freedom on a court-approved holiday of sun, surf and luxury'. Under the headline 'BEACH BAIL' the reporter wrote that police were 'appalled that Mr Williams, who is also facing charges of threatening to kill an officer,' was 'enjoying the high life'.

Carl was enjoying parading his wealth and disdain for authority. He felt he was too clever for the cops assigned to chase him. They could follow him all they wanted, listen to his phone calls and harass his friends, but they wouldn't pierce his well-constructed wall of alibis. In the meantime, they would know he 'was sipping on drinks out of pineapples by the pool' while they 'sipped on warm cans of Coke in squad cars', as the *Herald Sun* noted.

Like a handful of reporters, I met up with Carl and Roberta shortly after they returned from their beach bail in January 2004.

Carl believed the media coverage had blackened his good name. In his view, he wasn't doing much wrong but this negative portrayal might impact on his upcoming drug trials. He believed the cops had leaked his holiday plans in Queensland to embarrass him. He had long been self-conscious about his weight and he hated seeing himself on the front page of the newspaper, wallowing in the ocean like a baby dugong. And it would only get worse as the cops fed more nonsense about him to their captive media mates. They had charged him with two sets of drugs charges and making threats to kill but he was confident he could beat all that. When the citizens got wind of what police officers were doing in the drug trade with vile scum like the Morans, they would give Carl a medal for taking out the rubbish.

He prided himself on the fact he had been able to spot the set-ups. He was taking advice from an old lag, who was a self-styled expert in PR. He advised Carl to get out and speak to journalists whom he felt would give him sympathetic coverage. By the time he was finished, there would be no juror in Victoria who wouldn't know about his case. Then his lawyers could argue that Carl wouldn't get a fair trial in the state. Perhaps it was simply delaying the inevitable, but extending his bail for as long as possible was an end in itself. He would have to do some jail time eventually, but if he could tie the system up in knots that might be a long way in the future.

He didn't need to sell himself too hard to the press. Carl's war was the hottest story in town and reporters were queuing up for interviews. His lawyers felt more like publicity agents as they fielded requests daily from media outlets all over the country. There were already film producers trying to buy his story, even as the war raged on. Police were surprised at how fast Carl had learnt to court the media. Purana reportedly scrutinised the connections of the journalists he was meeting, hoping to find some leverage to stop the press reporting his statements. In the middle of a gang war with hot lead flying around public streets, Purana apparently had time to run background checks on journalists. It underlined how much Carl had embarrassed police and how personally the investigators took the adverse comments he made in the media. And the cops could always rely on the mean spirit of journalists to spread nonsense about those who did speak to Carl. As if they wouldn't have spent time with Carl if they could have. But of course that might have displeased key police handlers on whom the leading crime journalists in Melbourne relied for many of their scoops.

Meanwhile Carl was loving his notoriety. One morning inside the County Court, a police officer asked him if he had any identification on him. To which he replied, 'You don't know who I am?'

When Carl and his entourage came to court, city workers and passersby gathered to watch them do 'the walk of shame' into court through the throng of media. The camera crews and photographers even recorded them eating lunch in a nearby café. He felt like a fair dinkum celebrity, he told friends.

Mostly, he would say nothing to the media and just stare through them like he was above all this but he wasn't always so cool. Once, outside court, Carl was asked if he feared for his safety. He sidestepped the questioner, but managed to walk into the oncoming city traffic.

Carl was amused at how competitive and treacherous the press pack was. Some journalists were prepared to write whatever the police told them, he said. The police had protected the Moran clan for years, so he expected no sympathy from the media, which he believed was happy to parrot whatever line the cops wanted out there.

Carl cut a most unusual figure as a crime boss. It was hard to reconcile what he was accused of doing, with his soft baby face and easy smile. But behind the gormless fat boy image, there was a calculating and shrewd character. It was easy to dismiss him as a bogan in his polo tops and long denim shorts, but he captured the attention of the media. Journalists were used to gangland figures looking the part. In earlier times they were fearsome men with names like Freddy 'the Frog' Harrison, or Mark 'Chopper' Read. They had sallow complexions, sunken cheeks and hollowed-out eyes, the hallmarks of men who did their best work at night.

But Carl was different. He looked like a guy you would meet at a suburban footy ground with a beer in his hand or at McDonald's, flipping burgers. He was now prepared to meet journalists to protest his innocence.

With Roberta at his side they looked every inch the suburban couple. This was the front they showed to the square-head world from whom they sought acceptance. Roberta, with her glittering diamond rings and designer outfits, would tell people that her maternity sleepwear business was doing really well. Carl's nightclub and footy friends knew that he was moving a bit of gear, but they had no idea of the scale of his operation.

For a man said to be marked for death, Carl was remarkably relaxed and jovial when he met reporters. Home from his Queensland holiday, he was beaming with vitality and good humour. His face was deeply tanned but for a pale patch on his nose where zinc cream had protected him from the sun. Williams could fall to a bullet that year but not to skin cancer.

Carl looked like a guy who took good care of himself, except when it came to food, where almost anything would do. While self-conscious about his weight, he was apparently very proud of his smile and perfect teeth. The white-blond hair of his childhood had dulled to mousey brown, so Carl ritually had streaks added to keep his youthful look.

If Carl had one message for the press in this period, it was that he was the victim. Anything that he was alleged to have done was more or less justified because of the heinous things that Mark and Jason may or may not have done to him. He was confirming nothing but hinting at everything.

Roberta was acutely aware of how their story was being told. It was never clear exactly how much she knew of Carl's murderous activities. She professed to know very little, instead focusing on the hurt that her family and associates had suffered. They were being harassed and persecuted by police and the media, she said. They were just 'an average everyday family who got up in the morning and took the kids to school'. But it all got a bit hazy after that. Roberta claimed to feel shock and concern at the steady demise of Carl's fellow drug dealers. They were friends of Carl, many of them, she said. Perhaps the police should look at their own, the bent cops who had worked with the Morans.

There was no war from their side, Roberta said blithely. It was all media hype, just like the stories that Andrew Veniamin was Carl's bodyguard. The press had written that the 'well-muscled' Benji stayed by Carl even when he went into the surf. The truth was Benji had stuck to Carl because he couldn't swim. Carl was looking after him, Roberta said. Benji had made Carl stay between the flags in the shallows. Benji was terrified of drowning when the water got over his waist.

Benji was nothing more than Carl's friend 'and a good friend at that', Roberta declared on national television.

Roberta was convinced the police, with the help of certain media, were hatching a plan to kill Carl and Andrew. 'Then all this killing can be blamed on them and no one will ever know the truth,' she said.

Roberta just wanted life to go on as it was, before all this bullshit took over their lives. She wanted to go travelling with the kids on

Carl's money, throw parties and go shopping. Yet privately she knew it was all coming to an end soon. Carl couldn't go on killing people for much longer, without someone knocking him, or his being locked up forever. So she would ride this thing out to see what was left at the end, if anything. Bizarrely, Carl began to blame Roberta for all the drama in his life. He had decided that it must have been Roberta's ex-husband Dean that had paid for Mark and Jason to shoot him back in 1999. From that moment, his life had changed. It was all her fault. If he hadn't hooked up with Roberta, none of this would have been happening.

Roberta would do what she had to for her children. Everything in life so far had ultimately disappointed Roberta, her marriage to Carl included. But she would fight for him, if it meant her kids had a roof over their heads and a private-school education. Then it would have all been worthwhile.

The feud had got right out of hand over the summer. There were persistent references in the media connecting Carl and Benji to the murder of Kinniburgh. People were getting in Mick Gatto's ear, suggesting that it was only a matter of time before his little mate came for him. Mokbel was said to have put a $400 000 contract on Mick's head after the beating he took at La Porcella in 2002.

On 22 December, Gatto asked Carl and Benji to a meeting at Crown Casino to clear the air over Kinniburgh's death. Gatto had initially suggested meeting in Carlton but Carl wanted a place where there were plenty of witnesses about and CCTV to tell the story if it all turned to shit.

After the obligatory kisses and hugs, Gatto came straight out and asked whether Benji had been involved in Kinniburgh's death. Benji denied it, saying he had heard that Asian crooks had been behind it. This failed to satisfy Gatto. According to lip readers asked by police to analyse the tape, Gatto calmly told Carl and Benji that he wanted to be left alone, but if they sent anyone to him, he would send someone to them. According to Roberta, Carl fired up, suggesting that Gatto and the Carlton Crew were 'not the only cunts who can turn on the drama'.

As far as Carl was concerned, the die was cast with Gatto at that moment. The fact that Mick thought Benji had been behind Kinniburgh's death meant that his days of sitting on the fence between the Williams and Moran camps were over.

After the casino meet, Carl and Benji went to ground for a while, spending most of their time in their thirtieth-floor apartment at Regency Towers. Soon after, Roberta moved the kids into an apartment on the nineteenth floor of the same building. They had by this stage officially broken up but the relationship carried on almost as normal, whatever that was. Carl still wanted a home life when he needed it. He still wanted someone to cook and clean for him and look after his kid. But he wanted to live large too.

Benji had introduced Carl to a gorgeous young socialite he knew from the club scene. She was from a good family that hailed from south of the river, a mark of respectability in Melbourne. Her father was managing director of a leading Australian company. She knew who Carl was but fell in love with him anyway.

Barb was overjoyed. Finally, here was a woman that deserved her boy. She was looking forward to Carl divorcing Roberta and marrying this girl. Barb naively believed that Carl had a future. He was smart enough to stay one step ahead of the cops. She believed the drugs charges would fall away when the public learnt of the rampant police corruption. Then Carl would be regarded as a hero.

High atop the city skyline, Carl felt safe, the emperor of all he surveyed. But he knew that his day might be coming soon. He and Benji had alienated powerful forces. These were people who had run affairs in Melbourne for decades. Benji believed he was on his final run, that all the bad things he had done would catch up with him soon. He told associates that he was going to take down as many of the dogs as he could. He had no fear of dying. Benji was already planning his own funeral: he and Roberta went shopping at a funeral home for just the right coffin.

In the meantime, he would stand by Carl. Benji had once been intent on killing him, and had switched sides for money. Yet the relationship had changed and deepened. Now Carl promised that he would share everything with Benji, and the survivor would keep the lot. But now the money didn't seem all that important. It was like they were in some kind of movie, the pair of them against the world, and the climax was fast approaching.

25

GUNS FOR HIRE

The Purana Taskforce took its name from a class of Sanskrit writings of the eleventh century recounting the birth and deeds of Hindu gods and the creation, destruction, or recreation of the universe.

To Assistant Commissioner Simon Overland it conjured up an appropriate image. It did seem that epoch-making events were unfolding in Melbourne. In this volatile atmosphere, criminal legends were being made and others destroyed. By early 2004, he knew virtually all the elements of the story.

'Some of this is about revenge, some of this is about bad business deals, some of this is about personal animosities and some of this may well be about power plays in organised crime whereby people see that there is an opportunity to position themselves within a market place and they are executing that in a very ruthless way,' he said on the Nine Network's *Sunday* program.

Yet Purana seemed powerless to prevent the bloodletting. Overland had offered police protection to Lewis Moran, Carl and others but it had been refused. They would take their chances, they said. To hide behind the police would be seen as an act of cowardice or surrender. So the players tried to behave as if nothing was wrong, maintaining their routines and parading their defiance. Lewis Moran and Bert Wrout could be found at the Brunswick Club every evening with their seven-ounce pensioner-special beers in hand. Mick Gatto still did business daily in his office, La Porcella, a quiet little restaurant off the main strip in Carlton. Tony Mokbel was still regularly entertaining friends and associates in the nightclubs that he had an interest in. Carl and Benji would hold court in the foyer of the Marriott Hotel adjoining Regency Towers or at Carl's favourite KFC nearby. If he wasn't in the city, he was at Barb's place in Essendon. Nobody was hiding, no one wanted to be the first to flinch. Meanwhile, through February and March tension steadily built, fuelled mainly by a press pack that was breathlessly speculating on who would be the next to go.

On 23 March, Gatto was the one who broke the stand-off. He had been told that Benji was coming for him, so he decided to head him off.

Earlier in the day, Benji and Carl had been in court supporting the Raptor at a hearing on the Marshall murder. Television pictures showed them leaving the court building together, in animated conversation as they ran the media gauntlet outside. They walked out onto the road without looking for traffic and Carl put an arm out to stop Benji.

'Now who's the bodyguard, buddy?' he said. They got to their car and Carl dropped Benji off in the city. He was due to meet Roberta and later they all planned to celebrate Roberta's birthday over lunch. An hour later, Roberta and Carl went to Regency Towers, missing Benji by just minutes. They even thought they smelt Benji's aftershave in the apartment.

At 1 p.m. Benji had called Roberta, bright and bold as always. He had wished her happy birthday and said he loved her. Benji had quickly become the most important man in her life. These days she often couldn't even stand the sight of Carl. Once he had sought to meet her needs, now it was all about him. In Benji, Roberta thought she had found a friend who accepted her for who she was. Maybe Benji wouldn't let her down like everyone else, the dogs she had called friends over the years. Maybe she could trust him.

It was clear that Roberta was falling in love with Benji. Police, the media and even Carl already believed Roberta was sleeping with him. She denies this steadfastly, she always has. She seems to have little reason to lie about it. She now wishes that she had rooted Benji to pay Carl back for all his cheating.

Just after 2 p.m. Mick Gatto telephoned his former protégé. A police bug in Benji's Merc recorded a short and friendly, but somehow guarded, exchange: 'Hello ... Hey, buddy, what's doing? Yeah ... What? ... Where's that? ... The same place? I'll see you soon ... See you soon, buddy ... Affirmative, bye ...'

Benji wound his way through the lunchtime traffic en route to La Porcella, on the corner of Rathdowne and Faraday streets in Carlton. The days when he had been at Mick's elbow down there at the big fella's office must have seemed a thousand years ago. They had been close then, like father and son.

Benji took another call two minutes later from an unknown party. 'Yeah, mate ... Yep ... Nah, nah, I'm not ... I've just got to catch up with someone, just rang me, the big bloke. I'm just going to catch up with him ... I'll ring you when I'm done ... All right ... See ya.'

There was nowhere to leave the car, so, as usual, a double-park outside Mick's place would do. He would only be a minute, and if he got a ticket, what did it matter? The car wasn't in his name anyway.

Gatto and Benji talked amicably for some minutes at a table in the restaurant before the hit man kicked his former mentor under the table. He said he needed to talk in private, so they moved into a passageway that led from the restaurant to the kitchen. Only the living man can tell the story of what happened next and Gatto gave his version in court and in his own book, *I, Mick Gatto*.

Gatto claims that when they moved into the passageway, Benji turned to him and said he had a problem. He was hearing that Gatto believed he had something to do with Kinniburgh's death.

Gatto agreed, saying that everyone was saying the same thing. Benji may not have pulled the trigger, but Gatto still suspected that he was a part of the conspiracy.

Benji denied the allegation, protesting that Gatto was a friend; he wouldn't hurt anybody who was a friend of Mick. Gatto knew this was bullshit. Benji was in the frame for several killings, including those of his former friends Dino Dibra and Paul Kallipolitis.

Gatto claims that Benji confessed to those killings. 'They were fucking dogs anyway,' Gatto alleged Benji told him. 'They deserved it.'

Gatto then told Benji that he no longer wanted him in his company, he couldn't trust him.

Benji lost his temper, took a step back and pulled out a handgun, according to Gatto. As Gatto lunged for the weapon, Benji fired, and the bullet whizzed past Gatto's ear.

There was a short struggle before Gatto turned the gun on Benji. He lay dead on the ground in the passageway, three gunshot wounds in his head and throat.

Gatto walked from the room, holding the gun, trying to maintain his composure but he says his heart was jumping out of his chest.

He told the owner of the restaurant, 'You'd better ring the police and an ambulance. He just tried to kill me and he's finished second best.'

Gatto then called his friend and business partner Mattie Tomas, who was with Gatto's two sons at a building project. Fearing that Carl might strike back at his family, Gatto told Mattie to send his kids home for the day without telling them why. From Mick's tone, Tomas knew not to argue or even ask questions.

After making the call, Mick sat and waited for the cops to arrive. Gatto was charged with Benji's murder but quickly presented a plausible story of self-defence. Later Gatto reportedly told investigators that, far from locking him up, they should have been pinning a medal on him. Killing Benji was a public service.

When they heard from a journalist there had been a shooting involving Benji, Carl and Roberta drove straight to La Porcella, though they knew the place would be swarming with journalists and onlookers. Carl stood behind the wall of cameras and reporters outside the restaurant for a few seconds before somebody noticed him. There was the villain of the piece in his stone-washed jeans and red polo top, his face dripping with nervous sweat.

After dealing death for three years, Carl's team was finally on the receiving end. The story had come alive again and Carl had arrived on stage with immaculate timing. The reporters saw there was fear in Carl's eyes for the first time. The cocksure matinee gangster who had walked from court with Benji that morning was gone. He had lost Roberta in the crowd, and alone and disoriented from the shock of losing Benji, Carl decided he had to get away. Where he was going to run to he hadn't a clue – he just needed to be away from everything, the ambulances, the bystanders, the cops swarming everywhere, the media and all their stupid questions.

Carl's mind was in turmoil as the media pack surrounded him. He suspected that there could be someone lurking nearby who meant to kill him. What had happened to the rest of the Carlton Crew? If they could kill Andrew in a café, then why not him in the street? Anything was possible right now.

In his panic, Carl randomly flagged down a passing car. The driver of the Mazda 323 had to stop or it would have run him over. Carl got in and, to his relief, found that he knew the driver – he was actually the cousin of a friend. Unfortunately, he was going only to the service station less than 200 metres up Rathdowne Street. When the reporters and camera crews spotted Carl getting out of the car, the pursuit resumed in earnest. They chased him around the petrol pumps, firing questions at him. Finally, he gave them the quote they needed for the news that night.

'You fucking vultures! Don't you know someone's just died?' he cried. Then he locked himself in the staff toilet and rang for Roberta to come get him.

That night Carl downed most of a bottle of whiskey and sat

staring into space, according to Roberta. Still he couldn't sleep. He lay thinking about Andrew all night. Perhaps he didn't really know that person lying in the morgue. Why would Benji go to La Porcella to meet Mick without telling him or Roberta? The idea he would meet with their greatest foe alone troubled Carl. Had Benji been true to the end, or was he in the act of betraying him when he met Mick at La Porcella? Part of Carl wanted to say that if Benji had been in the act of somersaulting Carl, he had got his just deserts. What did that say about their friendship?

On their Queensland holiday, Carl had rediscovered feelings he had thought lost and forgotten. In the four years since Jason had shot him, there was a kind of numbness in his soul. Where once he had been fun-loving and accepting of people, he had become anxious and paranoid. He had self-medicated with alcohol and crack cocaine and that had worked for a while. When Dino Dibra had been murdered in 2000, most likely by Benji, Carl was unmoved. They had been very close but Carl hadn't even gone to Dino's funeral. It was bizarre that Benji had been the one to lighten his mood. The cocky little hit man had killed Dino and even had a contract to kill Carl and his family, and yet they had become best buddies. During their short friendship, they had shared everything, including girls, drugs and murder, not to mention the shared knowledge that they could be killed anytime.

It seemed impossible that Benji would sell him out after all they had promised each other. Carl would never get to the bottom of that now, so he tried to block it out of his mind.

He wrote death notices for Benji that spoke of the desire for revenge he harboured:

We mourn the loss of a soul whose life was taken in the blackness of deceit. Only in good faith did you attend but were wounded by the Judas you thought a friend
– Your friend Carl Williams

> *To Andrew my friend. It has taken me years to finally experience a broken heart. You were a sensation. This great loss is only God's gain. You put a roof over my head when I most needed one. Your generosity could not be matched by anyone. If I was not convinced before I am now that only the very special are taken before their time. Till we meet again. Thanks for being such a special friend. All my love to my friend.*
> – Carl Williams

In the days before Benji's funeral, there was talk that Carl would be ambushed on his way from the city to St Andrew's Church in Sunshine. The night before, he told reporters that he'd heard the same thing. Looking out at the lights of Melbourne from his high-rise apartment, Carl might have been forgiven for feeling alone, or even a little scared. The next day he would bury his friend, and now he was apparently marked for death in the morning. Yet he was calm and cool as he discussed how he might spend his last night on earth.

He would just spend a quiet night at home. There would be no pizza for him, 'not even home delivery'. It was his attempt at black humour. As if he would go to La Porcella where Gatto had killed his friend. At least there would be plenty of tables. The place was deserted now but for reporters trying to catch the flavour of the moment that Benji died. At least Carl was still living high on the hog, while his rival Mick Gatto had to make do with prison food while he awaited his trial.

His best friend lying cold in a funeral parlour across town, dressed for a date with eternity, Carl was still trying to make light of everything. He and Roberta had spent time with Andrew at the funeral home. Carl had noticed the bullet wounds in his head and throat. This was how violent death looked. His brother, Shane, had looked at peace in his coffin after his heroin overdose, but Benji's last brutal moments were plain to see.

Carl had ordered several murders prior to this, and they had all been done by remote control. Until now, Carl had watched the results of his decisions on television, like any other disinterested viewer. Now it was up close and personal. This was how a man looked after he had been shot in the head and throat at close range. The mortician's makeup couldn't conceal the powder burns from the muzzle flashes.

From his window, Carl could look westwards to the endless expanse of suburbia he had left behind. He wondered if it had all been worth it, but the story was not over yet. Even if they threw him in jail for all the murders, it wouldn't bother him. You did time easy when you were among friends, and he was popular in jail. There were mates. He told reporters that Gatto was going to do it tough considering how strong his network was.

'He might have a few problems inside,' said Carl. Clearly he was already thinking of revenge. Carl was struggling to keep the feelings of fear and anger under wraps. 'Of course it affects you. He was a good, loyal friend to me,' he told me in a phone call. But he had an image to maintain. He resolved to remember the good times he'd had with Benji, rather than sooking about losing him.

Carl wanted to blame the media for what had happened. The media had pressed the false story that Benji had shot Graham Kinniburgh. The constant pressure of the allegations had put everyone on edge since Munster was killed.

Benji had been 'tried by the media and sentenced to a public execution', he said.

The press believed that Carl's time was fast running out too. Sydney's *Daily Telegraph* newspaper published a picture of him running from La Porcella, with a bullseye superimposed on him. The screaming headline read: 'THE NEXT DEAD THING'.

Carl was outraged. 'How would people like it if I did the same thing to them?' He wasn't afraid of his enemies, but he was becoming worried that a nutter might want to make a name by shooting him.

He may have been afraid but he wasn't going to hide away. 'If they want to kill me, they're going to have to work for it. You know what I mean: they're going to have to put in the hard yards. I'm not going to fall for any set-ups. Not going for no pizzas, no meetings, nothing,' he said. 'I don't go nowhere for no one,' he told me.

Police were amazed at Carl's bravado. He had taken on Melbourne's underworld establishment; now he had no choice but to see it through. How he hadn't been murdered before this was a modern miracle, said one officer.

Carl told himself that he would come out on top if he held his nerve. If he died at least he could say he hadn't run. He adopted a saying he had heard on TV: 'It's better to be a tiger for a day than a sheep for a thousand years.' The line came from Italy's wartime fascist leader, Benito Mussolini, but it seemed apt.

There was no point in trying to run away or staying holed up in the apartment. If someone's out to get you, they'll get you sooner or later. Benji had told him that and, being a hit man, his late friend had been an expert on such matters.

26

A DYNASTY DONE AND DUSTED

After the deaths of his sons and Graham Kinniburgh, Lewis Moran was a spent force. Racked with pain from arthritis and gout, he was now physically incapable of firing a pistol, it was said. Lewis had lost the last remnants of his dash with the deaths of Mark, Jason and the Munster. He blamed himself for everything. If only they had dealt with Williams early on, none of this would have happened. His life now was nothing more than a daily routine of reporting to the police to satisfy his bail conditions and then going to the Brunswick Club.

At six o'clock on 31 March, eight days after Benji's death, Lewis had been at the Brunswick for a couple of hours with Bert Wrout. It was a set routine for them: a half-dozen seven-ounce beers, a few bets on the horses, a chat with the locals. Lewis always stood in the same place at the bar, with a view of the front door and anyone coming in off Sydney Road. After the club, he would go to rent a DVD, and then the rest of the night would be spent on the couch, watching some old gangster film.

Moran had spent that day with friends, enjoying a long lunch at a Middle Park restaurant with a few mates from the racing industry. He had said openly he was living for nothing since the deaths of Jason and Mark. The murder of his best mate Kinniburgh was just a dismal epilogue to his wasted life. At fifty-eight, it was as if he was waiting to meet his death. He had even refused police protection.

As the two hit men in balaclavas, Noel Faure and Evangelos Goussis, strode in the door of the Brunswick Club, Wrout remembers Lewis saying, 'Looks like we're off here.' But when Goussis, his executioner, loomed it seemed Lewis wasn't ready. His survival instinct kicked in and he ran down a passageway, past the toilets into a gaming area. As he passed a line of poker machines, he pushed over a bar stool in a futile attempt to thwart Goussis's inexorable pursuit. The agile former boxer simply leapt over it and caught up with Lewis after he'd run into the arms of the club's manager, Sandra Sugars. To her horror, the killer levelled his shotgun at Lewis, but the weapon misfired. Drawing a handgun from his coat, Goussis put two rounds into Moran's head at point-blank range.

Lewis Moran now lay dead by the pool table. On the bar he had left a half-full beer and a betting slip – two items that summed up his life in recent years.

Wrout went for the front exit only to confront the other gunman, Noel Faure, who was covering the street. If Wrout had stayed at the bar, he might have avoided a bullet. The killers were only there for Lewis, but Wrout had unwittingly run into the line of fire. Bert had stuck by Lewis for some insane reason and had paid the price for his misguided loyalty. The killers ran around the corner to a waiting getaway car and disappeared into the night. A couple of patrons were seen arguing with police for the right to play pool as Moran's body lay inconveniently by.

Carl had his now-familiar nonchalance in place when the press began calling within half an hour of Lewis's murder. He had not known in advance when the killers were going to strike; it made it easier to pretend the whole thing was news to him. He was just having another 'quiet one at home', he said. He had heard about Lewis on the radio. It was pretty brazen: 'They just walked in off the street and gave it to him, eh?'

Of course he had no clue who was responsible. Lewis probably had lots of enemies.

Carl had been at his mother's house in Essendon at the time of the shooting. He had been spending a lot of time at Barb's since

Andrew's death. At the precise time Lewis was getting shot, Carl reckoned he had been getting his dinner from the local KFC. He had bought 'a Zinger burger, chips and a Coke', he told me.

The conversation moved to fast food and cholesterol. Carl was always trying to lose weight but it was difficult when he loved junk food so much. But then again, he said, his fast-food belly had probably saved his life the day Jason shot him. His gut fat had absorbed most of the force of the bullet. It had been slowing dramatically when it struck a layer of muscle. It had deflected downwards and missed everything important.

'No, mate, no worries. It came up good as gold. Anyway, gettin' shot didn't hurt that much,' he said, as if discussing a trip to the dentist. 'It didn't even bleed that much.' He said he'd heard the shot so he knew he was all right: 'If you don't hear the shot, you're in trouble . . . It means you're dead.'

Carl was trying hard not to show his pleasure at the death of Lewis Moran. Lewis's demise meant nothing to him, he said, save for the fact that the police and the media had been wrong. All along, newspapers had carried comments from unnamed investigators that Carl would be the one lying in the morgue but he was still standing. One of the killers later told police that Carl had called him to arrange payment, telling him: 'You've got $150 000 reasons to smile.'

It was the end of the Morans. The killing of Lewis ended a feud that Jason had sworn would last forever; they had been destroyed in just under four years. And they had barely fought back, paralysed by arrogance and their penny-pinching. Only Lewis's brother Tuppence remained, and the next day it was reported that he had cleared out of the city just in case the killers wanted to take out the last of the male line in the family.

Only a handful of people turned up for Lewis's funeral, held a few days later at St Therese's Church in Essendon. In 2000, hundreds of Mark's friends had gathered for his send-off, but for Lewis only a few drinking buddies and mates from the racing industry turned up. Judy Moran made a great show of grief, even though everyone knew it was an act. She had hated Lewis and only kept her married name for the status it brought.

The hangers-on from the glory days were long gone. There was no one even prepared to act as a pallbearer for Lewis's cheap coffin. So the undertakers wheeled him out of the church on a gurney. The mourners moved away quietly for a few drinks to send Lewis off.

Meanwhile, the advisers who had hidden the Morans' ownership of pubs and other property behind front companies and nominee directors quietly pocketed what was left of the empire.

It had been the most dispiriting week of Purana's year-long existence. After Lewis's death, the taskforce chief Simon Overland had gone to the Brunswick Club and held an impromptu press briefing. The strain was clearly taking its toll on him. His was no longer the voice of a dispassionate investigator following the evidentiary trail, but a man shocked at the violence that was unfolding in his city.

The killing had 'reached new depths of stupidity, to be quite frank', he said.

'It is just stupid, wanton killing. And we are committed to doing everything that we can to stop it and to bring this to an end.' Overland's first duty was to prevent the further loss of life, so the latest killings had hit the squad hard. Months of diligent police work, surveillance and forensics now seemed to have been to no avail. The credibility of Purana was now under serious question. This investigation was looking like all the others into previous gangland wars: a perfunctory effort and nothing more. One cartoonist depicted Overland's squad as an old toothless piranha in a police cap swimming haplessly through a sea of dead gangsters in concrete boots.

27

LOOSE ENDS

The Morans had been reduced to widows, orphans and a few men with no stomach for the fight, but still the killing wasn't over yet. In fact, a new front was opening up. With Mick Gatto in jail, Mario Rocco Condello believed he was in charge in Carlton, and he was going to fix Carl once and for all.

He was a fifty-two-year-old former lawyer, disbarred after he showed a predilection for villainy over justice. As a tertiary educated professional man, he had long felt superior to his associates. He believed he had the vision to lead his people out of the present circumstances and restore order. Once in a generation comes a man with the wit and integrity to unify the rabble of the underworld, he liked to say, and Mario had no doubt that he was that man.

Condello was renowned in Melbourne as a highly effective money launderer but he also had convictions for drug trafficking and insurance fraud. He had deep, serious ties with the Mafia in the Calabrian region in Italy, where his family had originated; he was a student both of the Classics and the history of the Mob. There were also some bizarre stories told about Condello. He was afraid of violence and would pass out at the sight of blood. He had others for the rough stuff, but liked to be on hand when they went to work on the victim, notwithstanding his squeamishness. It was said that Condello had once arrived at the beating of a rival dressed like the 'gimp' character from Quentin Tarantino's *Pulp Fiction*, clad in a leather mask and gloves.

Condello had begun by suggesting a peace summit. He had

even toyed with the idea of approaching a member of parliament to be a mediator. The last thing he wanted to do was to spend his money protecting the Morans. If and when the threat came to him, he would act.

After Lewis Moran's death, Condello met Carl Williams and George to talk peace. Carl told Condello that he didn't want any trouble and that his team would take on anyone in Melbourne except the Calabrians.

'They came and offered peace and goodwill,' Carl told me in an interview. 'At first it seemed a little vague, but like any situation, you've got to give it a chance.' But both sides knew that this thing had gone way beyond that. Condello recognised some things could only be settled with blood. And there were willing assassins queuing up for an earner.

The Rat was a third-generation crim with a penchant for changing sides when it suited him. The gangland war would be a financial bonanza for him, if he played his cards right, he told people. He had put together a little kill team of his own. He had organised Noel Faure and a mate, Evangelos Goussis, to kill Lewis Moran on behalf of Carl, but Carl hadn't paid the full whack of the promised $150 000. He was still owed ten grand, the Rat told police later. Apparently, in early 2004, he also tried to step up for the contract on Gatto but Mick had discovered this and quickly suggested that the Rat make other plans.

Meanwhile, Carl had allegedly contracted another gunman, Lewis Caine, to go after Condello. Caine was a bar-room brawler who had killed a man in a moment of drunken misjudgement. One night in 1989, in Lazars nightclub, a fight became a killing and Caine suddenly moved up the criminal pecking order. In Melbourne crime circles, a murderer is worth more than an armed robber, but Caine was a square-head who fantasised about being a gangster. He came to Carl through his new lawyer, Zarah Garde Wilson, who was also in a relationship with Caine.

On the evening of 8 May 2004, Caine accepted a ride from the Rat and Ange Goussis, and ended up dead in a lane in Brunswick. Carl didn't seem overly concerned. There were others who could replace him. But the quality of Carl's assassins had dropped off dramatically after the Raptor had been jailed and Benji shot dead. He still had the Savage on hand but he was busy on other matters.

In early May 2004, Carl began to take an interest in Terry Hodson during conversations with me. Hodson was the small-time drug dealer who had been approached by Lewis Moran in 2002 to find a hit man to kill Carl and George for the paltry sum of $40 000. Carl said he had received a leaked police information report that had showed details of the plot. He was outraged that police hadn't shared the knowledge with him. It was their duty to do so, he bleated. To Carl, the IR had no doubt justified his decision to have Lewis Moran killed. He wasn't being paranoid: there was a plot to kill him. But the fact that no one had picked up the contract showed it was a fruitless search. Why would someone kill Carl for $40 000 when they could pick up $150 000 for killing on his behalf?

Hodson had another significant role to play in the drama of Carl's life. He was due to give evidence in the committal hearing of Detective Sergeant Paul Dale, who had been charged with involvement in the grand final day drug-house burglary in Oakleigh. The courts, with the full support of police command, were out to make an example of corrupt police. Dale's co-accused, Senior Detective David Miechel, would go on to receive a sentence of fifteen years' jail, with a minimum term of twelve years. If the Crown could prove that Dale was the instigator of the plot, he was looking at a heavy penalty.

On 16 May 2004, Hodson and his wife, Christine, were found shot dead in their East Kew home. Their killer had ordered them to lie face-down on the floor of the living room, and then he executed them with shots to the backs of their heads. There were no signs of forced entry into the house, and the Hodsons' two German shepherds had been locked up in the garage. To make the scene even more suspicious, the murder had been carried out just 200 metres from a police station.

When Carl was called by reporters, he said he was shocked at yet more murders. However, he made the point that being a police informer was an exciting but often short life. He denied to me that he was responsible. He was hurt to be even accused, he said. He had offered reporters copies of the police report that detailed Hodson's informing in years past. Why would he tell the world about the police report if he intended to kill them?

It was a performance for the police, who were listening to every phone call. Carl complained that he might as well take himself down to police headquarters and give himself up.

Days after the murder, ABC radio broadcast details from the police report that Carl had been hawking. It had been compiled by David Miechel. With the death of the Hodsons, the police report took on a much more sinister meaning. It was later revealed that Miechel had been sleeping with Hodson's daughter. After he was busted for the Oakleigh job, Miechel had sent Hodson a card with a picture of Tony Montana from the movie *Scarface*. The meaning could not have been less ambiguous. Miechel had unwittingly made himself a murder suspect.

The emergence of the police report changed the complexion of the gangland war, even if the underlying facts were far from clear. It suggested there were much deeper links between police and organised-crime figures than had been previously imagined.

A bloody gangland feud now had the potential to become a serious issue for the state of Victoria. Police were dealing with crime organised as never before and their own were up to their necks in it. Now the killing was a problem for the state's ruling class. The state Opposition leader, Robert Doyle, had been looking for a link between the gangland murders and police corruption, and this was it. Doyle and the Victorian Bar Association called for a judicial inquiry into corruption in the police service. This could be nothing less than a royal commission or a standing crime commission.

It was unclear how far this stain of corruption had spread. If further evidence emerged, then a far-reaching inquiry could bring down a government if the momentum got going. There were select senior Labor figures, both state and federal, who had known links to underworld figures. They had plenty to fear from a public forum into organised crime. Gangsters had long contributed to the election campaigns of some politicians; and they had greeted each other warmly at party functions.

Premier Steve Bracks had flatly refused to hold a judicial inquiry, but now the police response was being called into question. The failure to stem the violence was becoming a political issue. The press began to ask what vested interests lay behind the poor performance of the police. Perhaps authorities had too much to lose, if crooks like Carl finally told their stories.

Remarkably, Simon Overland stepped into the political arena, calling for a public debate into the establishment of a crime commission. Now even the cops were putting pressure on Bracks. But to create a crime commission or a judicial inquiry would mean losing control of the debate. Instead, Premier Bracks would go only halfway, giving the police ombudsman the powers of a royal commission, while the police commissioner would become as powerful as a standing crime commission. The ombudsman would be able to subpoena witnesses and make them answer his questions or face jail. The police commissioner would be empowered to seize the assets of suspected mobsters and freeze their bank accounts. There would not even have to be any charges laid.

Later, in her 2011 book, *Fair Cop*, former chief commissioner Christine Nixon wrote what many other police had previously thought. Gangsters killing other gangsters had little significance for the public, beyond the strictly voyeuristic. But throw in some bent cops and the whole system of law enforcement and justice could be called into question.

The gangland slaughter had become 'part of the scenery' in Melbourne. But the execution of the Hodsons had raised 'the most serious questions' about whether Victoria Police could be trusted to do its job. The safety of witnesses and informers, and the confidentiality of sensitive information was in doubt.

Carl knew the information he had was of value to authorities. It was a bargaining chip he could hold back until he needed it. For the moment, he wasn't thinking about jail, but his survival.

28

BEHIND BARS

At 7.20 a.m. on 9 June 2004, Carl was at his mum's place, sleeping off a hangover. Barb was thinking of the cooked breakfast she would make him sometime later that morning. Only a week before, Carl had told his mother that he wanted to turn back the clock to a time before he was shot by the Morans. He no longer knew who his friends were. This was not the kind of life he wanted. This was not how he wanted his daughter to remember him. He was tired of looking over his shoulder all the time and wondering when the bullet was coming for him. But his greatest concern was for his family. If Barb or George suffered as a result of what he had done, he would never forgive himself. He didn't regret his actions, but he just wished it hadn't come to all this.

Carl had won the war, as far as Barb was concerned. The Moran men were dead and buried, but still there seemed to be no peace.

She wondered whether there could be life after this gangland war, whether Carl and all the barristers could make it all go away somehow. It worried her, but as long as Carl was in control of things, Barb believed it would all work out. She was happy that her boy was out of Roberta's clutches. Apart from providing a grandchild for Barb, Roberta had ruined Carl's life, she believed. Now he was free again, there would be time for the two of them. She would make his favourite: eggs, baked beans and chips. He'd smell the fry-up and get out of bed and they would have a little time together.

But Carl's wake-up call was already on its way. At 7.30 a.m., a posse of cops descended on the house and hauled Carl out of bed and down to the St Kilda Road headquarters. Barb would never again see her son as a free man, let alone cook him a meal. Whatever family life the Williamses had left ended that morning.

Ten minutes earlier, another team of police, including members of the special operations group he had swooped on two men, Sean Jason Sonnet and Gregg Hildebrandt, around the corner from Mario Condello's fortified home in North Road, Brighton.

Sonnet and Hildebrandt were caught with the usual kit of the assassin, including handguns, balaclavas and two-way radios. Around the corner, they had parked a stolen Mazda 626, containing a drum of accelerant which would be used to torch the vehicle after the getaway. Witnesses later told the media pack that they had seen one of the suspects sobbing as they lay handcuffed on the footpath. He was in such a state of terror that he had apparently crapped his pants. In Wantirna, Carl's cousin Michael Thorneycroft was also arrested. They would all be charged with conspiracy to murder Mario Rocco Condello. Of the hit men that Carl had used in the past four years, this was the least professional team. Originally, Thorneycroft had been the driver for the operation but was so addled by drugs Sonnet was forced to replace him with Hildebrandt, a former schoolmate.

Detectives from Purana had eavesdropped on the unlikely assassins via telephone intercepts and listening devices between 29 May and 9 June 2004. While Sonnet was a career criminal, Thorneycroft was just a complete liability.

'You don't understand, mate,' police heard Sonnet tell Thorneycroft.

'This is not a stick-up. I'd rather you on smack [heroin] than like this. I'd rather you stoned than like this, mate.'

On another occasion, Sonnet said, 'I can tell you now, you're off your fucking 3KZ [head]. There's no way you'll be right. Fuck, you can't even sit still.'

Sonnet suggested Thorneycroft substitute alcohol for the hard drugs he was using. 'Listen, drinking's fucking not good, but it's the best of the worst. And smoking bongs, they're the best of the worst. We can't have heroin and you can't have fucking speed.'

Thorneycroft was highly emotional, often breaking down in tears.

'Oh, fucking hell. Do I need to hear these fucking waterworks again? You're pissing me off by fucking breaking down all the time,' Sonnet told Thorneycroft.

Just two days before the hit, the pair had a furious public row after Sonnet told Thorneycroft that despite stealing the getaway car he was incapable of driving on the day.

SONNET: 'Why the fuck did you ever agree to do this?'

THORNEYCROFT: 'Dunno. Cos I'm a fucking idiot, that's why.'

SONNET: 'If we were robbing a bank or something I wouldn't give a fuck, you know? We go look at a bank, run in, bang! If I get caught, five or six years. This, mate, forget about it. I'm thirty-five years old.'

THORNEYCROFT: 'You get pinched, you're fucked. You never go home. That's all there is to it.'

SONNET: 'Well, that's what I'm trying to stress to you, Mick. That's why I say, mate, I'll put holes in ya. I'll fucking shoot you if you're stupid enough to get us all caught.'

'I was waiting for them,' Condello said in an interview with me, although it later seemed that he had been staying at an apartment in the city. 'If they had set one foot on my fuckin' land, at least I would have had a fuckin' defence to say, "Mate, he tried to come into my fuckin' house with a fuckin' gun." Is this self-defence or not? What does it take to fuckin' cause self-defence? Coming into a fuckin' property with a gun and confronting me and next thing you know I pull out a fuckin' shotgun or something and fuckin' kill the fuckin' dog.'

All the expletives and threats in the world could not hide the fact that Condello was scared out of his wits. He knew that Carl was not afraid of him, and could not be bought off. For years, he had covered his faint heart with a big mouth and a ruthless coterie of thugs to do his dirty work. Now he stood alone.

Roberta was at home sleeping, amid the rubble of home renovations, oblivious to the arrests. When she learnt of Carl's arrest, she raced downtown to the St Kilda Road Police Headquarters and got into a minor scuffle with the Purana officers. Later that day, she told me her greatest regret was that Carl's daughter might now have to grow up without a father. The previous weekend Carl had taken Dhakota and they had spent some rare time together. Now it was back to normal: her dad was behind bars again.

The next day, Carl and his co-accused made their first appearances in court on the charges. There was intense security; a police chopper had shadowed the Corrections van that brought the men to court. Carl was shackled hand and foot; they were taking no chances that other associates might try to spring him. The court was filled with media, Purana detectives and even a group of Year 10 school students on work experience.

Roberta complained that Carl and the lads were being treated as animals, kept as they were behind a sheet of security glass. Sonnet was in a feisty mood, threatening to kill any journo who took notes on proceedings. Thorneycroft complained he had been locked up naked in a cell with no blankets and that he had done nothing wrong.

'Why can't my mates be naked with me?' Thorneycroft shouted.

Sonnet responded, 'I don't want to be naked with you.'

Carl sat in the dock smiling impassively and chuckling at the antics of Sonnet and Thorneycroft. Sonnet had a history of playing up in court.

According to *The Age*, Sonnet faced the County Court in 2000 with four co-accused, including one Matthew Charles Johnson, over the jailhouse bashing of murderer Greg 'Bluey' Brazel. Two of his co-accused bared their buttocks in the dock and one threw a bag of excrement into the jury box. Sonnet egged them on by making animal noises.

Two days later, Mario Condello met me at an outdoor café near the Queen Victoria Market. He had no protection with him, no bodyguards and he sat with his back to the street. He was a tall, distinguished figure wrapped in a long black overcoat. He wanted to say the war was over and his side had won. Condello said that this was a war that 'didn't have to be'. He had broken his customary media silence to call for an end to all conflicts.

He hated talking to the media. He hailed from 'the old Calabrian school'. Calabrians never revealed secrets to outsiders like journalists, even if you were 'hanging by your fingernails suspended by violin strings'. However, as an educated man, he believed it was his duty to speak out. There was no one who could do it quite so eloquently as he, Condello believed.

He wanted to counter the idea that the Carlton Crew was battling Carl's team for control of Melbourne's amphetamines market.

'We really don't have a problem with them, because we are not in the line of business they are in. We don't have anything to do with their line of business and, quite frankly, we despise anyone who has anything to do with that line of business,' he said. Of course, Condello didn't want to be reminded that he had done time for drugs, namely cannabis, and that he had at one time tried to sell kilos of heroin around Melbourne.

'No one wants any further destruction of life. No one wants any further traumas, stress or anything of the like – least of all . . . taking a life. It's absolutely absurd,' he said.

Not that he was taking Carl's threats lightly. 'Put it this way. I have my finger on the pulse and I was pretty focused about matters that were going on . . . Once they reached the other side of the road where my place was, they would not have been able to walk back to the car. I can assure you they would not have been able to return.

Now, you make your own assessment of what I'm saying and thank God it turned out the way it did. Thank God for them and thank God for me.'

But Mario Condello was not about to let divine providence determine his fate. On 17 June, Condello and two others were arrested over a plot to kill Carl. According to police, Condello had offered a hit man a contract worth up to $450 000 to eliminate Carl, George and a third unnamed man. On police intercepts, Condello was recorded saying that only Carl's death would bring this blood lust to an end.

'Until this fucking cunt is put in a hole, there will be no peace,' Condello told a co-conspirator. But the hit man he had contracted was in fact a police informer. Condello was charged with conspiracy to murder, but another hit man visited Mario Condello on 6 February 2006 before he could stand trial. A gunman, thought by police to be the Savage, was waiting as Condello drove into his garage at home. He shot Condello before he could close his roller door. Police say Carl had nothing to do with it; the tip was that the murder had been an in-house affair.

29

HOTEL ACACIA

Well into his twenties, Carl had liked nothing better than to while away the hours at home in his small bedroom. It was cramped but everything he needed was close at hand. There was a single bed, a wardrobe with all his clothes and shoes, a shelf for his TV and many aftershaves and colognes. Everything was neatly arranged.

He could spend most of the weekend in there, just lying on his bed, watching the races and the footy, reading the form, the mobile phone going to bookies and friends. He might go out to get Red Rooster or drop by Moonee Valley races but he liked being at home best. His mates came to visit him and, with Barb around, he didn't have to lift a finger. Everyone else, he could pay. Carl, along with Ozzie the dog, had grown fat and content in there.

Now in the Acacia Unit of Barwon Prison, he was back to lying on a single bed, watching telly all day. He had once again chosen to make his world small, and his reality was a 4-by-3-metre cell made of concrete and steel, with what the *Herald Sun*'s Terry Brown would aptly describe as 'the feel of a public toilet'.

Carl had always boasted that he could do jail easily, 'on his ear', as good crooks say. Port Phillip Prison had been the making of him, he said. He had thrived in there, making friends and learning how to work the system.

But Acacia was designed to deprive a man of his spirit and identity. Victorian Supreme Court Justice Bernard Bongiorno once said that conditions were 'such as to pose a risk to the psychiatric health of even the most psychologically robust individual. Close confinement, shackling, strip searching and other privations to which the inmates at Acacia Unit are subject all add to the psychological stress of being on remand, particularly as some of them seem to lack any rational justification'.

Carl was on twenty-three-hour lockdown, with just a one-hour 'run-out' daily in the exercise yard. He spent that time with the Raptor, planning their defence to the Marshall murder charges and making his allowance of fourteen telephone calls per week.

Acacia had been designed to exert exclusive disciplinary and coercive control over the system's most high-risk, unruly and dangerous prisoners through the use of high-tech security devices and electronic controls. The daily routine was founded on sensory deprivation and solitary confinement.

The stark fluoro-lit atmosphere of Acacia was something that Carl had never experienced before. It played on his pride and self-regard, making him feel anonymous and inadequate. This was not a place he could ever feel comfortable, let alone call home. On the outside, his possessions had defined his self-worth but in Acacia there was nothing and he was nothing.

In letters to me, Carl tried to deal with this crushing reality by pretending he would not be there long. Miraculously, he was going to beat four murder and sundry drug charges and re-emerge onto the street.

Sunday 11th July
Hello Adam,

Well it was good to hear from you as it always is. As for me, I'm back here at HOTEL ACACIA, just taking a break for a while, everything's good no problems.

Time goes quickly here, if you don't keep track of it, it seems to get away from you. A good way to look at it is things always get better and I will be back to have a drink with you. Just not sure when, but it won't be too long.

Acacia ground its inmates down day by day. Chronophobia, or prison neurosis, is a recognised form of mental illness, literally a fear of time, where events seem to move too fast for the sufferer, who can make no sense of them. In Acacia, this was the desired outcome. What police interrogators could not accomplish would be achieved simply by putting them in there.

In a cruel irony, prisoners were allowed televisions and newspapers but news from the world outside only sharpened the sense of isolation in there. Nothing ever changed in Acacia but the date on the calendar, yet there was a constant sense of unease and fear. 'It's Hannibal Lecter stuff, mate. A jail inside a jail,' Mick Gatto said after his release.

Acacia was home to many of the players in the gangland war, including Gatto, the Rat, Goussis, the Raptor and others. Michael Thorneycroft had been the first to crack as soon as the horrors of heroin withdrawal began to claw at him. He gave a statement in which he told police that Carl had confided that he had killed seven of his rivals. Police believed Carl's tally was up to ten, but also that more of Carl's friends and enemies would soon follow Thorneycroft's example. A few months in this cage and they would open up like ripe watermelons falling off a truck. It pleased Carl to know that Mario Condello was doing it tougher than him.

Sunday 8th August
Hey, buddy, lucky you never got shot with me at the MARRIOT. I would have jumped in front of you anyway. But we live another day. Every day above ground is a good day. And that bloke's [Mario Condello] trying for bail. He has a headache. Why don't he just see a doctor? I've never seen on Panadol packets if pain persists go for bail. It says if pain persists see a doctor. Some of the new Australians (WOGS) aren't too bright. Might be good at standing over hardworking family people, that's not something I'd like to be known, or remembered for, but that's ME.

In Acacia, Carl's sense of identity was fading almost as fast as the peroxide blond tips in his hair. Roberta noticed the difference in Carl after just a few months away. He needed her again, emotionally, physically and spiritually. He was no longer indifferent to her needs as he had been. The minutiae of other people's lives had always bored Carl but now he gobbled up every morsel of news. He became acutely interested in the state of relationships he had taken for granted on the outside.

Wednesday 1st September
I always thought people were brought up to tell the truth, sometimes the truth hurts, and some people shy away from that, and prefer to believe they belong in the movies, they could be right, but just have the wrong scene.

You are my friend, well I consider you as a friend anyway. You've always paid me respect and I will always pay you the same right back. We will be having a few drinks again before we know it, don't you worry about that.

Tough men last, tough times don't. As much as the POLICE want to keep me here they are wasteing there [sic] time, doing their heads in over me, because I will be back out there when I finish these court cases, no rush at the moment, but I have no doubt that everything will work out, time tells everything.

Well only a short letter today to say thanks for writing to me, as its [sic] always good to hear from you. Until I hear from you again, 'be good or be good at it'.

Take care, your friend always.
Carl
He who searches for friends with faults will never have a friend.
A good friend is hard to find, hard to lose, and IMPOSSIBLE TO FORGET.

The only respite Carl received were day trips to court for hearings. In October, he was sentenced to seven years on the drug charges dating back to 1999. He told himself that at least now his jail time was defined. He was still going to beat the rest of the charges. In the meantime, he could torment the police by penning letters that he knew they were sure to read.

Acacia HMP Barwon
Dear Mum and Dad,

Gee it's grouse in the Victoria Police Force, sorry Service, Purana Taskforce. My very first day at the station at the St Kilda Road Complex, Sergeant Stuart Bateson says: 'Don't just sit there counting money son, come on the beat with me.' So I buckled up my pistol and truncheon and radio and capsicum squirter and handcuffs and electric pod and thermos and brown paper bags and chased after him. We went down Lygon Street, which is in Carlton, to see what information we could gather from the Carlton Crew, the likes of Mick (the Don) Gatto, Mario (the Bull) Condello just like the opening credits of The Bill. Big Boots, moving slow, plus the use of the hips as they taught us in the academy, like a Friesian cow smuggling parrots in condoms through customs, and we took an apple off a fruit store for free, just like in the NYPD, because fruiterers know we are looking after them. And then we got a coffee for free and a donut for free and a side of lamb each for free, and a um, massage for free and heaps of money in brown paper bags and we're just coming up to the trattoria at lunchtime and the Sarge says, 'This is real community policing.' Then the Sarge says, 'Strewth, what day is this, Lightning?' (They call me Lightning, I'm not sure why – give me time and I'll work it out.) And I says, 'Tuesday' and he says, 'Cross the road now. We need some brioche, urgently.' So we just settle down to some free brioche and the front of the trattoria over the road explodes in a hail of gunfire and there's blood everywhere and screaming and there's these blokes laid out on the pavement in a pool of veal parmigiana and blood and I say to the Sarge, 'Those blokes look dead!' And the Sarge says, 'A good copper never jumps to conclusions. Wait for forensics.' And I say, 'Sarge what about those blokes in balaclavas? Are they the killers here?' And the Sarge says, 'Don't jump to conclusions about balaclavas, son. It's nearly the start of the ski season. Or perhaps they tan easily. Have some more of this uncommonly good brioche.' Then he got on the radio and placed a couple of bets. So, to reassure the civilians, I crossed the road and stepped over the alleged bodies and booked a bicycle courier for angle parking.

Dear Mum and Dad,
Me and the Sarge went undercover to the alleged crim's funeral. It wasn't very undercover. We parked across the road with the lights flashing and the cones out and we had some donuts and some chips and brioche and pizza and KFC, but the Sarge has certainly got the drop on the crims. He showed me how to spot them. They were all in their uniforms, black suits with wraparound sunglasses, guns, drugs and photographers. And also they all waved, and the Sarge waved them over. The Sarge placed a couple of bets on the car radio, and a couple of the crims came up and asked him to put a couple of monkeys on for them. I said, 'Sarge you've got them where you want them. They can hide but they can't run.' The Sarge said, 'Lightning your [sic] two pizzas short of a patrol car.' Then some blokes in balaclavas ran out of the mourners and shot the Sarge's mates. Sorry allegedly shot them. Blood everywhere, sorry alleged blood everywhere. In the carwash, the Sarge said, 'The first rule of good policing is this. Avoid domestic disputes.' OK I've got stuff to learn.

Dear Mum and Dad,
Back at the station, in a quiet moment when people weren't placing bets, I asked the Sarge about Organised Crime. Everyone knows who the crims are and what they do, and is this Organised Crime?

'Organised Crime,' he said, 'is when thugs stand over people and demand their money, with no return in goods or services.' Then he showed me some Sydney newspapers about the Carr and Egan mini-budget, and all I could do was whistle, just like the people in NSW have to do. He said that this was the work of the mob, the mates of Bob, going through people's pockets, and also, strictly speaking, this was disorganised crime. The NSW ALP is not so much The Sopranos as The Falsettos, or possibly The Castratos. So I said, 'What about the multi-million dollar trade in amphetamines and stuff that has led to so many shootings there?' And the Sarge said, 'Alleged shootings of alleged dead people, in alleged pools of blood, in alleged public places. Given the usual lawyers, these may never have happened. Lightning, who makes and takes and sells these drugs? Heavily armed bikie gangs? Heavily armed crims? Huge wired truckies? Sparking party goers?' I thought this was likely. And Sarge said, 'What do these people have in common?' And he helped by answering 'lawyers' and 'Bracks' Judges. Then he took some more bets over the phone and I went out for Maccas and brioche. Oh, and he also said, 'If these people trouble you, you try to bring them in.'

Dear Mum and Dad,
I'm learning. And apparently, the Sarge's book is on who gets shot next. I got the trifecta! Also when there's the next gangland slaying, I get to stand out the front of the police station with a sign saying, 'HE WENT THAT WAY'.

P.S. I hope you had a laugh.

> *Your friend always,*
> *Carl*

By December 2004, Purana had a new star witness, Goggles, who had agreed to give evidence in the Michael Marshall murder trial against Carl and the Raptor. Goggles' identity had been suppressed by the courts and couldn't be mentioned by the media; at this point he was being referred to as '161'. Carl believed it was time to call in the debts of friendship.

> *Wednesday 15th December*
> *Adam,*
>
> *Hope you are well, as for me im [sic] fine. Received your letter today dated 6-12-04 and it was good to hear from you. The media don't really care about the truth as long as they can make up a good story what sells.*
>
> *They don't care whos [sic] life they put at risk, whos [sic] trials they make hard to win by poisoning the protential [sic] jury's mind. They are the lowest of Low.*
>
> *The media people no [sic] about witness known as 161 prior conviction of dishonesty, different stories to POLICE and proven lies but yet wont [sic] report on any of those stories, as they don't suit the police, the media is an outlet for the police and most reporter are worse than the lying Police.*
>
> *I was once told the public needs a true portrayl [sic] of the FACT but no-one wants to report the facts [in fact, it was me who told him this], when someone with any balls [does] that they'll get and earn my RESPECT. Hopefully you can do something as I thought you were my friend, if I could ever HELP you I would and I believe you no [sic] that.*
>
> *A few reporter should watch a good movie I seen the other week VERONICA GUERIN.*
>
> *All the best regards Carl*

The movie Carl referred to starred Cate Blanchett as Irish reporter Veronica Guerin, who was murdered in 1995 after investigating a drug lord with links to the IRA. Despite this hint of menace, I stayed on Carl's Christmas card list that year.

Adam,
I could think of better holes to be stuck in over the x-mas period.
   Merry Christmas and Best Wishes for the New Year
   Your friend Always Carl

30

DEAL OR NO DEAL

In mid-2006, Carl's pal Snalfy had decided it was time to opt for his own survival. After nearly two years in the maximum-security hell of Acacia, Snalfy was at breaking point. The police were threatening to charge him with three murders. He hadn't been the shooter in any of the killings, only an accessory before or after, but the police promised he would get life with no minimum.

After some reflection, Snalfy decided he wasn't going down for life just for sourcing some guns for Carl. He summoned members of Purana to see whether they would cut a deal for him, like they had promised earlier.

'The reason why I got youse here, right . . . I plead to something I haven't done but I want youse to put it all as a package deal. Whatever I know, I tell yas. What I want is if the cops can look after me,' he said. 'I've had enough. I can't fight any more. I got no more fight in me. Look, I should have listened to you from the start and a lot of crap wouldn't have come out. I should have said something, and Moran wouldn't have been shot, no one would have been shot.'

But Snalfy had not suffered an attack of conscience. The police had told him that Carl's hit man, the Raptor, had already had his own appointment with Purana in March 2006. He had fingered Carl over all the murders and a good deal besides. The Raptor had also spoken of Snalfy being up to his neck in several of the murders. With willing witnesses, police could make almost any construction of the facts stand up before a jury. The villains were almost interchangeable. They had all been involved or had knowledge of the murders so it was easy for investigators to suggest they would promote certain players to starring roles.

'I'm telling you now, I know for a fact [the Raptor] is lying. I can't fight it.'

Snalfy made sixteen statements in all, which provided a comprehensive insight into the workings of Carl and Tony Mokbel's empire.

Snalfy told the story of how Tony Mokbel rose to prominence, including the methods he had used to import cocaine and ecstasy. He explained how he had helped Carl and George set up a press in the garage of the Williams family home in Broadmeadows. He implicated George in a plot to kill Lewis Moran in jail. He lagged a range of players in the speed trade and showed the cops where to find their assets. He provided fine detail of murder plots, how he had supplied two sawn-off shotguns to Carl for the murders of the Moran brothers, how he had helped lure Nik Radev to his death. He would also provide evidence on how Paul Kallipolitis was murdered and play a key role in other prosecutions for years to come.

Purana had amassed more than 53 000 hours of electronic bugging and 20 000 hours of physical surveillance in just over a year. But this intel alone did not produce a single conviction. It was merely corroborative material for what the snitches were telling them. Now the crooks were falling over themselves to help, competing to show they had a mortgage on the truth. It was a brilliant execution of the age-old tactic of divide and rule.

Like many of them, Snalfy insisted that only he was telling the whole truth and nothing but the truth.

'No one else wants to do the right thing and put their hand in and tell 'em the truth, so what else am I gunna do?' he asked. Many crooks believed that Snalfy was lying and had concealed many of his own sins, but police kept getting results on his evidence, so it hardly mattered whether he was telling tales or not.

The Raptor had hung tough for longer than he'd thought he could. He and Carl had been close and it was Raptor's fault that the team had begun to unravel. If he had acted on Goggles' warning about the police bug they'd found in the car used for the Marshall killing, perhaps they would still be out there, having fun and killing people.

Carl and Raptor had become staunch mates in jail, but Acacia was no ordinary boob. In Port Phillip, they'd set up a supply line of drugs, mobiles, food, alcohol – basically anything you wanted – through a dodgy contact in the outside catering company that served the prison. The Raptor didn't mind jail. He'd been in custody for most of his life. In fact, he'd found it hard to know what to do with freedom. In a year out of jail, all he had done was kill people, drink and punt. The weekly visits to see his ageing mother were the only semblance of normality in his existence.

Jail held no terrors but he had never been in a jail like Acacia, he told me in a telephone call. In fact, he openly admitted that he would probably break under the 'protracted torture' he was being subjected to.

'The will of the individual becomes overborne by the torturous conditions in here,' he said. The screws hadn't let any mail in or out for weeks. I had arranged to be at Carl's mum's place when the boys were due to call. When prison authorities worked out a journalist was speaking to their prize inmates, the call was cut. The Raptor called back and talked of his daily routines inside Acacia Unit and the phone was cut again. He called back. 'See how petty they [the prison officers] can be? Surely I have the right to discuss my daily routines!' he raged down the phone.

Six calls were terminated in the space of ten minutes. The screws stripped Carl and the Raptor of their telephone privileges for a month after a story quoting the discussion was published in *The Bulletin* magazine. Carl no longer had the right to make comments to the media. He would speak only with those approved by Corrections.

Now they spent all day watching TV, reading piles of legal briefs for their upcoming appearances. Whenever they felt even the slightest sense of comfort, a screw would shake them down again with strip searches or a move to a new cell. The system was designed to keep them off-balance and to destroy any sense of camaraderie between inmates.

It would take another year for the Raptor to betray Carl. He only turned on his mate after he learnt that Carl was trying to have his charges on the Moran–Barbaro murder heard separately from the Raptor's. Carl believed he would do better at trial without the Raptor, who had actually pulled the trigger. On his own, Carl might have a chance of beating it.

Carl was now being slowly crushed between the cell walls, as they closed in on him. His writing now reflected a man coming to terms with the possibility that he would not get out of Acacia. The loss of status and identity was appalling to him.

'The moment you become a prisoner, you lose all sorts of legal rights and social respect. Even the value of your life is downgraded in one big thud,' he wrote. I suspected that someone, perhaps his lawyer, had helped Carl put this together. However, the sentiment was all his, even if the words weren't. He was predicting his own demise with, what seems now, chilling foresight.

'Prisoners are not considered as people. Your death or mutilation does not particularly concern the judges, prosecutors, police, prison officers or other state officials, providing it does not cause too much embarrassment . . . Very few people in society even want to hear about the dozens of people that commit suicide or are killed in jail. Death in jail is such a common occurrence that it is rarely reported in newspapers and even other prisoners find it too painful to dwell on.'

On 3 February the Raptor was ready to cut a deal with the Director of Public Prosecutions. He wrote to the DPP with a proposition. 'Before anything can be discussed my mother would first have to be relocated and I would also have to be moved from my current placement . . . I would then provide you with some explosive allegations in relation to numerous matters involving and not exceeding ten individuals.'

The combined testimony of Carl's former associates was enough for the police to convict him of four murders (Jason Moran, Mark Mallia, Michael Marshall and Lewis Moran) in addition to the attempted murder of Mario Condello. They held back from charging him with at least two more (Nik Radev, Willie Thompson). As if Acacia wasn't enough, this was another pressure point on Carl, an incentive to roll on the corrupt cops. They could make sure he never emerged from jail. In May 2005, he was convicted of Mark Mallia's murder and sentenced to twenty-seven years' jail. The grind had begun.

31

JUDGEMENT DAY

On 28 February 2007, Carl was in the back of the prison van, returning to Barwon after another day in court. He was assessing his options. If he fought the three new murder charges he was facing and lost, he'd be looking at life with no minimum sentence. Roberta and his mother had urged him to fight on, but he knew it was over. Another trial would just waste more of his dwindling fortune. Purana had also suggested it might charge Roberta and George with a few more things, possibly even murder. He had been seeking advice from other prisoners, even staff.

He knew his best chance was to cut a deal on assisting police with the Hodson murders. He had dangled that carrot a few months earlier to test their appetite. They had bitten hard. Assistant Commissioner Simon Overland's pursuit of corrupt police had become all-consuming. Carl could afford to wait and make the decision to talk when it best suited him. The media focus was turning away from gangland murders to corruption within the police force. He would pick his moment. Carl banged on the back of the van.

'Take me back into court,' he said to the guards.

He wanted the court reconvened but first he had to talk to his mum and dad. Barb was dead against him pleading.

'Once you say you're guilty, that's it: you're guilty,' she said. Deep down she could never accept that he had done anything wrong.

George was more practical.

'If you ever want to see the light of day, plead guilty,' he told Carl. That was enough for Carl.

He couldn't bear to think of Purana locking up Roberta and George, tearing his family apart in the process.

His relationship with Roberta had reached an interesting plane. They were in the process of divorce and Carl regularly blamed Roberta for ruining his life. He had fallen in love with a pretty twenty-one-year-old blonde, Renata Laureano, who had begun visiting him. Nicole Mottram was still on the scene as well. There were yet more women writing letters to him, some enclosing saucy photographs of themselves. He would tease Roberta, saying that even in jail he could still pull chicks. But that didn't stop him becoming jealous when he heard Roberta was seeing a prominent underworld figure of Middle Eastern heritage.

Former Purana chief Jim O'Brien remembers listening to tapes of telephone calls between Carl and Roberta about this time.

'Roberta and this bloke had been on a trip to Darwin and she was telling Carl that they were just friends and they had slept in separate bedrooms on the trip. He didn't believe her at all. He cross-examined her for about twenty minutes, like he had seen barristers do. I had a new admiration for him after that,' says O'Brien.

On Monday, 7 May 2007, Carl's entourage gathered in the Victorian County Court for what would prove to be his final public appearance. Carl's sentencing had been moved from the Supreme Court to the more modern and secure County Court as a safety measure. Who knows what stupid desperate finale Carl might have dreamed up with the media on hand to farewell him?

Justice Betty King had already barred Roberta from the court after she had made a scene a week earlier during the sentencing hearing. So Roberta, wearing a beanie after her new Muslim beau had ordered she shave her head, waited in the forecourt for the arrival of Carl's supporting cast. She looked rough, tough and ready for anything.

Judy Moran, dressed in a black outfit with matching gaucho

hat, could have been auditioning for the part of Carl's executioner. She told friends that she dreamt of throwing the lever on a hangman's trap for Carl or giving him a lethal injection. Carl had destroyed her family, she said in a witness-impact statement, without mentioning all the evil that her own brood of psychopaths had inflicted on so many others.

Ironically, Judy later trained her own murderous impulse on her family too, ordering the murder of her brother-in-law Des 'Tuppence' Moran in June 2009 after a squabble over the remnants of Lewis's estate. She showed that ultimately all the killing had taught her nothing. For now, she played the grieving widow and mother.

Carl's jail penpal Renata Laureano was enjoying her brief moment of celebrity and turned up to lend a little glamour to the proceedings. She walked into court bathed in camera flashes like a starlet walking the red carpet at a premiere. But Roberta wasn't going to let her have the limelight so easily. To get into court Renata had to first get past Roberta, who unleashed a torrent of abuse. Roberta called her every name under the sun and threatened to cave Renata's head in. Most of all she wanted Renata to know how this thing ended.

'Stupid sluts like her fall in love with gangsters and think it's all glamour and glitz but they are going to be bringing the kids to jail, running errands for their man,' she said later.

Roberta had warned Carl that he wouldn't be seeing his daughter again if he continued to allow Renata to visit him in prison. She found it intensely unfair that Carl had cheated on her relentlessly during their marriage and still she was expected to remain loyal, doing whatever Carl asked without question, while he cosied up with 'sluts and bimbos like Renata'. Roberta suspected that Carl was secretly giving Renata and other 'slags' money that should have been going to her and the kids. All she got for staying loyal to Carl was public humiliation. So be it, but everyone else was going to cop it too, she decided. In a letter, Carl had pleaded with Roberta not to act up at court but that was just further provocation. Carl had treated her like shit and she wasn't going to keep quiet about it.

After giving Renata her serve, she turned on Judy Moran, calling her a fat ugly cow. Judy would never see her loved ones again because Carl had put them all in the cemetery, she said.

Barb got hers too, mainly because she had arrived with Renata. Barb had never accepted Roberta into the family; she was always encouraging Carl to leave her for other women, even though she had given Barb a grandchild. Roberta terrified Barbara so much she couldn't stop her knees shaking until she sat down in the courtroom.

Carl was oblivious to the pantomime playing out in the forecourt as he waited to face the most important woman in his life at that moment – Justice Betty King of the Victorian Supreme Court. When she appeared, King peered over her glasses at Carl with a look of pure disdain, as if to say: I don't care what you were on the outside. In my court you are just the defendant and nothing more.

Carl maintained an attitude of studied defiance as Justice King sentenced him to life imprisonment with a minimum of thirty-five years, commencing immediately. With nearly three years already served, it was effectively a thirty-eight-year sentence. He would be eligible for release in 2042, when he would be aged seventy-one.

Justice King threw in a withering condemnation and character assessment, free of charge. She was appalled that this mass murderer had become a folk hero to many in the community.

'You are not [a hero],' she said. 'You are a killer, and a cowardly one, who employed others to do the actual killing whilst you hid behind carefully constructed alibis. You should not be the subject of admiration by any member of our community.' It was repugnant to her that Carl could have revelled in his notoriety. It was deeply disturbing that he should be giving media interviews, when he had such a callous disregard for human life.

Carl tried to pretend that he was impervious to her words but the flush in his cheeks gave him away. Nobody had spoken to him like this for a very long time, if ever.

He did not get 'to be judge, jury and executioner', King told him. 'You acted as though it was your right to have these people killed.'

In his evidence Carl had been 'a most unsatisfactory witness virtually incapable of telling the truth', Justice King said.

'The manner in which you gave evidence was arrogant, almost supercilious, and you left with me the strong impression that your view of all of these murders was that they were all really justifiable and you were the real victim.'

She got that part right. Even when faced with life in prison, Carl had not managed to find any remorse in his heart for what he had done. Justice King might have knocked two years off the sentence if he had shown even a flicker of contrition. Earlier, in a letter, he had ordered his counsel to stop Justice King describing him as the boss or the head of a criminal organisation. He expected people to believe that when his co-accused referred to him as 'the big fella' or 'the big bloke', it was only a reference to his 'build' not to him being 'a crime boss or anything like that'. It was not surprising that faced with life in jail, Carl no longer wanted to be known as 'the Premier'.

In terms of remorse, the best Carl could manage was a feeble wish that all these terrible things had never happened. However, it was obvious that he felt he could justify everything because the Morans had started the war.

He had agreed to be photographed in the dock (one shot could be published) and left a goofy smile as his parting image to the world.

As Justice King adjourned the court after sentence, Williams leapt to his feet and asked to address the court. 'I have something to say,' he began, opening a clipboard which contained a prepared speech. The judge forbade him to speak but he pressed on.

'I expected nothing better of you. You are not a judge. You are only a puppet of the police. You are a puppet for Purana —'

Justice King angrily cut Carl's final soliloquy short, ordering that the prisoner be removed. But Carl would get the last word in his relationship with Justice King.

'Aah, get fucked!' he shouted as Corrections staff led him away.

With a dismissive gesture of his hand to the judge, Carl Williams' final public act was done. Yet Carl wasn't ready to slink off into anonymity.

He wrote a letter to the media, claiming he was not guilty of the murder of Lewis Moran, but only said so to cut a deal to keep his father and Roberta out of jail.

'The prosecution threatened me if I didn't plea[d] that they'd charge them both and strongly oppose them getting bail, so I thought to myself it's better to sacrifice my life to save there's [sic] & hopefully give them some peace,' he wrote.

He accused a senior member of the judiciary of making a drunken sexual advance towards a member of his legal team.

'You're a drunk who can't handle your liquor. [You] were out drunk talking shit about me and conversation that you had out of court with the police and the prosecution to my [then] barrister ... you also tried to fuck [them], little did you know that [they] would come running back to me telling me what you said and done. [They] knocked you back for sex and called you a disgrace directly to your face.'

Williams also said a Supreme Court official had been involved in his drug-trafficking operation.

'[To] this day [the individual] works at this court as [name deleted]'s associate despite the fact the court are fully aware of his past drug trafficking activities,' he said.

His sentencing judge, Supreme Court Justice Betty King, had prevented him from having his defence barrister of choice by scheduling his trial when his senior counsel, Peter Faris QC, was unavailable.

'I feel you only done this after Faris told you in open court that he would be subpoenaing the police to give evidence at my upcoming trial, simply to prove that the Crown witnesses . . . were liars and they've told lies in other murder investigations about me that the Police know are 100 per cent lies.'

Justice King had not given him a fair go, Carl complained.

'I knew that you were placed here for a purpose, and that purpose is to convict anyone who comes before [you] in this so-called Gangland stuff despite what the evidence is. [How] can you come from the County Court with not very much experience, and be given the biggest, highest profile case this state has seen in a long time?

'Last but certainly not least, you might have taken my freedom, but one thing I can assure you, you haven't and you will never be able to break me,' he wrote.

'I can look in the mirror and I'm proud of the person who I see, my family can always hold their head up high as I stood up for what I believed in, and I never sold my soul to the devil and I never will. Life isn't about waiting for the storm to pass, it's about learning to dance in the rain.'

32

THE SOLO SAILOR

The youthful spark that had always glowed in Barb went out after Carl was sentenced. It was like the years that Betty King had given Carl were piled onto her. She withdrew from the world, spending most of her time shut up inside the townhouse that Carl had built for her in Essendon. She was seeing a married man, who swore he was going to leave his wife for her, but he never did.

George was in jail, having been sentenced to seven years on the 1999 drug charges. The police had lied to Carl, he said. They promised George would get a suspended sentence if Carl signed up for the murders, but the judge had other ideas. Betty King had told all the gangland players on remand they had a choice: they could turn Crown witness and be rewarded or expect no favours whatsoever. They could get aboard the bus, or be run over by it, she said. The only concession was that George was in a hospital unit at Port Phillip Prison, close to medical attention. Still Carl found plenty to moan about in letters to Barb.

'His TV was permanently fixed on one channel (SBS), he didn't even have a kettle to make a cup of coffee or tea, he wasn't aloud [sic] to purchase a radio and on his canteen he was only aloud to purchase toiletries and stationary [sic], he was virtually on a loss of privileges regime. Yet he had done nothing at all to warrant that. He was kept there for six–seven long weeks, god only knows how a man of his ill health survived those tortuous [sic] conditions. I believe it is blatantly obvious, if you are isolating a man with ill health who also suffers from stress and depression, and who has previously had three open heart bypass operations, his health will dramatically decline. Yet that's exactly what Correction Victoria [sic] did, knowing full well that stress and anxiety can bring on a heart attack. I believe without a shadow of a doubt they tried to kill him, otherwise why did they have done what they did [sic] to him. It certainly weren't to look after him.'

Somehow George survived this ordeal of one TV channel and ended up serving only eighteen months of a seven-year sentence.

Despite George's discount, Barb felt that they had been betrayed yet again. Whatever the family had managed to attain in the years since leaving the slums of Richmond was now gone. They had broken the law but they had paid such a terrible price. All the hard work they had put in to make something of their family had come to nought.

Everything was in ruins as far as Barb could see. Shane was long gone and Carl was as good as dead. She could see him behind the glass on visits but she could never hug him, she could never cook a meal for him nor have a conversation that wasn't recorded and listened to by the screws.

Now television viewers had their own image of Carl, courtesy of the *Underbelly* series on the Nine Network. While initially it was banned in Victoria as it threatened to derail various underworld trials, Carl was becoming a national celebrity. The screenwriters portrayed Carl as the unlikely hero triumphing over the evil Moran empire.

Even if he didn't enjoy his portrayal by actor Gyton Grantley, how many inmates could say they had a TV series made of their lives?

Dear Mum
I must say I am extremely pleased that Underbelly won't be shown for at least the next three months, after that I can only hope that it gets put off again. I don't mind them telling the truth about me but telling lies and painting me out to be some dickhead who is brain dead well that's bullshit. They have me

*associating with people I never met before, such as Alphonse.
They also have me committing crimes that I have never even
been suspected of, what a load of crap.*

*Yes I did what I did. I am guilty of defending myself and
my loved ones from being killed, that I am and I am the first
to admit that, but please try putting yourself in my shoes for a
moment. It was my 29th birthday, as far as I was concerned I
didn't have a care in the world, life was good. That is up until
I went & met someone whom (MARK MORAN) and ended
up getting shot by him and his brother, what for you probably
ask – because they were money hungry greedy control freaks
who I would not bow down too [sic].*

Barb could see the toll that prison was taking on her son. The once happy-go-lucky kid was gone. In his place was a much slimmed down, pale shadow of his former self.

*Some people would say that the chances of me remaining fit or
sane for that long in prison are slight, but I will do my best to
prove them wrong. The system, the authorities are being aloud
[sic] legally and systematically to destroy my body and mind,
and they say that this is a civilised society we live in – I beg to
differ. Many would say that I deserve what I cop; fair enough
they are entitled to their opinion.*

*However, what about those who worked alongside me,
whose crimes were every bit as bad as mine. Was it really fair
was it justice that they got away so lightly – and in some cases
without any penalty at all – in exchange for my liberty. I think
not. In many cases against me, authorities forgave these men
for there [sic] crimes, which in some cases included murder
which to this day remains unsolved in exchange for evidence
which, in many cases, was a pack of lies. Fair enough I have
lost my freedom but should I really have to serve my time in*

solitary confinement, which I have done for the past 3¾ years since the day of my arrest?

To give a little bit of an insight into what solitary confinement can do to ones [sic] mind, take a look at the likes of Francis Chichester, who, after a year alone on his yacht, could not converse properly on his arrival home. He was suffering a sort of personality disorder brought on by being in total solitude. There is also the case of the Englishman who was arrested for spying in Russia. He was in solitary confinement in a Russian prison for 18 months and nearly went insane. He wrote a book about his experiences and fight against insanity.

Now if you compare his 18 months in solitary confinement, with a life sentence with a minimum term of 35 years on top of the three years I had already served prior to receiving the minimum term of 35 years, which was all served in solitary confinement, you will have an idea of what I am up against. It is one hell of a hill to climb, and one hell of a battle to fight.

However I have no doubt that I will continue to fight it day by day, month by month, year by year. I know the authorities won't be happy until they have pushed me over the limit. But they are wasting there [sic] time, they won't succeed that I assure you. With my loss of freedom comes the loss of a lot of other things I will never get to see such as I will never get to see either of my parents as a free man. I weren't there to see my daughter's first day of school; I won't be there to see her start high school. I certainly won't be there for her 21st birthday, I also doubt I'll be there to walk her down the aisle if she gets married.

Although I wish what happened had never happened, I still believe I had no choice but to do what I did, as I said earlier I was in a kill or be killed situation.

No matter what happens from here on in, I will always be able to see & talk to my loved ones whether that be on the telephone or face to face, and that is a lot better than what the scum bags who shot me can do.

I will always be able to look in the mirror and be very proud of the person I see, unlike a lot of other people who I doubt could even look at themselves in the mirror, but they have to live with that not me!

He told Barb that although she had to visit him in Barwon, Judy Moran had to visit her family in the cemetery. But that was small consolation. At least the Morans had peace in death. That seemed preferable to the purgatory that Carl was living in.

The only thing Barb was living for was the weekly visits from Dhakota. She looked so much like Carl, it was painful. Otherwise, she was alone and isolated.

On the evening of 21 November 2008, Barb spoke to Dhakota on the phone, asking her as always to sing her favourite song. Dhakota obliged and Barb told her only granddaughter she loved her.

Then Barb poured herself a glass of champagne and, taking a black eyeliner pencil, wrote 'I'm sorry' on the mirror of her ensuite bathroom. She washed down a handful of sleeping pills with champagne and lay on her bed and slowly drifted away.

Everything had gone wrong. All of Barb's silly, girlish dreams had been shattered one by one. She had grown up in the embrace of a large, close-knit family. The Denmans had got by with nothing so Barb had this faith that life was going to work out when the money started rolling in. For a long time, she ignored the evil, violent things that Carl had done but the thoughts and images of his deeds had crowded in on her. There would never be any relief in this life.

George was allowed out of prison for Barb's funeral but Carl would get no favours until he signed up to help the police. He hired a cameraman to film the service and watched it later.

Carl watched Roberta give the eulogy. 'Barb stood up to our enemies, the police and even Supreme Court judges because she believed loyalty was a lifetime thing, not just a luxury for when things were going well. She knew loyalty was a sacrifice and she was prepared to pay the cost. She loved us unconditionally,' she said.

Carl had written a death notice for Barbara in the newspaper: 'There's nothing in the world I would not have done for you. Losing you is the hardest thing I have ever had to deal with.'

Now Carl was alone too. All the friends that had once flocked around, gorging themselves on drink, drugs and food at their wedding and Dhakota's christening were gone. All the money was gone too. The police forensic accountants had not located any assets beyond the family home in Broadie and Barb's townhouse. There was talk that Carl and George still had a cache of pseudoephedrine tucked away somewhere, but no one ever found it. Carl couldn't even afford to pay for his mother's funeral. Everything had fallen to Roberta. She had helped pack up Barb's house too.

Roberta had found letters Carl had written to his mother or that she was supposed to forward to others but had forgotten. There were nasty, mean letters in which he had urged Barb and her boyfriend to get prepaid telephones and harass Roberta with anonymous calls. There were also pathetic, needy letters to Renata in which he told her that he wanted to have a child with her. He asked her to organise to go on IVF like Roberta had.

By this stage, Renata was long gone, replaced by a new penpal, Stacey Vella, a twenty-one-year-old hairdresser from the western suburbs. The *Sunday Herald Sun* reported that Carl had asked her to marry him, and sent her a diamond ring.

Having fallen in love with the *Underbelly* Carl, Stacey had written him a letter, which the newspaper had obtained.

'Hello how are you going? Listen you don't know me, or at least I don't think you do, anyway my name is Stacey.

'I'm from the western suburbs. I'm a hairdresser.

'Well anyway this is weird enough as it is, so I'll leave it to you but feel free to write back, or just tell me to piss off. But I do look forward to hearing from you (just for the record I'm 20, not 10 or anything and I think you're sexy) take care, would be good to get to know you more. Stacey xx.'

But Carl would only ever be a figure behind the glass to Stacey, a curiosity she could compare with the Carl she had fallen in love with on the telly. At least visits from her broke the monotony and the occasional raunchy photograph gave him something new to beat off to.

By this stage, Tony Mokbel had fled the country for Greece after learning he was to be charged with Lewis Moran's murder. Tony had helped Roberta and the kids for a while, but in the end everyone chooses themselves in this life. It had been a great party while it lasted but it was over.

Growing up, Shane had drummed into Carl the importance of staying staunch, of keeping your mouth shut. A man wasn't judged by his possessions but by the contents of his heart, his elder brother had told him. But look at how Shane had ended up. All the friends he had stood by, even did time for, had deserted him.

In 2007, before George went to jail, Purana chief Jim O'Brien had visited him at home. He was sitting in the empty house in a singlet and shorts, reading the form, as always. The cop saw the livid scar down George's breast bone, where surgeons had opened him up for three separate heart operations. He was all out of lives, the detective told George. Another heart attack and that would be it. He would never see his son as a free man, he said. George nodded.

But, of course, there was one option left, said O'Brien. If Carl helped police solve the Hodson murders, there was a chance to make a deal. Carl might even cut a third off his sentence. The detective saw that George was uncertain. Giving up anyone, even a police officer, was a dangerous move in jail. But George agreed to think about it.

Now after Barb's death, Carl's resistance crumbled. In 2004, he had given a statement to police on police corruption but it was a rambling contradictory document with no evidentiary value. Now Carl was ready to tell a story and for the right price he would make it a good one.

33

SWAN ISLAND

It was supposed to be a top-secret operation. On 22 December 2008, detectives from Petra Taskforce, investigating the murder of the Hodsons, planned to spirit Carl out of Barwon for a few days. Not even the warden of the prison was to know the destination. Carl would be taken to a secure location, where he would spend up to a week downloading his story of police corruption and involvement in murder. There was to be no record that the sojourn had ever happened, beyond the taped interviews. Police members on the detail were instructed to write in their diaries that they were working in an 'undisclosed location'. If the media got hold of the story, Carl would never be able to return to Barwon; his life would be in danger.

At the time, George was in the low-security Dhurringile Prison at Murchison, 200 kilometres north of Barwon. He was taken by prison van to Barwon, where he spent the night, unaware of what was afoot. The next day he was blindfolded and put in the van again. George got the feeling they were driving round in circles for about an hour just to disorient him. Finally, the van rumbled down a narrow causeway and George had the smell of the sea in his nostrils.

He was reunited with Carl in a lounge room, where they were left alone. Carl was equally clueless as to their location, until George flipped over the *Foxtel* magazine sitting on the table. There was the address: PO Box XX Queenscliff Victoria. They were on Swan Island, an ultra-secret training base for the Army's Special Air Service regiment and various intelligence agencies. The 140-hectare island was connected to Queenscliff by the causeway and was bristling with barbed wire, electronic security and highly trained, heavily armed commandos. They would be housed in a military brig on the island while spending their days with the Petra detectives.

After nearly five years locked up in Acacia, Carl must have felt like he had been reborn on Swan Island. This was life with the rest of the Crown witnesses, the former mates who had betrayed him. Now it was his turn. Carl had plenty to say. He had seen how the other dogs had worked their deals. They gave them what they wanted even if they had to make up some of it.

The Rat, who had organised the killing of Lewis Moran for Carl, had served up his co-accused Evangelos Goussis in two murders. All went to plan even if it took the Rat three statements to tell a satisfactory version of the truth. Flushed with success, he proceeded to allege that serving and former police had helped him in another contract hit, the 2003 murder of male prostitute Shane Chartres-Abbott. Operation Briars, a joint operation between Victoria Police and the Office of Police Integrity, was launched on the Rat's information. It cost more than $20 million and achieved not a single conviction, wrecking careers and lives in its wake.

Carl would have no trouble making things up if he needed to. When Justice Betty King sentenced him, she had drawn attention to his loose relationship with the truth.

In a few months' time, Simon Overland, the former Purana frontman, would succeed Christine Nixon as the Chief Commissioner. Operation Briars was his disaster, but still he was prepared to put everything on the line to solve the Hodson murders. It became his number-one priority. Carl told his father he believed that detectives were told to host him on Swan Island as long as he kept talking about Paul Dale and his links to the Hodson story.

'Dale, Dale, Dale, all youse want is Dale,' Carl apparently said at one stage. Over nine days, Carl gave them chapter and verse. He was beginning to trust his handlers, including Detective Inspector

Steve Smith. He still had to sign the statements, but for now he was talking freely.

Carl said he met Dale following his release from prison in July 2002 when Dale asked for a meeting through another criminal.

'I first met him at the Brunswick Club, where Moran was killed,' Carl said. 'He [Dale] was telling me he could keep an eye out for me.

'In return, Dale expected to be paid for any information that he gave to me . . . I think we were both suspicious of each other at that time and remained so.'

Early on, Dale showed him a police report that revealed an Asian crook called Jimmy had been informing to police on Carl, called 'Fat Boy' in the document.

'As a result of reading the report, I dropped off Jimmy and did no more business with him.'

As the trust between them grew, they began to meet more often. 'On most occasions when I met with Dale, I would give him an envelope with money in it. The money I paid Dale usually ranged from $2000 to $5000 each time.'

One day, Dale asked him if he wanted any help dealing with Jason Moran.

'It was pretty widely known that Jason and I had problems at the time,' Williams said in his statement. 'I didn't know whether they [Dale and a fellow detective] were fair dinkum or trying to set me up. Dale said he could kill Jason for $400 000. I told them they were dreaming.'

Dale told Carl he had fixed internal systems so he could leak sensitive intelligence to Carl. 'He told me he did this so that he could keep up to date with any investigations against me.'

They had met once in a swimming pool near Seaford.

'We met at the swimming pool because he was paranoid of me and I was paranoid of him,' said Williams. 'Dale had two pairs of shorts or swimming togs. We put these on and got into the pool and walked up and down in the water.'

On this occasion, Dale told Carl to warn Tony Mokbel that police were getting close to a drug laboratory he was operating.

In April 2007, Carl had said he did not know who killed the Hodsons but now he was ready to spill his guts.

'There were a number of reasons I did not tell the police all I know about the Hodson murders in my last statement,' he said.

'I did not think police would be able to charge anyone because of the lack of traceable phone calls. [The killer] was still out of jail and because I did not want to get charged with the murders. I didn't want to be a dog and be a protection prisoner, but my attitude has changed.'

Dale had to 'get' Hodson before he could testify at a committal hearing about his alleged involvement in the Oakleigh East drughouse robbery of 2003, Carl told police.

'Dale said he didn't want to go back to jail. He said he had been in isolation and it was tough.

'He said he had someone on the job but it was taking too long to get Hodson. Dale asked me if I could help him out.'

According to Carl, Dale said the job was worth $150 000.

Carl said he organised a shooter with 'a reputation as a fairly ruthless bloke'. This turned out to be the Savage, Williams' favourite hit man. They met in the lobby bar of the Marriott Hotel.

'I told him there was a contract there for Terry Hodson and I told him the amount of $150 000. There was never any contract on his wife and I never mentioned Terry's wife to [the hit man].'

Carl said he wasn't aware of exactly when Hodson was to be killed, and he had heard of it through the news. A few days after the Hodsons' deaths, Carl said Dale telephoned him to say, 'It's been dropped off.'

'I knew he was talking about the money for the Hodson murders,' Carl said.

'I was at my mum's when Dale made that call to me. I went and checked the bin. It was a large green wheelie bin that Mum kept inside the gate. Inside the bin, I saw a plastic bag and I took it out of the bin and went back inside.'

Carl said he counted the money, which was bundled in $10 000 amounts with rubber bands around them. 'It might have been $100 or so short but effectively the money was all there.'

A few days later, Williams met the hit man at the Marriott again. 'I left the bag containing the $150 000 on the ground next to our seats and he collected it.'

'[The hit man said,] "Quick, hey?" and smiled and chuckled.

'I said to him, "What happened with the sheila [Christine Hodson]?" He said, "That's not for you to worry about." That was the end of the conversation.

'I asked him about the sheila because I didn't think she needed to die and she wasn't a part of the contract. Having said that, I didn't push it any further.' The job was never mentioned again. 'It is an unspoken rule that once a job is done, you don't mention it again so you don't get caught out on a listening device or something.'

It was powerful evidence, enough for a jury to convict, with the corroborating evidence of others. Yet still Smith wanted more. He arranged for Stacey Vella to meet Carl in a boatshed for a visit. George maintains there was no sex and no hookers during their seaside adventure. But there was plenty of food. After the miserable fare of Barwon, the spread of pizza, burgers, Chinese and more was almost better than sex to Carl.

George says Smith asked them to stay another week on Swan Island, but Carl was done for now. Word of his absence would soon be spreading through Barwon. It was time to get back. If Simon Overland was as good as his word, he would sign the statements. But there were a few conditions.

Victoria Police would pay Dhakota's school fees at Penleigh and Essendon Grammar School. They would also pay off a tax bill of $750 000 that George owed the Australian Tax Office. (The ATO had made a guesstimate on the tax owing, coming up with a very modest figure, considering the enterprise had been valued at $20 million in 1999. Obviously, Carl and George had not kept receipts.) There would also be a reduction in Carl's sentence of up to seventeen years; he might yet get to take his daughter down the aisle as a free man.

But surviving the inevitable backlash against his decision to turn dog was a more pressing consideration. Carl needed people with him whom he could trust. In Acacia, the two men you ran out with had the best chance to harm you. George would do the rest of his time in Acacia with Carl. That left one spot vacant, at least until George went home.

Carl had wanted to run out with Tony Mokbel and Ange Goussis, but the request was denied, says George. In June 2007, Mokbel had been arrested in Athens and was facing a series of trials. The Crown couldn't afford to have Carl mingling with his old partner, especially if he could help them to lock up Mokbel for financing Lewis Moran's murder.

Carl's next choice was Matthew Charles Johnson. In Melaleuca Unit over 2007–08, the screws had observed Carl and Matty chatting intermittently through the mesh of adjoining exercise yards. They appeared to get on well and Johnson had no links to the gangland war.

On 23 January 2009, Johnson shifted into Melaleuca with Carl and George, a move supported by almost all, including Victoria Police. The only dissenting voice was Acting Commissioner of Corrections Rod Wise, who cited three reasons as to why Matty posed a risk to Carl. There could be financial incentives – potentially offered by people against whom Carl was giving evidence. There might be an opportunity for Johnson to enhance his reputation within the prison population. And, of course, he was already facing a 2007 murder charge so, if he was found guilty of that, any further jail sentence would run concurrently. He could effectively kill Carl for free.

In April 2012, the Victorian Ombudsman noted in a report into Carl's death that 'notwithstanding these identified risks, [Corrections Victoria] had supported the placement of Mr Johnson with Mr Williams. However, this was conditional on the basis the placement be carefully monitored'.

It seemed an odd decision, given Matty Johnson's violent track record, especially with police informers. In 1998, Johnson had been involved in the savage bashing of triple murderer Greg Brazel in the Acacia Unit. Brazel had apparently used the metal stem of the seat from an exercise bike to defend himself while his attackers had gone to work on him with a sandwich maker.

There would be no situation or cellmate in Barwon that police could guarantee would be risk-free. Other Crown witnesses had been taken right out of Victoria for this reason and housed in interstate prisons. However, that was never a serious consideration for Carl. There was talk of taking Carl to Ararat Prison but that was still under renovation. The decision was taken that Barwon, the most modern penitentiary in the state, was the best option. Confidentiality was the key to Carl's safety. When Steve Smith had taken Carl and George out of Barwon, prison staff had not been informed of their destination. However, on the pair's return a senior screw came up to them and asked, 'So, how was the holiday on Swan Island?' It was only a matter of time before everyone would know there was a new dog in residence.

34

A SECRET FOE

Over the next year and a half, Carl's relationship with his police handlers grew closer. He had once dreamt of becoming a policeman, now at least he had the chance to solve a murder, albeit one that he had set in train. He was speaking to Petra's Steve Smith, whom he called 'Coach', five or six times a week as momentum gathered for the committal hearing for Paul Dale on the Hodson murders.

On 13 February 2009, Dale had been arrested at a service station he was managing in Wangaratta, in central Victoria, and he was charged with the murders of Terry and Christine Hodson.

A committal hearing was set down for March 2010. Now it was a question of getting Carl to the witness box. All Carl had to do was give his evidence at the committal and his part of the bargain would be fulfilled. It might have been easier to convict Dale had Carl not been available for the trial. There would be no witness to cross-examine. Either way, it seemed Carl was ready to play his part. He would sacrifice himself, to ensure his family's future would be taken care of. He trusted 'Coach' Smith and vice versa. One former Petra detective says it was too strong to suggest that a friendship was developing between them, but they had certainly become allies.

In the context of Carl's previous friendships, his relationship with Smith was as honest and transparent as any other. Smith had found that Carl was not as stupid as he had been portrayed by other police and in the *Underbelly* series. As Smith later told a court, 'He was very clear as to what he sought to obtain from our relationship, as it was with us.' And Smith kept his side of the bargain.

Soon after their return from Swan Island, George was moved from Dhurringile to Barwon, where he joined Carl in Melaleuca Unit. Johnson soon made up the trio, and they were moved into Acacia Unit One in May. Carl was said to be happy with the new arrangement, despite still making requests that Mokbel be put in with them.

In June 2009, George was released from Barwon on parole and a month later Tommy Ivanovic moved in. On the face of it, it was a strange placement. Tommy had links with Dale going back a number of years. Whatever qualms police had about Tommy's friendship with Dale were counterbalanced by Carl's insistence that Tommy be put with him. If there was one person who had stood by him through it all, it was Tommy. He knew plenty of what Carl had been up to, but had never breathed a word.

It was already common knowledge in Barwon that Carl was assisting police. The *Herald Sun* had quickly learnt of his Swan Island break, reporting in January 2009 that father and son had enjoyed fast-food feasts and the services of prostitutes on their 'coastal holiday'. Matty Johnson had been perfectly happy with Carl's cooperation, says George. He had even wanted to get on board, but he had nothing as valuable to offer.

As usual, Carl had been keeping Matty sweet, organising for money to be put into his prison-canteen account each month. Johnson was a force to be reckoned with. Physically imposing, with a reputation for wanton cruelty and violence, Johnson had most recently been accused of killing a man over a $50 drug deal. Johnson had been a leading member of the jailhouse gang the 'Prisoners of War'. POWs regarded punishing police informers as a duty of membership. There were fears that if Johnson were to learn that Carl's cooperation went beyond lagging corrupt police, his life would be in extreme danger. But as long as Carl and his police handlers raised no concerns about Johnson's placement, nothing would change.

But the prison authorities had already missed or ignored obvious clues that Carl's cooperation was causing disquiet among the prison population. In March 2009, an officer reported that an inmate had told him everyone knew that Carl had been paid $1 million and he'd had ten years cut from his sentence for helping police. The inmate had said that Carl couldn't hack doing time in prison and was poised to inform on others. Carl would 'only end up doing five or seven years, just you watch, because he will rat on everybody'.

In December 2009, Victoria Police received information that an associate of a high-security prisoner in Barwon would be murdered. Tommy Ivanovic was moved out of Acacia for three weeks, and Carl and Matty were isolated from each other for eight days. But the threat was not substantiated and the trio was reunited in Acacia in late January.

Meanwhile, the 'Coach' Steve Smith was anxious to prepare Carl for his star turn at Dale's committal hearing, set down for March 2010. He requested that Carl be removed from Barwon again for another few days. But Carl could feel the temperature rising around him. As much as he craved the opportunity to get out of jail, he had reservations this time. Carl had told Johnson that his cooperation with police was just a ruse. Johnson said later that Carl had told him he planned to string Smith along until it was time to give real evidence. He planned to shaft the police by withdrawing his statements, having enjoyed as much preferential treatment as he could. Perhaps Carl reasoned that to go out again would raise suspicions that he was actually fair dinkum about testifying.

Two weeks before he was due to go out once more, Carl called his father to share his concerns.

CARL: 'When you speak to Steve [Smith] tell him there's no headaches or anything but it's too risky to do it out there [outside the prison] that's all . . . but you agree, don't you? – it's too risky?'

In a telephone call with George on 20 February 2010, Carl again raised concerns about the impact his removal from Barwon Prison might have had on Matty Johnson and Tommy Ivanovic.

CARL: 'He [Steve Smith] wanted to do this thing out [of prison], but I think it's too much, Dad. He wants to work it out . . . you know, rather than here. Yeah, but I think it's too much. What do you reckon?'

GEORGE: 'He said that to me.'

CARL: 'I think when it affects . . . for me, it doesn't really, but the other two [Johnson and Ivanovic] it does, you know what I mean. I gotta respect their . . . space, you know, a little bit.'

Carl rightly sensed that resentment towards him was growing and was spilling over onto his cellmates. Tommy voiced those concerns in a telephone call to an associate on 24 February.

'They [Victoria Police] don't care about us, at the end of the day they could [not] care less about us but at the end of the day we all gotta work together mate because . . . Carl lives with us, I live with him, Matty lives with him and it's a reflection on all of us at the end of the day.'

Despite the growing tension in the unit, Steve Smith insisted on taking Carl out of the prison for another session. On 27 February, Carl was taken to a safe house in a suburban location – Swan Island being no longer an option after the media had exposed it in 2009. It was just one night out for Carl but Steve Smith was apparently confident that his prize witness would keep up his end of the bargain.

There were others who doubted that Carl would get to testify; some were amazed that he was still breathing.

In a later interview with the Victorian Ombudsman, the Supervisor of Barwon's Intelligence Unit said that Carl 'was very high-profile but at the end of the day he had no prison sense'.

'And then all of a sudden Johnson comes out of nowhere. And Johnson wasn't part of the gangland set-up; he was a prison thug . . . [H]ow they [Corrections Victoria] ever let it happen I will not know. Because basically as soon as Johnson found out that Williams was cooperating with police to either get years off his own sentence or help his father out, he was doomed. "He appointed his own assassin" are the words that I've used, and I stick by it,' he said.

35

CODE BLACK

On 19 April 2010, the *Herald Sun* splashed its front page with the headline: 'YOU PAY KILLER'S SCHOOL FEES'. The story, by reporter Padraic Murphy, detailed how Victoria Police had paid Dhakota's school fees.

Other journalists had been aware of the story for some time but only Murphy had managed to make the claim stand up, obtaining a letter written by the Victorian Government Solicitor that showed the police had paid $8000 in fees.

The *Herald Sun* was unable, for legal reasons, to explain the reason behind the school fees being paid, but everyone in Barwon knew exactly why.

Considering how fast the *Herald Sun* had got onto the Swan Island story, it had been surprising to the Williams clan that Carl's deal had remained a secret for so long. Carl had known a story was coming, making enquiries of me a couple of days earlier. Yet he seemed unconcerned when prison staff had asked how he felt in response to the revelation. A prison officer remarked to Carl that he had done well to make the front page.

'Well, it's either page three, page five,' Carl reportedly replied. 'It's just which page I'm going to be on. Yeah, I'm fine. I'm fine with it.' Carl was of course no stranger to publicity.

While the big news of Acacia Unit One that morning was Carl's front-page story, prison staff missed a more significant event unfolding. Earlier, Johnson had taken his mattress out into the day room and placed it over the exercise bike. It was a common practice: the thin foam mattresses would become saturated in a man's sweat overnight and prisoners would dry them in the day room. But this day the mattress obscured the view from surveillance cameras of Johnson unscrewing the stem of the bike seat and taking it into his cell.

Later Carl went off to the visitor's centre for a box visit with George. Nothing was amiss, according to George. It was just a normal visit, like so many others. If he had known it would be the last, he might have said something more profound.

At 12.48 p.m., Carl was back in the day room at Acacia, perusing the newspaper again. He liked to take his time and work his way through the paper from front to back. It was one of the pleasures of his day. Tommy Ivanovic was nearby in the kitchen area, with his back to Carl.

Carl sat resting his head in his right hand, oblivious to Johnson's approach from behind. A grainy CCTV picture released to the media shows Johnson standing in the doorway of his cell, holding the bike stem in both hands. He looks the very image of a grim executioner.

The first blow to the side of Carl's head dropped him to the floor and was probably enough to kill him. But Johnson followed up with another seven strokes to the left side of his head as Carl lay motionless beside the table. It was all over in ten seconds.

The closed circuit television system at Acacia had been state of the art in the mid-1990s when it was installed. By 2010, it was practically a museum piece. Three monitors displayed live images from inside and outside the unit. One monitor displayed live split-screen images from eleven cameras inside the Acacia Unit for four seconds at a time, rotating in a preprogramed sequence between a number of cameras inside and outside the Acacia Unit.

Staff said later that, as each camera view reappeared at approximately forty-five-second intervals, there might have been only one or two images of Carl's death visible to anyone monitoring the system.

As it turned out, no one saw anything. Even Tommy Ivanovic, who must have heard the terrible sound of the metal bar shattering Carl's skull, did not turn around until it was all over.

At first, Johnson covered Carl's head with a towel, and then soon after dragged his victim's body into his cell and closed the door. He then placed the towel over the spreading pool of red on the blue vinyl floor.

At 12.54 p.m., Tommy telephoned his sister and said, 'I can't talk for long . . . something's happened here . . . I think he's [Johnson] . . . [just] done something to him [Carl] . . . He [Johnson] just went crazy . . . He's all right with me; we're good friends . . . I don't know what happened; he just went crazy.'

SISTER: 'What did he do to him?'

IVANOVIC: 'Oh, he [Johnson] hit him. I don't know what happened; I wasn't looking. I don't know . . .'

At 12.58 p.m., Ivanovic telephoned an associate.

IVANOVIC: 'I'm shocked, mate . . . Something just really terrible just happened. I think Carl's dead . . . I think Carl's dead, mate . . . Matty just went crazy . . .'

ASSOCIATE: 'What happened?'

IVANOVIC: 'I don't know, mate. The screws haven't come yet or nothing, so we're going to get locked in . . . I think he just started threatening Matty . . . I just heard some noise and I turned over and seen Carl on the floor.'

Ivanovic and Johnson then walked laps of the exercise yard, waiting for the inevitable alarm and lockdown, but still the screws did not appear.

Finally, at 1.15 p.m., twenty-seven minutes after the attack, Johnson alerted a female screw, saying she should push her panic button as Carl had 'hit his head'.

Soon after, forty screws descended on the crime scene. It was a shocking moment. The highest profile prisoner in Victoria had been killed in the state's most secure facility. In spite of all the security, the high-tech surveillance and the psychological controls built into this jail within a jail, nothing could prevent Carl's murder. The inmate code of justice had prevailed in Acacia after all.

That night, after news of the 'Code Black' in Acacia had spread across Barwon, the sound of prisoners howling like dogs echoed through the jail.

36

VIOLENCE AND MERCY

The autopsy showed that Carl had been in the best shape of his life on the day of his death. He had been grossly overweight, around 120 kilos, on his admission to Barwon in June 2004. The forensic pathologist noted that the deceased weighed in at just 87.5 kilos with a body mass index of 26.85, just above average for a man of his height. There was no sign of disease in Carl's body or his blood, not even high cholesterol. Ironically, Carl was physically much better off for his six years in jail. But the state of his mind was something else.

Moving to his injuries, the pathologist observed that it was fairly certain that Carl had suffered little, if at all.

'The injuries present are judged to be non-survivable and are likely to have been rapidly fatal. In this instance, given the extent of skull fractures present, the overall degree of force is estimated to be extreme,' the autopsy read.

Johnson's aim had been to dispatch Carl as quickly and cleanly as possible. There was seemingly no rage here, no desire to make his victim suffer, to prolong the agony. This was a cold, detached act of violence, the way someone might put down a dog.

Johnson refused to answer questions from police, saying only that he had acted alone.

In the days after Carl's death, Corrections staff and police sifted through the telephone calls and correspondence of the inmates of Acacia Unit One. While prisoners assumed that the screws listened in on every telephone call live and read every letter as soon as it was written, the reality was they were weeks behind in vetting their communications. There had been several clues as to what was brewing in Acacia.

In a letter dated 5 April 2010, Johnson warned his cousin 'there will be media attention soon', 'just don't want you to worry . . . I'll be sweet so don't stress'. On 12 April, in a letter to another prisoner, Johnson said, 'I know the Khoon [Williams] is getting baked everywhere, he doesn't believe it or care? I told you the bloke has gone insane. He's not well in the head.' One day before Carl's death, Johnson appeared resigned to another long prison term: 'As for myself I think that now I'll have to hang around for a while longer. Doesn't matter but coz I love this shit. I am the true general so I must keep things in good true order.'

In his trial, Johnson pleaded not guilty, on the grounds of self-defence. He came up with a story that Carl intended to kill him. He claimed the day before the murder, Ivanovic had told him that Carl was going to attack him. The day of the murder, Ivanovic claimed that Carl planned to sneak up on Johnson while he was eating, with a sock filled with pool balls. Anyone who knew Carl doubted this far-fetched story. Carl would never have had the heart to do his killing personally, even with a gun. The idea that he would risk doing it close up with a cosh was ridiculous. Killing was something that other people did for him.

Predictably, there was intense speculation that an outsider had ordered the killing. With Carl's death, the Crown's case against Paul Dale for the Hodson murders collapsed. If Carl had made it to the committal hearing, his evidence could have been used in the trial, but now his statements were just pieces of worthless paper. It was a devastating blow to the Petra Taskforce: now the alleged links between the underworld and corrupt police could never be tested.

Curiously, Johnson sought to repair Carl's reputation in death. Despite claiming that Carl had planned to kill him, Johnson wanted everyone to know that his victim was not a dog after all. Johnson claimed that Williams was 'pulling the wool over the eyes of police' and was going to 'shaft' them.

In sentencing Johnson to life with a minimum of thirty-two years, Justice Lex Lasry expressed revulsion at Johnson's actions.

'This was an appalling murder,' he said. 'It was a killing which appears to demonstrate your belief that you have some special entitlement to kill when you think it is appropriate, or your ego demands it according to some meaningless underworld prison code.'

But those close to Carl eventually came to a different view. When the shock of his death subsided, they began to realise that Matty had done Carl a favour. This terrible act of violence was also, perversely, an act of mercy. Carl could never have hacked his thirty-five-year sentence. He was prepared to throw away the only principle that mattered to a crook, staying staunch. He was prepared to let his associates, Matty and Tommy, not to mention his family, wear the stain of his informing, because Acacia had chopped him into small pieces.

Now, as George says, Carl is free again. The case against Paul Dale for the Hodsons' murder would be dropped and Carl could go to his rest with his reputation rehabilitated. No one would ever do a day's jail because of him.

They laid him to rest in a garish gold coffin in the best underworld tradition. But just like the funeral of his brother Shane, the friends who had flocked around him in the good times were absent. It was family and his childhood mates from Broadie who turned up to walk the gauntlet of cameras and microphones into St Therese's Church in Essendon, where the funeral of his mother had been held, not to mention the send-offs for two of Carl's victims, Lewis and Mark Moran.

All the girls who had written to Carl or visited him had long since disappeared. Only Roberta was there at the end, organising the funeral while dealing with her own grief. Carl had never really let go of her, even when she took up with Rob, her new partner. Carl thought they could get married again, maybe even have another baby through IVF. She played along; she didn't have the heart to tell him that finally she was moving on.

By the end, Carl was becoming the bloke that Roberta had known before all this had begun, before Jason Moran had shot him, setting off a decade of blood and revenge. She could look into her daughter's face, so much like her father's, and see the best of Carl. Matthew Charles Johnson would always be 'a maggot' but true to his 'meaningless prison code', he had put things in 'good true order'. The story could now finally come to an end.

George Williams shuffled out of the restaurant into the bluestone lane, squinting his good eye against the bright afternoon sun.

'Thanks for lunch; you take care of yourself,' he said.

'Yeah, you too, George. We'll stay in touch . . .'

But after nine years of these steak lunches, this felt as though it would be the last.

'You know, the more we talk, the further from the truth we seem to get,' I said.

George tilted his head back and grinned.

'Don't matter what the truth is. Carl's story is how the young ones want to see him from here in. He belongs to the world now,' George said.

He got in the old Mercedes Carl had bought him and drove through the city, past the courthouses where the media pack had swarmed around them years before.

He followed the tramline out of the city, down Flemington Road to the freeway, passing the old grounds of Camp Pell. He took the exit at Pascoe Vale Road and trailed it all the way to Broadie, passing through the exhaust plumes of the fast-food joints where Carl and his associates had met to plot the fate of friends and enemies. Cross Keys Reserve flashed by, where Jason and Paddy Barbaro had their brains blown out in front of all those kids, on Carl's orders.

George came home to the old commission house he and Barb had bought back in 1973.

It was just him and Kath living there now but they kept the place nice. He always mowed the lawn and cleaned the pool. It looked like his boys and their mates could descend any moment. He and Kath would settle down to read the form guide and watch the races on Sky, even if there was no dough to bet with.

They would retire to the bed that Barbara had in the past always made for George. He would lie awake most of the night, processing his regrets while the monitor on the wall rolled through images from the security cameras outside.

CASUALTIES OF MELBOURNE'S GANGLAND WAR 1998—2010

16 January 1998 – **Alphonse Gangitano**, forty, shot in his Templestowe home. Coroner Iain West finds Gangitano's associates Jason Moran and Graham Kinniburgh are 'implicated in the death'.

3 August 1998 – **John Furlan**, forty-eight, bombed in his car in North Coburg.

23 November 1998 – Notorious criminal **Charles 'Mad Charlie' Hegyalji**, forty-two, shot in the front yard of his home in Caulfield South. Main suspect is Dino Dibra.

9 January 1999 – **Vince Mannella**, shot outside his North Fitzroy home.

28 May 1999 – Bankrupt fruiterer **Joseph Quadara**, fifty-seven, gunned down in a Toorak supermarket car park.

9 September 1999 – Brighton businessman **Dimitrios Belias**, thirty-eight, shot in an underground car park in St Kilda.

20 October 1999 – **Gerardo Mannella**, thirty-one, shot in a North Fitzroy street after talking to and trying to escape from two men.

8 May 2000 – Melbourne Fruit & Vegetable Market wholesaler **Francesco Benvenuto**, fifty-two, shot dead at the wheel of his car in Beaumaris. Andrew 'Benji' Veniamin is the main suspect.

16 May 2000 – Career criminal **Richard Mladenich**, thirty-seven, shot in a St Kilda motel room in front of three other people. Case remains unsolved despite the offer of a $1-million reward by Victoria Police.

15 June 2000 – **Mark Moran**, thirty-six, facing drugs and firearms charges, shot getting into his car outside his Aberfeldie home. Carl Williams was the main suspect but charges were later dropped. Remains unsolved.

14 October 2000 – **Dino Dibra**, twenty-five, shot outside a Sunshine West home. Andrew Veniamin and two unnamed associates suspected of involvement.

1 May 2002 – **Victor Peirce**, forty-two, a career criminal acquitted of the murders of police officers Steven Tynan and Damian Eyre in South Yarra in 1988, shot in his car in Bay Street, Port Melbourne. Andrew Veniamin was the main suspect.

15 October 2002 – **Paul Kallipolitis**, thirty-three, found shot dead in his Sunshine West home. Andrew Veniamin was the main suspect.

15 April 2003 – Bulgarian migrant **Nikolai Radev**, forty-seven, formerly jailed for assault, burglary, attempted arson and drug-related offences, shot in the head and chest in Queen Street, Coburg. Raptor and Andrew Veniamin alleged to have carried out the hit for Carl Williams.

21 June 2003 – **Jason Moran**, thirty-six, and **Pasquale Barbaro**, forty, shot to death in the front seat of a van in the car park of the Cross Keys Hotel, Essendon North, while five children watch from the back seat. Raptor, Goggles and Carl Williams convicted.

21 July 2003 – **Willie Thompson**, thirty-nine, shot in his car in Waverley Road, Chadstone. Andrew Veniamin was the main suspect but the case remains unsolved.

18 August 2003 – The charred remains of **Mark Mallia**, thirty, an associate of Radev, found in a drain in Sunshine West. Carl Williams and others convicted of his torture and murder.

9 September 2003 – **Housam Zayat,** thirty-two, a violent criminal, forced from his car and shot in a paddock near Werribee, southwest of Melbourne. Nicholas Ibrahim charged with the murder.

25 October 2003 – **Michael Marshall,** thirty-eight, kickboxer and hot-dog dealer, shot in front of his five-year-old son outside his South Yarra home. Carl Williams, the Raptor and Goggles are convicted of the murder.

13 December 2003 – Semi-retired crook **Graham Kinniburgh,** sixty-two, ambushed and shot outside his home in Kew.

23 March 2004 – 'Person of interest' to police, **Andrew 'Benji' Veniamin,** twenty-eight, gunned down in self-defence by Mick Gatto in a Carlton restaurant.

31 March 2004 – Crime patriarch **Lewis Moran,** fifty-eight, shot at the Brunswick Club in Sydney Road, Brunswick.

8 May 2004 – Williams associate **Lewis Caine,** thirty-nine, shot and dumped in a Brunswick lane.

16 May 2004 – Police informer **Terry Hodson,** fifty-six, and his wife, **Christine,** fifty-five, executed in their East Kew home. Former drug squad officer Paul Dale was charged but the case is later withdrawn. Remains unsolved.

6 February 2006 – Carlton Crew elder **Mario Rocco Condello,** fifty-three, shot in the garage of his Brighton home. Case remains unsolved.

19 April 2010 – **Carl Anthony Williams,** thirty-nine, bludgeoned to death by Matthew Charles Johnson in the Acacia Unit of Barwon Prison.

Acknowledgements

I would like to thank a number of people, some of whom would not like to see their name in print. Those whom I can publicly thank include the dedicated team at Penguin, including Publishing Director Ben Ball, publisher Andrea McNamara, editor Bridget Maidment, not to mention all the other staff who have worked hard to turn a manuscript into a book in a very short space of time. Former publishing director Robert Sessions, who first brought the idea of another book on Carl to me, deserves special recognition for his support over nearly a decade.

It's been a long journey for me with the people whose voices are heard in this book. I'd like to thank them for putting up with my persistent and often intrusive questions. These include George Williams, the late Barbara Williams, Roberta Williams, Deana Falcone, Travis Day, Bert Wrout and a host of others. I hope there will be peace for one and all from here on in.

Most of all, I would like to thank my family for sticking by me as I covered this story over nearly nine years. It has occupied a large amount of my time that I would have otherwise devoted to them. It's time to repay their forbearance.

Thanks must go to my parents, Dr John and Robin Shand, and to Sekai, Noliwe and Jack. Thanks also to a host of good friends who have supported me, including Munch, Penal, Brendan, Brian 'Skull' Murphy, Teddy, Billy 'the Texan' Longley and a host of others.

Also by Adam Shand

BIG SHOTS

Carl Williams & the Gangland Murders
The Inside Story, Completely Revised

In 2003, Adam Shand, until then a finance journalist, naively set out to unravel Melbourne's bloody gangland wars. A few months' research, a guaranteed cover story. But his foray into the underworld took him deeper than that. He became embroiled in a complex world where feuds raged between rival families, and where a new generation was clashing with the criminal Establishment. Before long, he found himself counted as a friend by those who sometimes ended friendships with a hail of bullets.

In this fully updated edition, taking in the events of 2010, including the murder of Carl Williams, Big Shots takes the reader into the heart of the city's multibillion-dollar 'disorganised crime' scene, as Shand meets the key figures and suspects, including Carl and Roberta Williams, Mick Gatto and many others. He discovers the human drama behind the brutal slayings that were splashed across the front pages, and in the process comes to question his objectivity.

'Shand's effort is a real masterpiece. A standout in the literary true-crime genre, it gives us both a feel for the participants and their crimes but also delves into the murky side of journalism as Shand worries that he's getting far too close to his subjects. If you haven't read Big Shots yet, you're missing out – it's possibly Australia's best true-crime book ever'
— ILLAWARRA MERCURY

read more
my penguin e-newsletter

Subscribe to receive *read more*, your monthly e-newsletter from Penguin Australia. As a *read more* subscriber you'll receive sneak peeks of new books, be kept up to date with what's hot, have the opportunity to meet your favourite authors, download reading guides for your book club, receive special offers, be in the running to win exclusive subscriber-only prizes, plus much more.

Visit penguin.com.au/readmore to subscribe